BONATTI

ON ELECTIONS

Treatise 7 of Guido Bonatti's
Book of Astronomy

Translated by Benjamin N. Dykes, Ph.D.

From the 1491 and 1550 Latin Editions

The Cazimi Press
Minneapolis, Minnesota
2010

Published and printed in the United States of America
by the Cazimi Press
621 5th Avenue SE #25, Minneapolis, MN 55414

ISBN-13: 978-1-934586-09-9

PUBLISHER'S NOTE:

This reprint of Treatise 7 of Guido Bonatti's *Book of Astronomy* has been excerpted from the out-of-print 1st edition, published in 2007. The text reflects the original pagination, and has not been revised or updated to reflect new translation conventions or citations in more recent translations. The Table of Arabic Terms has been removed (a more recent version can be found at: www.bendykes.com/reviews/study.php).

Students should also consult *Works of Sahl & Māshā'allāh* (2008), which contains much electional material, now translated into English.

Dr. Benjamin N. Dykes
The Cazimi Press
May, 2010

TABLE OF CONTENTS

Book Abbreviations:

Abu 'Ali al-Khayyat:	*The Judgments of Nativities*	*JN*
Abū Ma'shar:	*Liber Introductorii Maioris ad Scientiam Iudiciorum Astrorum (Great Introduction to the Knowledge of the Judgments of the Stars)*	*Gr. Intr.*
	On Historical Astrology: the Book of Religions and Dynasties (On the Great Conjunctions)	*OGC*
	The Abbreviation of the Introduction to Astrology	*Abbr.*
	The Flowers of Abū Ma'shar	*Flowers*
Al-Biruni:	*The Book of Instruction in the Elements of the Art of Astrology*	*Instr.*
Māshā'allāh:	*De Receptione (On Reception)*	*OR*
	De Revolutionibus Annorum Mundi (On the Revolutions of the Years of the World)	*De Rev. Ann.*
Pseudo-Ptolemy:	*Centiloquium (Centiloquy)*	*Cent.*
Ptolemy	*Tetrabiblos*	*Tet.*
Sahl ibn Bishr:	*De Electionibus (On Elections)*	*On Elect.*
	De Quaestionibus (On Questions)	*On Quest.*
	Introductorium (Introduction)	*Introduct.*
'Umar al-Tabarī:	*Three Books of Nativities*	*TBN*
Vettius Valens:	*The Anthology*	*Anth.*

TREATISE 7: ELECTIONS

[PART 1]

Chapter 1: On elections, according to the sayings of the wise

After judgments, before all other parts of astronomy, we are in need of elections; and they are things which present themselves to us every day. Nor can we attain perfectly to the full degree of usefulness of the many judgments which it is necessary that we explain every day, without them. To me it seems appropriate to make a special Treatise on them, following in the footsteps of our sages.

But an election is a deliberate plan in light of a desire for something favorable.[1] However, electing is a desire of the intellect resulting from an act of the free will. And even if at some point many fools and tunic-wearing idiots rise up against me, saying an election has no strength and is wholly nothing, nevertheless elections and the other parts of astronomy remain in their fixity, nor is their truth diminished because of that.[2] For by elections we can apprehend many good things, and likewise we can avoid many bad things which are going to be according to the stars; nor however do I say that an election makes a thing, but it removes it, prohibiting it so that the matter does not come to be.[3] For if victory were judged by astrology for someone about to go against his enemy, concerning those things about which the question was made,[4] unless the querent had a good election in moving his army against his enemies, he could succumb on account of the evil beginning of his journey; or it could even destroy at least much of the good which will be signified for him by the judgment. And if he were to have a good election under a good Ascendant (and it will be signified more strongly for him by a judgment),[5] he will arrive at a good end of the matter, and he will overcome the enemy resisting him. For it is impossible for those things which come to be with correct advice, and lawfully, not to have firmness and to arrive at a good end. For the most high and

---

[1] *Prae consiliati appetitu consilium*, reading *appetitu* for *appetitus*.
[2] I.e., due to the objections of "fools" and "idiots."
[3] I.e., the election does not make things happen, *people* make things happen; and the correct election can help someone avoid an inopportune time to perform an action.
[4] *De ipsis super aliqua sibi facta quaestione.* I am not sure of the point of this clause, as it adds no information.
[5] I.e., by a horary judgment about the success of the matter.

glorious Creator of all things made the heavens and incorruptible stars from the fifth incorruptible essence, in order that they would rule and govern the corruptible inferior things made of the four corruptible essences (namely the elements); and He made the stars on account of men, in order that from the stars, assistance would be made available for men and other inferior things. For what is made for man ought to serve man—which if some people said it is not so, they are not to be argued with, when they know nothing and believe in nothing; but let them be dismissed, just like the teachers of error and the heretics to truth. For they are ignorant of the truth, because they are intent on pecuniary wealth, and it strips them and their minds of knowledge, and it blinds their hearts.

For the stars in the eight perceptible and moving heavens are set down [in place]; for those which are in the *primum mobile*[6] (which are called "fixed" by the philosophers), are virtually like matter; corruptible things are the forms.[7] Indeed the planets are and operate and employ a certain medium through which the superiors work in inferiors. Nevertheless however, they employ their operations formally; and because matter is a certain unlimited something, and forms come to be from matter; and that is the reason why the form of no rational thing is likened simply to the form of another, and still less [are] individuals; but even species are practically unlimited to us.

Since therefore God has made the stars for man, the which utility they pursue from them, if they did not operate and imprint in diverse inferior things, now this, now that—which we see them do clearly every day: for they operate good in one place at some time, at another time we see them in the same place [doing] the contrary of what they had done at first, which does not happen except by the diversity of their motions and locations.[8] Wherefore on account of the diverse qualities of their motions, and the diverse locations of their bodies, diverse changes come to be in the world. For we see the planets moved by diverse motions, and according to those diverse motions they imprint into inferior things in diverse ways, and [inferior things] are changed and alter in diverse ways according to those diverse impressions. For they are made hot and are chilled; they are dried and moistened. For if Mars and the Sun were joined together, if it were summer, heat rises. If it were winter, cold is driven back, and

---

[6] I.e., the "first movable," or the sphere of fixed stars.

[7] This may have to do with Bonatti's belief that changes caused by the fixed stars are not lasting if their wordly phenomena are not of the right type—see Tr. 5.

[8] As usual when Bonatti waxes theoretical, his sentences suggest further arguments and hypotheticals, but never quite complete themselves satisfactorily.

it is restored to temperate [weather]. If indeed the Sun were joined with Saturn, and it were winter, [cold] is indicated. If however it were summer, heat is driven back.

Whence if an astrologer, through his investigation, came to know the diversities of motions, and were to know the impressions which they impress in inferior things on account of those motions, and the motions were sometimes of a good quality, sometimes of a bad one, he could elect something good when the qualities of the motions are good, and take it up. And then [he could] elect something bad which is signified by the qualities when they are evil, and avoid it. Because just as was said elsewhere, a planet does not signify the same thing when it is retrograde as it does when it is direct; not the same when it is slow as it does when it is fast; not the same when it is stationary as it does when it is progressing; not the same when it is combust as it does when it has escaped [the beams]; not the same when it is void in course as it does when it is joined to another; not the same when it is in strange dignities[9] as it does in its own; not the same when it is in an angle as it does when it is in a cadent; not the same when it is free as it does when it is impeded.

Whence if it is known when a planet is well disposed through someone experienced in this science, an election can then come to be for the good; and when it is known by him when a planet is badly disposed, an election can come to be and be avoided in accordance with how the astrologer perceives it to be. And it can be elected in a good hour from a bad one, according to how our Lord Jesus Christ himself elected when he said, "Let us go again to Judea," *etc.*,[10] and evils can be avoided which are going to come in accordance with the dispositions of the aforesaid motions, and the evil things signified by them in all beginnings of those things which we intend to do, as much in journeys as in the betrothals of women and the celebrations of weddings; as much in building things as in destroying them; as much in planting things as in digging them up— and in exceptional things which we wish to do or intend to be avoided. And so it shows that the stars do diverse things in inferior things, in accordance with the diversity of their diverse motions; and that the astrologer can avert many evils by good elections which, unless someone were to make precautions, would happen to him according to the motions of the stars.

Whence they cannot diminish astronomy nor the elections of some things in such a manner as they easily adopt; however they can in a certain way resist in

---

[9] *In alienis dignitatibus*, i.e., in the dignities of another planet.
[10] John 11:7*ff.* See also Tr. 1, Ch. 13.

those things which *seem* likely (even though they can all be defended)–namely, if they said that elections are not found for just any low-class person (and that is somewhat true, but not simply so).[11] Wherefore we cannot rely well on what any low-class person can do for himself, not always being elected with a question having been made;[12] but a question having been made about a matter [i.e.,] what could happen to him from it, we can well elect for him afterwards, a significator of the election having been taken from the question made by him: for through his question is restored what was already considered destroyed by what was signified by the root of his nativity, because it is about *that* that it is asked.[13]

And in a certain manner, elections seem to be common to everyone, because an election is not about a matter that is voluntary[14] or certain; nevertheless however it belongs to anyone who is advised by [someone], or whom another advises, and it is a matter whose deliberation was produced first, [and] reason and intellect vouches for.[15] But we can elect for magnates and noble men (namely those who are fit for a kingdom) and about nativities, and about questions, and always without them, and indifferently about all of their beginnings, both of journeys and other things. Indeed when you elect for low-class people without a question, and especially if there were many at once, just as sometimes happens with those wishing to go by land (provided there are more than one, as there is in pilgrimages and the like), you cannot elect for them as you do when you elect for one alone. Because the fortunes and infortunes of the roots of their nativities differ, so that a significator who is useful for one of them, can be the contrary to the other; and thus you could not have such an election which would be useful for all in one [and the same] hour. Because there is not something existing which can carry out two natural and contrary operations at one and the same time, according to one and the same matter and to one and the same signification. And that the situation works in this way is

---

[11] This is probably a reference to the opening sentences of Sahl's *On Elect.*.

[12] I have added a *non* to this clause, which seems the only way to make this clause make sense and to prevent its contradicting the following clause: *Quoniam non confidimus bene quod quilibet vilis persona possit facere sibi [non] semper eligi facta interrogatione.*

[13] Bonatti seems to be making two points here: (a) a horary question can serve as a proper root for an election; (b) an election based on a successful horary can overcome something not permitted by the natal figure.

[14] By "voluntary," Bonatti is drawing on an Aristotelian tradition. He means events that are under our (relatively) complete power and knowledge. One would not bother making an election for events whose success were already assured by the mere power of our desire to act–like electing a time to sit down in one's own chair.

[15] Somewhat uncertain about the exact meaning of this: *Cuius consilium fuit praeambulum, ratio & intellectus praestitit.*

evident by this: because we sometimes see some people go together at the same hour for the sake of some business matters, and it goes well for certain ones, [and] the contrary for certain ones. Whence if questions were had by all of them, it ought to be elected for those whose questions signified good; it ought not to be elected for those whose [questions] signified the contrary, like [it is] in the other cases. However it is true that a good election either brings profit or does not harm, provided that it is not contrary to the root of the nativity; nor however are elections to be rejected, but they are to be observed according to the order which I told you. Those whose significators are the benefic planets, rejoice on good days, and are happy in them; on bad ones they sometimes are made sad. Those whose significators are the malefic planets, rejoice on days in which they do not seem they ought to, and on good days they are made sad and it is bad for them; and this is not [so] except for the reason that the malefics were victorious[16] in the root of the nativity of each. For the malefics profit their own affairs only so much; they strive to harm others [or strangers]; indeed the benefics always profit their own affairs and strive to profit others [or strangers].[17] And this is the reason why elections are able to profit more strongly than to harm. Therefore you ought not to despise these things which I tell you, because if you were to consider well, and you were to look into it well, you would be able to perceive the usefulness of elections; and whence they have an origin, and how and when and for whom they are of value.

For I want you to know that Fortune rules in every matter, even if certain idiots in tunics might say that Fortune does not exist but only what God wills. Indeed of them, those wise in this disgreed in secret, even though in public they seemed to agree, which is more likely from fear that their ranks would be despised, than that they believed they spoke the truth. For if there is no Fortune, who would be of such foolishness who did not know due to his own free will how to acquire wholly necessary things for himself in abundance? But we see the contrary openly, every day. Do you not see certain wise men, honest and intelligent, who often do not have something to eat? And [do you not see] certain fools, who, if a wolf were to take away seven out of ten of their cattle,

---

[16] This could allude to having a malefic as an *al-mubtazz* in the natal figure–say, as the Lord of *al-mubtazz* of the 1st. Or perhaps as the *hīlāj* or *al-kadukhadāh*?

[17] There is some ambiguity as to whose affairs are meant–those of the planets or those of the inceptor. I believe he is saying that when malefics are the significators of the inceptor, they will still try to help the inceptor, while if they are the significators of the inceptor's enemies or other people in the chart, they will try to harm them. This interpretation is borne out in the chapters that follow.

would not know whether they were diminished or not, they being overflowing in necessities? For these liars impute rage to the Creator, saying he is not just; and they fall into abhorrent heresy.[18]

Chapter 2: On those things which are considered in this Treatise

For in this Treatise, which was stated to be about elections, it is necessary for you to know these five things, namely: [1] If the elections which we make contain something useful in themselves. [2] And likewise it is necessary for you to consider the beginning of each matter which someone intends to make or begin, [i.e.,] why it is. [3] And whether the matters which they begin are going to come to completion or not. [4] And if it were completed, whether its end which we begin is going to be good or bad.[19] For to Ptolemy (who more so than others was a reconciler of this science), the fruit of this art seemed to be judgments–not excluding elections, [but] rather by reckoning in the fruit of this science: for it is necessary that a great part of astronomy be the fruit of an election. Because when we elect the beginning of some matter, we can know the beginning, middle, and end of the matter (how it ought to be) through the election. For if we elect for someone (of an age fit for it) so that he may generate a child, or even if we do not elect for him, and we would know the hour of the conception (whether the conception is rational or not rational), we will know what is going to be concerning it in its maternal womb up until the day and hour of the nativity; and if we were to know the hour of the nativity, we would be able to tell him what is going to happen to it after the nativity up until the end of its life according to the natural order, and what ought to happen to it. For God gives to the native what the stars direct. And even though the matter is

---

[18] This argument is a "theodicy," an argument for how the existence of evil is compatible with the goodness of God. My reconstructed version of the argument runs like this: "(a) Either Fortune rules in every matter, or it does not. (b) If not, then either (1) there is only free will left, or (2) only God's will. (c) But if (1) only free will were left, then anyone could freely use their decision-making power to get what they needed. But this is not the case. (d) And if there were (2) only God's will, then God would be responsible for fools flourishing and the good and wise suffering. But that would make God unjust, which is false and heretical. (e) Therefore, (1) and (2) are excluded, and we are left with the fact that Fortune rules in every matter." Now, as stated, the argument is not very strong (and may not even be logically valid), because Bonatti is artificially excluding the traditional possibility that our lives have a *mixture* of Fortune and free will (even if our power of free will is so feeble that few are able to exercise it effectively). But clearly Bonatti is trying to argue in support of the existence of some form of fate to preserve God from being implicated in the evil all around us.

[19] Note that he does not list a fifth.

the same in them, still [their] operations are many and diverse, just as happens in limbs, to which the First Cause gave the virtue of each in like manner as their operations; for it is not in its interest to prohibit some matter, even if certain people ignorant of astronomy do not acknowledge it.

Likewise when we elect for someone wishing to sow seed or to plant, we will know what is going to happen concerning that planting or that seeding according to the administration and significations of the stars. Indeed Sarcinator seemed to want it that we not elect for low-class or middle-class people, unless upon a nativity or [horary] question of theirs; however he did not want us to refrain wholly from electing for them, but it seemed to him safer to elect upon [their] nativities or questions than otherwise, because it is good to elect upon nativities or upon questions.[20] But if at some time we cannot have one of those, still an election is not to be prohibited. And he said that we [ought to] elect even without them, nor are they contrary to this. Sarcinator wanted to be definite, so that he could not be reprehended, wherefore he wanted to elect concerning nativities (which are rarely had), or on questions from their nature.

Indeed al-Rijāl wanted[21] to be freer in this because he wished to bring profit to everyone, even if elections which do not come to be based on nativities or questions are not certain like those which do come to be based on them. However, he acknowledged concerning them that they ought to be effective, or at least they cannot do harm.

However, to me it seems that we can elect for everyone individually, provided that it is not a plurality for which we elect; nor should you understand by "plurality" something communally shared, but a plurality of private concerns, just like when some people go in a group at once on pilgrimages and the like, for indeed I believe someone of middle or low status has his own little root in a nativity, as for instance a magnate [has] his own root–because each one of them is born under an Ascendant. For if we were to adapt the Moon (who is a participator in every matter), we already have a part of the journey or other matter adapted universally, which is of rooted matters, and which does not permit the traveler to be put into danger easily, even if the Ascendant of the journey is contrary to the Ascendant of the nativity in which the Moon is a participator. And insofar as she is a stronger factor in journeys, she abolishes much of the contrary that could be signified by the other planets contradicting

---

[20] Again, a clear reference to the doctrine of a "root" (*radix*) mentioned in Tr. 5. This subject will come up repeatedly in what follows.
[21] Bonatti is paraphrasing from al-Rijāl's introduction to elections, pp. 297-98.

the [person] on the journey: because her signification in journeys is doubly greater than the signification of any of the other planets. Whence if she had so great a role in journeys, and of all other matters, and is a participator of the nativity of one journeying, and we were to adapt her in the journey, it seems that the side of the root of the nativity of the one journeying or beginning is adapted, so that there will be prosperity for him in the journey, even if perhaps all things do not go prosperously for him as he wishes. However, a good election diminishes and averts many evils which would be about to happen according to the significations of the stars. And he for whom it is elected will take hold of some good things which, without an election, he would not have taken hold of.

For those who avoid elections which do not come to be based on nativities or on questions, do not seem wholly wise to me: because if they cannot have something of the good which they want, still they should not spurn that of the good which they are able to have. For they who do this, seem to act like a certain actor who went to a wedding at which it was said there would be goose, but going there he did not find goose, but he found plover; and he was able to eat as much of them as he wanted; who, after he did not find goose, did not want to eat the plovers, but rather, led by foolishness, he stood back hungry. Indeed Trutanus[22] said that it is better to eat crickets than nothing, even if he had spoken in a misapplied way; however his intention was true, and so it is better to use elections than to dismiss them entirely.

Chapter 3: On the root of elections

For the root of our elections is adapting their foundations; and among these is the adaptation of the Moon, because just as is said elsewhere, she has participation and a signification in every beginning, in every journey, in every place, in every time, in every matter, and at every hour. And it is likewise with these, as al-Rijāl affirms:[23] the Sun, who is chief among the other planets, like a king; and the planet which signifies the matter which we want to begin–like if we wished to begin a battle or something else of those things which are carried out by iron and fire, we ought to adapt Mars (who naturally signifies that). If we wished to acquire money, we would have to adapt Jupiter, who naturally signifies it. If we wished to celebrate a wedding or similarly delightful things, we

---

[22] Unknown astrologer.
[23] Perhaps referring to al-Rijāl, p. 299.

ought to adapt Venus. And understand this about what is signified by every planet. Moreover, we ought to adapt the sign which is of the nature of the matter which we want to begin, and which signifies it: like if we wish to make a journey by land, we would adapt an earthy sign; if by water, we would adapt a watery one. And its adaptation is when it is free from impediments and from the malefics and their aspects, and you make it the Ascendant of your election (or you put the Lord of the Ascendant or the Moon in it–or both, if you can).

These are the things necessary in all common elections, both in elections which come to be based on nativities or questions, and in others, if it can be done; and certain other things are proper, even of not necessary (namely, that we adapt a masculine sign for a man, and a feminine sign for women).

Chapter 4: On the adaptation of particulars

After you have adapted the aforesaid universal things, it is necessary for you to adapt the particular ones, namely after you have adapted the luminaries and the Lord of the Ascendant, and the planet signifying the matter which the inceptor intends to do, [and] obviously the house which signifies the matter about which your election and the intention of the inceptor is. And this is twofold: for in those ones whose nativities you knew, and whose questions you have, you ought to adapt the house signifying that matter in the nativity or question. Indeed in those whose nativity or question you do not have, you will adapt the house signifying the matter in the hour of the election or beginning. You even ought to adapt the 1st and 4th and the Lord of each in every election: the 1st and its Lord so that the person of him for whom you elect will be kept safe and guarded, the 4th and its Lord so that the matter may be perfected and its end may be good and praiseworthy.

And al-Rijāl said,[24] adapt the house signifying the matter for this reason: because one and the same sign can make diverse houses, which will have diverse significations according to the diversity of the regions; like if Aries were the 1st house in Toledo, at that same hour the same sign would be the 12th house in Forlì; and at the same hour (that is, of the time then) it would be the 11th house in Corinth or a little close by, and so on up to the end of the habitable earth, by diversifying the houses according to the diversity of longitudes, regions, and the distance between them, by giving to each one 770 *miliaria* (according to how the

---

[24] Perhaps referring to al-Rijāl (p. 302) and the doctrine of "removal." Bonatti may also be thinking of Sahl (see Tr. 6, Part 1, Ch. 1).

ancient sages measured the earth, or perhaps according to the measurement as it is contained in their books). Whence I do not put great emphasis [on this] except so you might see the method of the diversities of houses, so you might see what is signified by them according to the diversity of the regions, for the reason that what the same sign signifies in one land, one can signify in another one different from it. And thus it seems that elections are not to be avoided in every respect, even if nativities or questions are not always had.

And if someone had said that "if we always make the benefics strong and the malefics weak in elections, and one of the malefics is the significator of the nativity of him for whom we are electing, we will do the contrary of what we ought to do, and thus we are made contrary to him, when we ought to be useful to him." To which it can be responded that we ought to follow the footsteps of nature, which is always directed toward what is better; and *we* ought to be directed toward what is better. For it is better (if we do not know the nativities, nor do we have questions) that we adapt the benefics and weaken the malefics. Because the weakening of the benefics is worse than the weakening of the malefics. For if we weaken all the benefics, it is possible that nothing of the good would remain in the election. If however, we weaken all the malefics, we cannot weaken them without something of the good remaining in it. Because none of the malefics (even if one of them signifies good in the nativity) signifies good universally and everywhere; for, of the benefics, there are many which naturally and universally, always and everywhere signify good: like Venus, who always signifies concerning betrothals and the celebrations of weddings, and other things done by women in every hour, in every land, and the like; and the Moon, who has a signification in things done by mothers, and in all other actions of ours, as is said elsewhere; likewise the Sun concerning what is done of dignities; and Jupiter, who naturally, always, and everywhere, in each hour, and in every land, is the significator of substance. And so, always when we strengthen the benefics or the stars signifying what we intend, we preserve something of the good for him for whom we are electing, which does not happen to him with the malefics.

Moreover, the malefics are naturally two: namely Saturn and Mars. Indeed the benefics are naturally five: namely Jupiter, the Sun, Venus, Mercury, and the Moon.[25] Whence, since the benefics are greater in number than the malefics, it is proper that they should conquer in strength; and so we ought more to

---

[25] In Tr. 9, Part 2, Ch. 5, Bonatti states that Mercury is only accidentally a benefic.

consider much good, than to have fear about much evil.[26] And in this, they who say that we ought not to use elections, err: for just as is said elsewhere, an election cannot harm, but it can bring profit. For it is impossible but that in a good hour there is good, and in a bad one there is evil. For since we can discern the good from the bad, why can we not take up a good hour, and avoid a bad one?[27]

If someone wishing to go into battle (who perhaps is in haste to go), were to ask advice of you so that you might choose a good hour for him, or were he to ask that you see for him if the hour is good or not, and you were to see the significator badly disposed in that hour (so that if he were to go to battle then, he would be killed), and you saw another hour in which he could go without danger, and you did not tell him that he should not go then, and that he should await the hour in which he could go safely; or you were to tell him, "Go, because this hour will not harm you, if God wills," haven't you committed murder, if he were to go then and were killed?[28] You should know that, just as I tell you, if you denied advice to him, it is your fault. This is if he wanted to recompense you; otherwise he is blind[29] (for you would not have to serve him for free if he could recompense you).[30]

For an election can be strong, so that it by no means averts the evil of him whose nativity is unknown, nor [whose] question is had; [it is] true [that] even if evil were signified for him by the nativity or question, it could be turned away from him[31] through a strong election.

Likewise if some traveler asked of you, concerning one of three paths, which would be better and safer for him: in one of which it was said publicly that robbers never stayed there; indeed in another there were sometimes robbers; in the third, say, there were always robbers, and you were to tell him, "go through this path," (namely the one in which there were always robbers) "because you will not encounter robbers, if God wills," if he went through that path and was robbed, would you not have to make restitution to him for what he lost, when

---

[26] Omitting *non*, which would have read, "than to have fear about not much evil."

[27] Again, his main argument is not that every time is equally good, but that it is so easy to tell a good hour from a bad one, why not take advantage of the knowledge we have? But there is a tension here between his oft-stated claim that elections cannot create positive evil (but rather just fail to do good), and his claim that bad things happen in bad hours.

[28] This is an extension of the earlier theodicy: putting all actions down to God's will is irresponsible in the face of other knowledge.

[29] Reading *caecus* (as in 1491) for *secus* (as in 1550).

[30] In other words, people who want free advice should not complain if things go wrong.

[31] The Latin could also mean, "he could be turned away from it."

you could have informed him about the one in which it was said there never were robbers (through which, if he had gone, even if he had been robbed, you would not have had to make restitution)?

For an election operates according to "more" and "less": for if we were to elect for him whose nativitity we knew, or whose question we had, and the nativity or question signified something good for him in its root, and the election were to agree with one of them, it signifies good and a perfected end of that matter and of that effect; if however if one were to disagree with the other,[32] it subtracts the good. And if the nativity or question were to signify evil, and the election were to signify good, the election will subtract good things from the evil that the nativity or question signified; or perhaps it would destroy it wholly, just like a good antidote decreases or sometimes takes the entire harm of venom; and we sometimes see doctors give medicines to certain people growing sick unto death, and for whom hope is not had that they can escape; still it is possible that the virtue of the medicine is sometimes so great that nature is strengthened thence, and likewise the sick person is freed. And if the medicine did not free the sick person, at least it will not harm him; and thus a good hour always ought to be chosen.

Chapter 5: That an election ought to agree with the nature of the matter for which it is chosen

However, take care that your election agrees with the nature of the matter for which you elect: because the effects and impressions of the superior bodies are not naturally adapted, except by subjects fit to be able to take them up.[33] Nor can an election give something to any subject unless it is his own, and [unless] it pertains to him according to the natural order of his kind. For one cannot elect for a man such an hour which would make him fly, nor make him run like a hare or roebuck runs; nor even make him walk 500 or 1,000 *miliaria* in one day. But it must be elected for him only for those things which can be adapted to him according to the natural order. For the most high Artisan of the world has ordained a rank [or order] to every creature according to its nature, and according to what was appropriate for it; for every creature and every individual has so much power as its own natural form permits; for indeed virtue must

---

[32] I.e., (a) the election with (b) *either* the nativity or question.
[33] See Bonatti's long exposition on this point in Tr. 5 (141st Consideration).

answer to shape;[34] for nothing can have something through its own nature unless it can be given to him through that [nature], unless perhaps it is monstrous.

Therefore you should not elect something impossible for someone, because the laity, and even certain tunic-wearers, and practically everyone indifferently, strive to deride astrologers, and they think to deride them with unheard lies. Do not elect an hour for an eighty- or ninety-year old woman so that she may conceive, because her old age prohibits it. Do not elect for a boy of ten or twelve years that he may generate [children], because his age does not suffer it nor permits it. Do not elect for someone wishing to ride a little horse of two or three months, because its tenderness will not suffer it [to be ridden]. In like manner, that which nature denies, no one readily dares. Nor should you elect for someone wishing to sow grain on the plains of Italy in June or July; nor for someone wishing to sow beans or millet in Hungary or in Germany in the month of October or November, because the region or disposition of the air is not inclined to it. Nor even should you elect for someone wishing to sow seed on the seashore, because the place is not fit for that. For an agent will not produce but what proceeds from its nature. Do not elect for someone who does not know how to swim [but] who wants to throw himself into deep water, because he will be drowned. Do not elect for someone wishing to throw himself into a burning furnace, because he will be burned up. Do not elect for someone wishing to throw himself from a tall tower onto the ground, because his neck will be broken. Do not elect for a hermit wishing to do battle with a lion, because he will be torn to pieces. Do not elect for a weak person wishing to do battle with someone much stronger than him, or for a few people wishing to do battle with many, because they will succumb (for violence will come to virtue),[35] but you should elect for someone equal or a little weaker. For natural reason does not incline except toward those things to which it pertains naturally; however sometimes it is well chosen for few against many, and the few win; still however, that it sometimes happens is not [a reason] to take it up as a general rule. For it suffices for him for whom you are electing, if you elect for him

---

[34] *Figurae.* Bonatti is using this standard term for an astrological chart in order to draw a parallel: just as a human has certain capabilities on account of its shape (*figura*), so an election has certain possibilities for the native on account of the chart (*figura*) for the time elected. The next paragraph makes it clear that Bonatti is drawing an analogy between (a) natural abilities and impossible tasks, and (b) the natal chart and impossible elections.

[35] *Fiet violentia enim virtuti.* Perhaps Bonatti is assuming that the few have a just and virtuous reason to battle the many, and it would be cruel to elect a time for a battle, knowing that they would be slaughtered.

against [someone] one-fourth or one-third greater than him. If however from thence it were to suffice, the election will not be secure; because power often makes reason turn back. For indeed the supercelestial bodies do not do anything else except what was presented them by nature. For they are of eight kinds—since each planet is of its own particular kind, the fixed stars likewise are of their own particular kind. And it could even be said that each fixed star is of its own kind, and because the kinds are diverse, so are their operations and significations (even though they are equally incorruptible).

It is true however, that I have elected for a certain Viscount[36] Guido Novello of Tuscany against the Florentines, who expelled him from Florence, and leveled all his castles which he had in Tuscany, and polished off all of his goods—which for his part he had 3,200 soldiers and perhaps 13,000 foot-soldiers and 300 *ballista*[37] men; and his adversaries had 5,300 soldiers, and perhaps 12,000 foot-soldiers and 5,000 *ballista* men and more. And nevertheless we vanquished them and conquered them completely; and this was in the valley of Arbia in the open mountains;[38] nevertheless I first had it by a [horary] question that we were supposed to win, and then we had the most powerful election going to battle; and I knew about their going out through private heralds sent to it, which was bad (or rather, the worst).[39] You however ought to consider in all of your elections according to how the nature and the condition of every matter seems able to suffer to become such-and-so, and you will not err.

For it is necessary in this, so that your election perfects what you intend, and that he for whom you are electing comes to a good end of the matter. Work so that you adapt all these things which I tell you, if you can—clearly, the 1st and its Lord; also the 4th and its Lord; likewise both luminaries; the Part of Fortune also; and likewise the Lords of the domiciles[40] in which they[41] were; and the house signifying the matter for which you are electing, and its Lord, and the planet to which the Moon is first joined after your election or beginning; and the Lord of the fourth sign from the sign in which the Moon is (because it has participation in the signification of the end of the matter); and even the Lord of the fourth sign from the sign in which the Part of Fortune is; and the Lord of

---

[36] *Vice comiti.*

[37] A kind of medieval catapult.

[38] This was the battle at Montaperti, which took place on September 4, 1260. See Bonatti's biography in the Introduction.

[39] I.e., this means either that, despite having a good election and horary figure, the army of Bonatti's patron started out badly; or that the battle was very bloody despite their winning.

[40] Reading *domorum* for *dominorum.*

[41] I believe this means the two luminaries and the Part of Fortune.

the domicile in which the Lord of the sign in which the Moon is–as much in all of the aforesaid as in the buildings of cities or castles or houses, and the like.

Therefore when you wish to adapt some election, insofar as you wished to build a tower or castle, or whatever other thing you wished to begin, it is necessary that you become intent concerning the matter and concerning the person of him for whom you elect: because the 1st and its Lord are to be adapted for his person; and you even ought to adapt the 1st and its Lord, and the Moon, and the Part of Fortune to the matter which is begun, so that its end will be good. Whence if some matter were undertaken (whether it were a building or journey or something else), and the significators were well disposed for you or for him for whom you are electing, it will be good. If indeed they were all impeded, it will be the contrary. While if the Lord of the 1st and the Moon were impeded and the Part of Fortune were safe, it will be good for the matter for which the election is, but not for him whose matter it is; still however the virtue of the Part of Fortune will not be so great (even if he does profit) that it could defend the business without participating with them in the impediment.

On tearing down some building[42]

If however your election were such that you wanted to tear down some building (namely a house or a castle, or some such thing), its significators must be weakened, and particularly the Lord of the fourth, and the planet to which the Moon is joined (on account of the fact that it signifies what is going to happen concerning the matter), and above all other significators Mars is to be weakened because he signifies the reinstatement of the torn-down building; and especially to the contrary of him who destroys the building or causes it to be destroyed.[43] If however the intention of the one destroying were that it be a repetition [or reinstatement] or his intention were to destroy it easily and with speed, or perhaps it does not matter whether the destroyed building will be rebuilt or not, let the Moon be separated from a malefic, and joined to a benefic which is oriental and direct; or let her be joined to the Lord of the domicile[44] in which she is, by a trine or sextile aspect, descending in her own circle.

---

[42] The purpose of this section is to remind us that elections are also made to destroy (and not just to build up)–so sometimes we need to *weaken* significators.

[43] Bonatti's point seems to be that Mars will work to the disadvantage of the inceptor. So if the inceptor wants to tear down a building, Mars will work to make the building rebuilt after a while.

[44] In this Treatise, I will always speak of the Lord of the *domicile* the Moon is in. As we will see, Bonatti and his sources are clear that the Lord of the Moon's sign is meant.

Chapter 6: That the beginning of a matter does not exist before the matter is begun

Know even that the inception or beginning of some matter cannot exist before the matter is begun; nor does it exist after it is undertaken, but it is in the beginning of the matter itself just as I will tell you: not when the beginning is made, not when it is not made, it does not even exist when it is in becoming; but solely when it comes to be, just as when we build a tower or house or any other building when we seek durability and lay down the first stone, and we place it in the required location; and such a first laying-down can be said to be the beginning of the building or process of building.

Which if someone said that breaking ground or measuring was the beginning of the building, it does not seem right to me: because every beginning fixes the origin, or it is the inward [aspect] of the matter which we want to begin or intend. But the external is what is not of it: because sometimes someone can build without digging, like when we build in stone or the like; but without the first stone we can never build the thing which we wish to build or intend to. Therefore[45] it is the manifest positioning of the first stone, and the first stone itself, and its required location [which must] be the intrinsic beginning of the matter and of the building which we intend to make or begin, and of its act of building. Measuring and breaking ground however, although they are preparatory for building, still they are not *of* the building except in terms of the gathering together of stones and the scattering of lime, and the like. Nor however would I reproach you if you could adapt all things.

And if it were necessary to found the building that we want to build over timbers (just as sometimes happens in bridges and the like), where sometimes the beginning of the building cannot come to be with stones, adapt [the chart for] the first timber that is put into place in the foundation: it is the beginning of that building, because it is *of* the building.[46]

---

[45] There seems to be a verb missing (or perhaps simply implied), since the accusative is present throughout.

[46] Bonatti's discussion here mirrors a discussion of conception charts and nativities in Tr. 9, wherein he implies a similarity between conception charts and elections. His point is that the elected time must correspond to an action which already has the the beginning of the result *in it*. For example, the elected time for building a building should be when the first stone is laid, not when the blueprints are commissioned or a model of the site unveiled. Likewise, the election for conceiving a child should be the "falling of the seed into the womb," not earlier in the evening when a couple, say, begins their date.

When it is built without making a wall

And if the building were something else than walls, I make the beginning the setting into place of the first column in a pit that is made, because it is the final and completed placing, and the like.[47] And because it seems practically impossible to adapt so many significators as I have named to you, if you could not adapt them all, adapt the ones you can adapt, because you will not adapt few of them without them profiting your election, even if not as many as you would want: for if you could adapt them all, it would be a matter blessed in every respect; however it will be blessed according to the quantity of the significators which you had adapted.

Whence, if you could, adapt the 1st and its Lord, also the Moon and the Lord of the domicile in which she is, and the planet to which the Moon or the Lord of the 1st is joined, and the Part of Fortune and the Lord of the domicile in which you were to find it, and the planet signifying the matter which you intend to do, likewise the Lord of the hour.

And if you could not adapt all those, adapt the Lord of the 1st and the Moon and the planet signifying the matter, and the Lord of the hour.

If however you could not adapt these, adapt all [of the following] again: the Moon and the Lord of the hour.

Which if you could not do that, consider on what matter your election is: for if it were a journey or going out to hunt, and the like, then you will adapt the Lord of the hour more strongly than any other, and make the Moon cadent from the Ascendant, so that she is not in it nor aspects it. If however it were something other than a journey or a hunt, adapt the Moon just as you are able, and it will profit you in the matter which you intended to do or begin.

---

[47] *Illa de causa locatione ultimata et debita.*

If however someone had said that we ought not to prolong[48] elections as I said, when nearly all would seem to want to say otherwise than that, it can be responded to him, "Because the wise wanted to bless their elections that they be perfect in every respect; and they considered elections which someone could not always anticipate, until the significators could all be adapted as they said."[49] But we often do not have time to wait, whence it is necessary that we elect within the interval we have, and commingle what of the good we have in our election.

On the strengthening of the Sun

However, let it always be of concern to you to strengthen the Sun in durable matters as best you can, and especially [in those of] of nobles and magnates (of which mention is made elsewhere), [and] even in other elections in which you can adapt him. Nevertheless, as I touched on for you elsewhere, elections are diverse, obviously according to nobility, according to the time, according to the age, according to the place, according to the office or magistracy, [and] according to the nature and kind of the matter to be elected. However, for those whose nativities we know, or whose questions we have, we ought not to weaken one of the planets which has strength in the root of the nativity or the question of some one of them.

And al-Rijāl said[50] that these things agree in every beginning, except that for certain men we ought to put certain of the following which are not universally to be put in all of the others, because they are singled out for them, and they are practically necessary in their actions, as will now be explained to you.

Chapter 7: How diverse planets are adapted for diverse people

In elections for kings, the Sun is to be adapted, and the 10th and its Lord (nor do these concern those who accompany [them], but they concern the necessary and rooted things).[51] Because whether you like it or not, it is necessary

---

[48] *Elongare*, which can also mean "to remove, to be aloof." Bonatti is making his point in an awkward way here, because he is recommending we *not* wait too long or prolong the inceptor's election. But the remainder of the paragraph makes it clear what his view is.

[49] For example, Māshā'allāh and his colleages were assigned the election for the founding of Baghdad years ahead of time.

[50] This is based on al-Rijāl, p. 303; see list below in the next chapter.

[51] *Nec sunt ista de illis quae exequuntur, sed sunt de necessariis & radicalibus.* Meaning uncertain, but based on comments below he might be saying that the Sun will not tell us the outcome, but it

that you adapt these things in the affairs of kings, powerful men, and the like—that is, the affairs pertaining to the kingdom and other lay dignities; the Sun is even to be adapted for the Babylonians and the Eastern Romans.

For scribes and merchants Mercury is to be adapted, for he naturally signifies writings and minds, and such things on account of their convertibility; and the Indians, because his strength is in that land.

For boxers, glassbowers,[52] bakers, smiths,[53] and the like, Mars is to be adapted because he naturally signifies contentions and those things which operate by iron and fire; and the Western Romans, because his strength is in those parts.

For the secular religious, and merchants wishing to conduct business justly, Jupiter is to be adapted because he signifies substance and particularly what is acquired in a good way; and the people of Iraq,[54] because his strength is in the areas of Iraq.

For women, Venus is to be adapted because she naturally signifies the affairs of women; and the Arabs, because she naturally signifies that people, and her strength is in those areas.

For Jews, farmers, old men, the religious,[55] those dressed in black clothing, and the like, Saturn is to be adaped, on account of the heaviness of his motion; and the Ethiopians, because he signifies that people.

Whence, just as has often already been said to you, adapt those significators which you can, even if you cannot adapt all that you would wish for this, so that our election can increase what of the good, and decrease what of the evil, that we can—even if we cannot do whatever we want.

---

must be adapted because it pertains to the fact that the inceptor is *already* a king—hence it belongs to the "rooted" facts surrounding the inceptor, not the facts that ensue after the inception.

[52] *Becariis*.

[53] *Fabris*, literally "workers," those who work in metal, stone or wood.

[54] *Alirach*.

[55] Here, Bonatti means monks and other members of Orders (i.e., not the "secular" religious).

Indeed al-Rijāl said[56] that in all of our elections we ought to consider the Lord of the Ascendant, and the Moon, and make the significator of our matter the stronger of them; and he praised this because it signifies what would follow from the beginning. And he said if the Lord of the Ascendant were made fortunate (namely joined with the benefics), and it were weak (namely cadent from an angle or from the Ascendant), and the Moon were strong (namely in the angle of the Ascendant or in one succeeding the angle), in the 11th or the 5th, aspecting the Ascendant, and were made unfortunate (namely joined to the malefics), that we ought not to judge evil because of it: but rather we ought to judge good. Because he says that then the Moon has little participation in the matter. But if the Lord of the Ascendant were then strong, and were not made fortunate, great emphasis must be put on the Moon; but rather he says that sometimes we ought to make her unfortunate, that is, weaken her, and to make the Lord of the Ascendant fortunate, as in hunts.

Nevertheless, Sahl and 'Umar seem to say[57] that the Moon is to be made fortunate in hunts; but what al-Rijāl said[58] (that the Moon is to be made unfortunate), was peculiar to him. For he said when he understood "being made unfortunate," that is, being *weakened*, because every planet can be strong and unfortunate, weak and fortunate (just as is said elsewhere); and what he said, that she is put with the malefics, she can even be put with the malefics without misfortune; and there are certain malefics with which it is necessary for us to place [the Moon] in hunting; sometimes it is necessary for us even to weaken her *and* make her unfortunate (just as in the searching for fugitives, as will be said elsewhere). Wherefore others said that she is to be made *fortunate*, [but] they did not understand that she is to be *strengthened*.[59]

---

[56] This seems to be a paraphrase from al-Rijāl, p. 299.

[57] See Sahl, *On Elect.*, Ch. 42, "An election on going out to a hunt."

[58] Bonatti's paraphrase of al-Rijāl is odd here: al-Rijāl says (p. 300) the Moon is evil or bad (*mala*) in *journeys*, and that she should be put in a place fitting for her so that she might make the Ascendant fortunate by aspect. The middle portion concerning "being made unfortunate," does not come from any definitional statement I have found in al-Rijāl. The latter portion, where Bonatti speak of planets being fortunate even when with the malefics, may derive from al-Rijāl, p. 301.

[59] In this awkward passage, Bonatti is trying to harmonize the texts by making two type of distinctions. The first distinction is that between a planet being (a) strong or weak and (b) being made fortunate or unfortunate (say, through aspects with the benefics or malefics). In this case he wants us to be careful about the condition we are trying to put a planet in. But he is also trying to distinguish between what is fortunate or unfortunate for a *planet's* effectiveness, and what is fortunate and unfortunate *for us*. For example, in trying to catch a thief (who is signified by the Moon), we want to make the Moon both weak and unfortunate, because it will slow down the fugitive and force him to make mistakes–but this is good *for us*, since we

Chapter 8: What kind of end may be hoped for concerning the matter which we begin

Indeed Abū Ma'shar said[60] that, moreover, so that we may know the end of our election, it is necessary for us to consider five things. And he made the first of them the Lord of the 4th; not, so to speak, like the preceding, but as something more dignified,[61] because it signifies the end, and the end is more dignified than the beginning. He made the second one the Lord of the sign in which the Moon is. And if the Moon were then in Cancer, she will be considered then (namely after the Lord of the 4th). And he made the third one the planet to which the Moon will first be joined in the first conjunction which she will have made with one of the planets after the matter is undertaken. He made the fourth the Lord of the domicile or sign in which the Part of Fortune is. He made the fifth, the fourth sign from the sign in which the Moon then was. And (as al-Rijāl said) a certain person wanted it that the Lord of the 4th from the place of the Part of Fortune be added.[62] But because all of these cannot be easily adapted at one and the same time, therefore I told you them. And even though the Lord of the 4th naturally signifies the end of the matter which someone wants to begin (whether it is a journey or something else) it sometimes happens that it does not signify the end, whence it is necessary for you to look for another. For example, the Lord of the 1st signifies the matter as one preceding the other significators; and beyond all the others (as I said) the Lord of the 4th looks toward its end—namely if it were to aspect the 4th. Whence, [if] some journey was undertaken, or some building, *etc.*, [if] the Lord of the 4th aspects the 4th, the end of the matter is sought only from it. But if it does not aspect the 4th, it is sought from the Lord of the domicile in which the Moon is; which if it were to aspect the Moon, it signifies the end of the matter; if not, not; wherefore then, [seek] the end of the matter from the planet to which the Moon will first be joined after the matter is undertaken (if she is joined, I say to some [planet] or seeks the conjunction of one). If however she were solitary, so that she would be joined

---

want to catch him, and it is good to catch thieves. These distinctions are key in elections, because the conditions we put the planets in are driven by the goal of the election. See also Ch. 12 below.

[60] These five points are found in al-Rijāl, p. 300; but al-Rijāl attributes them to "a certain portion of the wise."

[61] *Non tamquam praecedentem, sed tamquam digniorem.* I am not exactly sure what sort of contrast Bonatti is drawing.

[62] Al-Rijāl, p. 300.

to no one, nor would she seek the conjunction of another, seek then the end of the matter from the planet in whose domicile the Part of Fortune is; which if it were to aspect [the Part], it will be the significator of the end of the matter; if not, not. The signification will remain then upon the Moon and the Lord of the domicile in which she is; and he will be stronger than her in the participation, and even all the aforesaid significators will participate in such a participation, and the Lord of the 1st with them. But he (namely the Lord of the domicile in which the Moon is) will be more authoritative than all.

And al-Rijāl said[63] that if the signification were given by the Lord of the fourth sign from the place of the Part of Fortune, that it would be [counted as] less than all the others. And he said that if the Moon were joined corporally to some planet in the sign in which she is, degree by degree, that he will be the significator of the end of the matter, whether he has dignity there or not; and he will be preferred to the Lord of the sign in which the Moon is; wherefore if you were to find it so, then consider the participation of the aforesaid significators with the planet to which the Moon is joined corporally in the sign in which she is, degree by degree, and it reverts back to the Lord of the 1st (just as it seemed to al-Kindī),[64] because [the Lord of the 1st] signifies the querent or inceptor, and what happens to him from the beginning of the matter. And the Lord of the sign in which it is, signifies what happens to him from it in the middle. And if [the Lord of the 1st] were in his own domicile, he will signify the middle as well as the beginning. And the Lord of the sign in which he in whose domicile the Lord of the 1st is,[65] signifies of what sort the end of the matter is, and what happens to the inceptor from thence. Whence, see what kind of condition these three are in, and judge about the condition of the matter according to that, in each one of the aforesaid times.[66]

---

[63] I have not found all of this information in al-Rijāl. The sentences below about the significators that indicate the beginning, middle and end of matters are similar to a passage in al-Rijāl (p. 299), but Bonatti lists different significators. In al-Rijāl they are (a) the Ascendant, (b) the Lord of the Ascendant, (c) the Lord of the Lord of the Ascendant. Al-Rijāl also gives alternatives involving the Part of Fortune and the place of the matter itself. Bonatti may be referring to 'Ali al-'Imrānī.

[64] Source unknown.

[65] In other words, (a) the Lord of the 1st signifies what happens to the inceptor at the beginning; (b) his dispositor signifies the middle; and (c) that planet's dispositor in turn, signifies what happens to the inceptor at the end. If (a) is in his own domicile, he will be (b) as well. Bonatti does not say what planet would count as (c) in such a case, nor is he clear whether or not he is merely reporting or endorsing al-Kindī's position.

[66] I.e., the beginning, middle, and end.

However, our sages wanted to adapt so many significators (if what they said were possible), that we would have perfected all of our business to our liking. However, we cannot adapt all things as we can *say* they are to be adapted; nor do we always have the convenience of waiting as long as we are able to adapt them in that way: because perhaps for the whole time of our life we are not able to make one perfect election which lacks none of the aforesaid. Therefore it is necessary that we adapt our elections as well as we can; and if we cannot have everything that we want, we still might have something better than we can have, so that our labor is not more frustrated. Because just as our reverend predecessor Abū Ma'shar said (who was better in this art than any Latins were, [and] who studied in Athens, where study flourished),[67] as he confessed in a certain book of his, it is impossible for us to adapt the twelve houses, because the malefics cannot be removed from the sky; whence it is necessary for us to adapt those things which we can adapt, and do what we can of the good. And observe the method which I told you above in adapting the significators which you can adapt; and by doing thusly you will obtain the usefulness which someone can pursue from elections.

And al-Rijāl said[68] that the adaptation of the house [domicile?] of the end of the matter (namely the 4th) is very necessary, after you have adapted the other rooted matters (namely the Lord of the 1st, and the Moon, the Lord of the 10th, and the Part of Fortune). And he said that these are of the body of the inceptor. And the planet signifying the matter which someone intends to begin, and the house [domicile?] of that same matter, and the Lord of that domicile, signify whether the matter will be perfected–and therefore he said they are to be adapted.

Chapter 9: How a sign should be adapted

'Ali said[69] that we ought to adapt the sign signifying the matter which we intend to do or begin, and that its adaptation is when every impediment is

---

[67] Apparently Bonatti thought, on the basis of Abū Ma'shar's exposure to Greek philosophy, that he had studied in Athens. That is an odd claim to make–why and how would a Persian Muslim study, or be allowed to study, at a city in the Byzantine empire that was no longer the seat of the philosophical schools?

[68] I have not found this passage in al-Rijāl, but it is possibly a paraphrase of pp. 300 or 304. At any rate, it is a general enough statement about elections.

[69] This does not seem to be a direct quote from al-Rijāl, but rather a general statement with which he would obviously agree.

removed from it. That is, when it is free from the malefics and their square or opposite aspects; nor is it besieged by the two malefics or by their rays, but it is cleansed[70] of them; and in this way the sign will signify good. And it will signify a greater good if there were some benefic or its rays in it; and better than that if they were to aspect it by a trine or sextile aspect. And if many benefics were in it, or were to aspect it, [then] however more there were, by that much more will its signification for good be increased.

And he said that if the sign were made fortunate as was said, that even if it were cadent from an angle or were besieged by malefics, it could not be impeded for that reason; and if it were impeded a little, the impediment will be as though it harms a middling amount or not at all. But if the benefics were to aspect the sign by a square aspect or from the opposition, he said that it will not bring as much profit–and that is true.

And he said that if benefics and malefics were to aspect it, or they were in it at one and the same time, that the virtue of each one is to be commingled; and concerning the goodness or badness of that sign, it is judged according to the multitude of the strengths of the benefics or malefics.

If however the benefics and malefics were to aspect or be in it in equal amounts, one must speak about it as if there is no benefic or malefic in it. And if the planet who was to aspect it, or who was in it, were to have some dignity there, it will be good: because if it were a benefic it will increase the good; if it were a malefic, it will decrease the malice.

And he said that the Lord of that sign is to be adapted so that it has two significations there, namely one by the rulership[71] which it has in it, the other from the good place in which [the Lord] is.

Chapter 10: How a planet should be adapted

'Ali said[72] that the adaptation of a planet is [that] about which nothing evil is said,[73] and from which every impediment is removed, but it is so that it is cleansed of the malefics (namely from their conjunctions and aspects), and so

---

[70] The language of being "clean" and "cleansed" of impediments by the malefics, comes from Sahl and will be used much by Bonatti in this Treatise.

[71] *Dominio.*

[72] I have not found this passage in al-Rijāl, perhaps it is al-'Imrānī.

[73] *Aptatio Planetae est de quo nihil mali dicitur.* I think Bonatti simply means that the criteria for adapting a planet are more strict, with fewer negative factors being allowed, than when adapting a sign.

that it is direct, not retrograde; nor combust, nor cadent; nor in a sign that is cadent[74] or impeded in another way; nor weak by any other means. Which if it were so disposed, it strengthens and makes fortunate the matter which we want to do or begin, and the place signifying the matter and its end (if it were its significator, whether it were a benefic or not); and in every place it is and in every sign, the beginning, middle, and end of the matter will always be blessed. And if it were cleansed of the malefics, and disposed as was said, and strong and in a good place, it is said to be in the perfection of goodness. However if one of the benefics were to support it, it is said to increase its perfection. And if the aspect of that benefic were in front, it will be better again; if indeed it were from behind it does not increase as much, even though it does increase. If however one of the malefics were to aspect it, it subtracts something of its goodness from it, and it subtracts more if it were to aspect from in front rather than from behind.[75]

And if we were to adapt the sign and planets which signify the matter which we want to begin (as was said), our election and its hour will be good and perfect, according to how the sign or the planet were adapted. And it is even appropriate, if it can be done, that the sign and planet (or at least one of them) from which we take the signification, agree in nature with the matter which we wish to begin. That is, if we wish to elect for doing some matter in water or by water, or next to water (like going fishing, sailing, building boats, building a mill-house, digging wells, and the like), that we ought to adapt a watery sign and a wet planet, or one signifying wetness. And if the election were in earth or by means of earth, that we ought to adapt an earthy[76] sign and a planet which is more fitting for it–like when hunting by land, digging a ditch, dragging stones or rocks from a mine,[77] or building walls which they do not want to be greatly elevated above the earth, and the like. And if the election were on matters which pertain to the air, or which come to be in it, like hunting birds with birds (like with hawks, falcons, *ziri*,[78] hawks, and the like), or if we wished to build a

---

[74] Here Bonatti distinguishes between a cadent sign and a cadent planet. Could this distinction play a role in the historical transition to the use of quadrant houses for topics?

[75] I believe that "in front" means "in a later degree," so that the planet is moving towards the degree of the exact aspect by direct motion (and therefore closer to the benefic or malefic influences); "from behind" means "in an earlier degree," so that the planet is moving away from the exact aspect by direct motion. Probably the opposite would be true if the planet were retrograding: moving toward the degree of the exact aspect makes the influence stronger, moving away from it makes it weaker.

[76] Reading *terreum* for *tertium*.

[77] *De suis mineris.*

[78] Unknown word, but undoubtedly a kind of bird.

windmill, or other buildings greatly elevated (which pertain to the air), or the like, we must adapt an airy sign and a planet which agrees more with it. And if our election were on matters which pertain to fire or which operate by fire or with fire, we must adapt a fiery sign, and a planet agreeing with it–like electing for smiths or bakers, and the like.

And if it were a matter for which we elect, which we want to be perfected quickly, we will have to adapt a sign which agrees with quickness and with a matter which we do not want to be prolonged (namely a movable one), like in betrothals to women (because we want to celebrate the wedding quickly); and in works which we want to write[79] so that an action that is undertaken is perfected quickly; and in the seeding and planting of vines, and in the selling of wine *ad minutum*,[80] and in all of those things whose quickness we desire, and which we want to be perfected quickly.

And if it were an election such that we wanted to do something with quadrupedal animals, it is necessary that a quadrupedal sign be adapted, according to the species of the animal, and we make it the house signifying that animal: like if we wished to buy cows or other larger animals which have cloven hooves, or [we wanted] to do something with them like taming or castrating them, or something else which pertains to dealing with them, we would adapt the 12th and make it the sign signifying the aforesaid animals (if we can), like Taurus and the last half of Sagittarius. And if we wished to so something with small animals, we must adapt the 6th, and make it a quadrupedal sign signifying those animals, like dogs and birds with which we hunt; and even other birds and the like: such as Aries [and] Capricorn, which signify small animals with cloven hooves, and especially in smaller quadrupeds with cloven hooves, as are pigs, sheep, goats, and he-goats. And we can even attribute these same small cloven hooved [animals] to the 12th house when we do things with them, especially in selling them: because then they are signified by the 6th, just as other small ones are signified by the 12th: horses, mules, and donkeys, as was said elsewhere.[81]

And if you wished to go out hunting animals with cloven hooves, like deer, roe, and the like, one of those signs of cloven hooved [animals] would have to be made the house signifying a hunt [the 7th]. And if he were going out after other animals striking with their claws or teeth, like lions, bears, wolves, and the like, one of those signs which signify those animals would have to be made the

---

[79] I am not sure what Bonatti means by this.

[80] This seems to be an idiom: lit. "to the minute." *Minutus* generally means something very small. It could mean selling wine directly after it is bottled.

[81] I am unclear about what distinction Bonatti is trying to draw here.

house, if it could be done. But their Lords are not to be strengthened in a hunt, but it is better that they be weakened, as will be said below in its own proper place.

Al-Rijāl even said we ought to adapt Aries and Leo and Sagittarius in the actions of kings and magnates, because they are suited to them—and that is true.[82] Because that triplicity is more noble than the rest of the triplicities by reason of action, just like fire is the more noble element among the elements on account of its action; and because the lion is the stronger between these three animals, [Leo] is deservedly to be preferred in matters of kings on account their excellence among other humans. Aries is to be put second after him because among the other [fire] signs it is the first. Indeed Sagittarius is to be put last, because [this] last one in the triplicity is less strong in heat, on account of its dual form. Whence always if we can do it, one of those signs is to be made the Ascendant in the affairs of kings (where the Ascendant would be suitable to them), or the 10th (where the 10th is suitable to them). Likewise if we can, we must put in them the significators of the matters to be elected (provided they are not weakened by that for some other reason[83]): like the Lord of the 1st, and the Moon, and the place signifying the matter, and likewise the planet signifying it.

And al-Rijāl said[84] that the domiciles of the planets signify the same as their Lords—like the domiciles of Saturn, which signify obscurity and profundity [or depth] just like Saturn; [and] the domiciles of Jupiter, which signify goodness and honesty like Jupiter; likewise the domiciles of Mars, which signify wars and contentions just like Mars; [and] the domiciles of Venus, which signify games and gladness just like Venus; likewise the domiciles of Mercury, which signify writing and philosophy just like Mercury; [and] the domiciles of the luminaries, which signify loftiness and clarity just like the luminaries. For these, when they can become so, belong to the increasers of good and fortune, namely when it is the Lord of the house signifying the matter, signifying what its domicile does—or at least the planet should be the same nature with the sign. Which if it were not possible that a planet be of the same nature as the house signifying the matter, it should be of the nature of the Ascendant or its Lord, or it should signify the same as either one of them, or at least they should aspect with a praiseworthy aspect.

---

[82] Al-Rijāl, p. 303.

[83] *Ex hoc alia de causa.*

[84] This passage is based on a brief statement by al-Rijāl, p. 299.

It should even be watched out for with extreme diligence, in every election and in every beginning, if it can be done, that the nature of the Ascendant and that of its Lord not be contrary to the nature of the domicile[85] signifying the matter or its Lord. It is even good when the Lord of the hour is of the *haym* of the Ascendant, or at least of its Lord, if it can be so, and by however many of the significators are of the *haym* of the Ascendant or its Lord, or of the *haym* of the house signifying the matter, or of its Lord, by that much it will be better.[86]

Likewise effort should be made that a masculine significator of a matter be in a masculine sign; and if it were feminine, that it be in a feminine sign.

And if it were a durable matter, the end of which is not expected, nor does the inceptor wish that it be ended quickly, let the Ascendant be Taurus or Leo or Scorpio or Aquarius, and the Lord of the Ascendant and the Moon and the Lord of the house [domicile?] signifying the matter, and the Lord of the hour, and the Part of Fortune, and the Lord of its house [domicile?]–be in fixed signs. And if all of these could not be in fixed signs, let there be as many of them as can be: because all of these act for a good condition of the matter.

If however it were a matter which someone did not want to last a long time, let the Ascendant be Aries, Cancer, Libra, or Capricorn, and [let] its Lord be in such a sign, and let the Moon and the house signifying the matter be a movable sign, or [let] its Lord be in a movable sign, if it can be so.

If indeed it were a matter which someone wanted to be changed or shifted or repeated, like business partnerships and sharings, and the purchasing of things whose sale we desire, just like negotiators [or businessmen] or the like do, let the Ascendant be Gemini or Virgo or Sagittarius or Pisces.

It is even good if we can make (along with the other adaptations) the Ascendant one of the signs of direct ascension: because they help the matter, and particularly in the pursuit of truth when we want to investigate it.

And if you can put the Moon or the other significators in those signs which I have named for you, it will be good.

And make it likewise that the Lord of the domicile (or of the exaltation or two of the lesser dignities) in which the Moon is, aspect the Moon (or any of the

---

[85] I say "domicile" instead of "house," since domiciles (signs) have natures like the planets do, while houses *per se* do not.

[86] Al-Rijāl (p. 93) defines being in the "haiz of the Ascendant" as being "on [its] side" (*in parte*). Likewise he says a planet can be in the *haiz* of any angle, apparently by being on the hemisphere of the chart that the angle is on (i.e., above the horizon would undoubtedly be in the *haiz* of the 10th). But Bonatti could understand this to mean "of the same gender" of the Ascendant or its Lord, or even that they should be of the same sect.

significators you can) by a trine or sextile aspect, or at least by a square with reception; or at least let the Lord of the bound aspect her or one of the other significators. And if it did not aspect the Moon, it will be better that it aspect the Sun [rather] than one of the other significators. And if he who were to aspect the Moon (or the Sun or one of the aforesaid significators) were in a place which is aspected by the Lord of the domicile or exaltation in which it is, it will be better, and then its aspect to the Moon or Sun will profit more.

And let the Part of Fortune or its Lord be in the house [domicile?] signifying the matter which we want to do, or let one of them be in the 1st or the 10th or in the 11th; and let the angles be fixed (and particularly in matters which we want to last a long time), and let them not be removed: because they stand in the way of its durability. And if it were to happen that they were removed from the angles, let the Lord of one sign be aspecting the other. Like if Pisces were ascending by 28°, and Taurus is the second house by 3°,[87] this angle would be of only two planets, namely of Jupiter and Mars:[88] namely of Jupiter through the direct circle by equal degrees, and of Mars by the oblique one and by degrees of ascension.[89] Whence if Jupiter and Mars were to aspect each other, the removal of the angles will not harm, but the aspect will be good and perfecting; and more strongly and better if they (or at least one of them) were to aspect the 1st house. And if they were to aspect each other or were to aspect the 1st house from an angle, it will signify (if the election were for some magistracy or dignity or office, from which fame or honor is expected) exaltation and glory and a great name and loftiness. If however the Lords of these signs did not aspect each other, then you will consider the virtues of both of the signs, and you will say that Mars and Jupiter are participators of the election which you have made.

You will even consider the fixed stars (namely of those which signify fortune and the good), and you will see if you can put one of those which I have named for you in the Treatise on revolutions in the degree of the 1st house, or in the 10th or 11th, or in the degree of the house signifying the matter which we wanted to elect: the good will be increased beyond the other significators, and more

---

[87] Here Bonatti is obviously using quadrant houses, because he is allowing for an intercepted sign. Taurus could not be the "second domicile."

[88] Here is an indication that Bonatti, like Morinus, accepts the Lord of an intercepted sign to be a co-ruler of that house's matter.

[89] I.e., Pisces (the domicile of Jupiter) is the Ascendant as calculated from the right ascension of the Midheaven (standard practice), but due to the latitude of the place, Aries (the domicile of Mars) would be intercepted and Taurus the cusp of the 2nd quadrant house.

strongly and better than this is if it were of the nature of the planet signifying the matter.

Chapter 11: Again on the same topic

Again, Abū Ma'shar (who of all the other astrologers, except for Ptolemy and Hermes, was perspicuous in his judgments, and even more eloquent than them all) laid out more instructions for us.[90] And he said that if we wanted to elect something (whether it were a pilgrimage or something else), and we found its Lord (or the Lord of its exaltation) in the sign signifying the matter[91] to be elected, and it were strong (that is, free from impediments), we should not have any suspicion about the matter. Or let one of the luminaries be there, and if it is received it will be better than it could be otherwise. And [if] any one of the benefic planets were in it, it will be good and useful (nor is it to be of concern whether it has dignity there or not); likewise if a malefic were there which has dignity there (free from the aforesaid impediments). And he said that the Sun and the Moon should be received, provided that the Ascendant is not the sign of the detriment of one of them.

And al-Kindī said[92] the Moon is not to be put in the Ascendant, because she is contrary to it; but he allowed the Sun to be put in it, because he is not contrary to it: because he is of its nature, and he uncovers hidden matters and reveals them, just as the Ascendant uncovers and manifests for us those things which were covered and hidden below the horizon; and the Sun divides things joined together, and reveals secrets. And [al-Rijāl] said that in the case of the Moon, the opinion of Abū Ma'shar is more fitting and suitable to the sayings of Ptolemy than the opinion of al-Kindī; and [al-Rijāl] said that according to [Abū Ma'shar] the Moon is hot and wet[93] (just like Venus). And Abū Ma'shar testified to this where he speaks about pilgrimages.[94] And [al-Rijāl] said that Māshā'allāh and his associates prohibited the Moon from being put in the Ascendant for pilgrimages.[95] And [al-Rijāl] said that Abū Ma'shar did not assent to the sayings

---

[90] *Elargavit nobis magis habenas.*
[91] Here is an example showing that (for older authorities at least), *signs* signify the matter in elections, because we identify the *sign* with the *house.*
[92] The following statements are a paraphrase of al-Rijāl, p. 299-300.
[93] Reading *humida* for *fortuna*, following al-Rijāl's text, p. 300.
[94] Perhaps inferring from al-Rijāl's discussion, p. 300.
[95] Perhaps inferring from al-Rijāl's discussion, p. 300.

of Māshā'allāh in this.[96] And [al-Rijāl] said that they judged the Moon to be cold and wet, and the Ascendant hot, and therefore they were not suitable together. And he said (and it is true, as is said elsewhere) that she signifies concerning the beginning, and especially concerning the beginning of a pilgrimage; and therefore they said that she ought to be put in a place suitable for her, which I believe to be the 10th or 11th or 3rd or 5th (even though they did not specify the place).[97] And [al-Rijāl] said that they said the Sun was not to be put in the Ascendant, because the Sun is a malefic in the conjunction and prevention; and he said that many disagreed with their opinion.[98]

And[99] al-Rijāl said[100] if one of the benefics were in the Ascendant, not impeded and favorable, it will be very good. And he stated that which 'Umar al-Tabarī recommended more,[101] like when a benefic is in the first one-third of the house of the Ascendant, because he said it hastens the matter. However, he said that it seemed to him that if a benefic were in the first ascending degree, or a little bit after the rising degree, that it would be better and makes the Ascendant more fortunate. Nevertheless, that which 'Umar said, he did not say for any other reason except what happens most rarely, that a planet might be found in the ascending degree, and therefore he made more of its strength to be in the first one-third of the Ascendant rather than in the other two-thirds, nor however did he deny but that the ascending degree is stronger than the others. What al-Rijāl said about the ascending degree itself, he said for greater certitude and security. [As for] those who said the Sun is not to be put in the Ascendant,[102] their intention was [concerning] when he was malefic (and that would always be when he were joined to some [planet] corporally, or when he is in the opposition of some planet by 5° before the degree of the opposition or 2°

---

[96] Al-Rijāl also adds that he himself joins Māshā'allāh and al-Kindī against Abū Ma'shar and Ptolemy. Al-Rijāl accuses Abū Ma'shar of inconsistency, because in natal delineations of longevity, Abū Ma'shar says that the Moon "cuts off and abolishes life in the Ascendant" (probably by primary directions).

[97] According to al-Rijāl (p. 300), she ought to be put "in a place suitable for her, so that she makes the Ascendant fortunate by aspect," but he does not specify the aspect.

[98] Al-Rijāl says, "Those who shun the Sun in the Ascendant or in the house of the matter, say that the Sun is a misfortune in conjunction and oppostion; nor do all agree in this matter." Bonatti exaggerates this point because he disagrees with it–al-Rijāl does not say that "many disagree," only that "not all agree."

[99] Now Bonatti tries to harmonize the authorities, saying their apparently absolute statements were really conditional ones.

[100] This is probably based on al-Rijāl, p. 299.

[101] Cite unknown.

[102] Al-Rijāl, p. 300.

after). Whence, in order to avoid all impediment by him, they put him elsewhere rather than in the Ascendant.

This thing that al-Kindī said, [that] the Moon is not to be put in the Ascendant, and what Māshā'allāh likewise said[103]–their intention was for journeys and pilgrimages, because the Moon is naturally impeded by the Full Moon from before [it] up to the conjunction; and even before the Full Moon by 15°. For in those 15° she is impeded on account of her opposition. From the earlier opposition[104] up through the third quarter she is impeded on account of the dryness which flourishes in her then. And from the [end of the] third quarter up to the conjunction of the Sun she is impeded on account of coldness, and then she is not to be put in the Ascendant of a journey, because it afflicts the body of the journeyer. Whence for this reason they avoided putting her in the Ascendant (and so they would avoid all of her impediment, and so that perhaps occasionally elections would not be deceived in this).

[Concerning the fact] that al-Rijāl and Abū Ma'shar had praised the saying of Ptolemy (namely that the Moon is to be put in the Ascendant)[105] because she is hot like Venus: it is true that Venus (even though she is judged cold and wet), still has a certain hidden heat, which appears in the fact that Venus signies delights, gladness, and games: and these are not without an admixture of heat. Likewise the Moon has a hidden heat, and she even has it according to what is manifest: she has a hidden one like Venus, [and] she has a manifest one, because when she is in her first half, she is in the nature of wetness; in the second half, in the nature of heat, according to the Philosopher;[106] and therefore those who put her in the Ascendant acknowledged it, [and they], considering that heat and wetness are more noble than cold and dryness, and more harmonious with the operations of nature, they wanted them to be more able to bring profit than coldness and dryness could harm. Whence they did not put emphasis on that impediment but they they put her in the Ascendant.

Even though I will have told you elsewhere, still thus far I recall to your memory, [that] if you can adapt all the things which the wise told you, it would be the ultimate good in your elections–which seems to me something practically impossible. But if you could not adapt all that you want at one time, adapt those which you can; however, at least adapt the Moon; and if you cannot adapt her,

---

[103] Al-Rijāl, p. 300.
[104] That is, from the time of the Full Moon which has just occurred.
[105] But al-Rijāl does not agree with Abū Ma'shar and "Ptolemy" (see above).
[106] Bonatti undoubtedly means Ptolemy.

make her cadent from the Ascendant, and adapt at least the Lord of the hour, and it will be some help to you in your matter.

There are even other certain things which increase fortune and prosperity and the good–namely the degree of the conjunction and the degree of the prevention which was before your inception or the election which you wanted to make: like if it is made fortunate and cleansed of the malefics and their aspects (if you can do this), and its Lord. The place of the conjunction is the degree in which the Sun and Moon were joined together. Indeed the place of the prevention is the degree (and its minute) of the luminary which was above the earth in the hour of the prevention. And if one luminary were in the eastern degree and the other in the western degree, the degree of the prevention will be that which is in the east.

For al-Kindī said[107] the conjunction has signification over all things which come to be between the conjunction and the prevention; and the prevention has signification over all things which come to be between the prevention and the conjunction; and therefore it is necessary that, in every beginning, nativity, and in every election, if it is possible, it be adapted and the place of the conjunction or prevention be considered, so that we may know whether it is in an angle or in one following [the angle], or in one cadent from an angle, and which of the planets may be in the very degree of the conjunction or prevention, or, of the benefics or malefics, or of the aspects, [which is] in the same sign in which the conjunction or prevention was; and who they are which aspect that degree by any aspect, and likewise the Lord of the degree of the conjunction or prevention: like if it is under the rays of the Sun, or it is in its own light.[108] These are the things which signify what is going to be concerning the things which come to be between the conjunction and prevention, and between the prevention and the conjunction: which if they were sound, they signify the perfection of matters and their goodness, if indeed they were impeded, they will signify their weakness and instability.

It must even be considered lest the Moon be joined to malefics when she is separated from the degree of the conjunction or prevention; but let her [rather] be joined to benefics, and let the degree of the conjunction or prevention be with benefics in any angle. The Moon should even be going toward the conjunction of the benefics in the hour of the conjunction or the prevention, if

---

107 Based on al-Rijāl, pp. 300-301.
108 This undoubtedly is al-Qabīsī's sense of being in one's "own light," i.e., having gone out of the Sun's beams and not yet joined to any other planet. See Tr. 3, Part 2, Ch. 6.

it can be done:[109] because these will signify the exaltation and goodness of matters, and perfection and a praiseworthy end.

If however the place of the conjunction or prevention were impeded, and the Moon were joined to malefics after [her] separation from one of those two places, it signifies that even if the beginning of matters which were made within those times is praiseworthy, still its end will be evil; and the conjunction of the Moon with the planets is stronger than the degree of the conjunction or the prevention is. Whence if she were joined to benefics after [her] separation from those places, even though one of those places might be in an angle with the malefics, even if the beginning of the matters were not praiseworthy, still the end would be praiseworthy and good. If however the place of the conjunction or prevention were with the malefics, as was said, and the Moon were joined to malefics when she was separated from [the places], it signifies the beginning, middle, and end of the matters to be unpraiseworthy and evil, unless the Lord of the sign in which the conjunction or prevention was, were oriental in an angle, and in its own domicile or exaltation or triplicity or bound; or [if] it were to aspect that domicile;[110] because if it were so, it will break all the malice of the others; because it has greater virtue in matters which come to be in the aforesaid times than any one of the aforesaid significators does. Indeed if it were in one succeeding the angle, even if perhaps the beginning of the matter were weak, still its end will flourish and it will be good. If however it were occidental[111] or outside of its own aforesaid dignities, or cadent from an angle, or did not aspect that domicile, it will increase the malice of the others, and matters will become worse. And if the place of the conjunction were cadent from an angle, the matters which were undertaken in that conjunction or prevention will be evil and of no usefulness. All of this is referred back to the intention of al-Kindī,[112] but his intention was not unconditional, but it was so that we might make[113] a good election; and [so] those things which he said[114] were all well disposed, so that he said that the election will be aided thence, and the matter undertaken will

---

[109] These sorts of considerations remind one that some elections must be (or could be) planned out months in advance.

[110] I.e., the sign in which the conjunction or prevention was.

[111] I suspect this could refer to the "pertaining-to-sinking" version of occidentality, not "rising after the Sun."

[112] According to al-Rijāl, p. 300.

[113] Reading *fecerimus* for *fecerim*.

[114] Reading *dixit* for *dixerint*.

come to a better and quicker end.[115] And if they were not well disposed, [he said] that they will subtract something of the good, but will not be able to destroy the beginning of a well-elected matter; and if the election were bad, and it was poorly disposed, that the evil will be increased, and will come to pass more quickly.

And al-Rijāl[116] said what obviously increases the good is when we adapt the place of the Lord of the Quarter of the year in every election, just as was said about the place of the conjunction or the prevention. However he said that the adaptation of the place of the conjunction or prevention in this work is more appropriate than the adaptation of the Lord of the Quarter of the year; and the adaptation of the Lord of the Quarter is prior to the adaptation of the Lord of the Year of the world; however he said that we could adapt all of them that are not evil.

Indeed Abū Ma'shar said[117] if the Lord of the election were the Lord of the sign of the Moon in the revolution of the year, or the Lord of the Ascendant of the year were made fortunate in the hour of the election and of the revolution, it will signify the increase of the inceptor's honor, and a praiseworthy end to the matter undertaken. And he said[118] if the Lord of the Ascendant of the year did not testify in either one of the places of the luminaries, nor the place of the Midheaven, the matters undertaken will be low and middling and minute.[119]

Indeed al-Tabarī said (as al-Rijāl reports)[120] if the place of the conjunction or prevention, and its Lord, were in a praiseworthy place,[121] the matter (namely which was begun then) will be durable and firm. And likewise if someone were

---

[115] This interpretation of Bonatti's may refer to al-Rijāl's own summary (pp. 300-01), where he says that we ought to try to elect as many of the appropriate Lords as we can.

[116] Al-Rijāl, pp. 300-01. To summarize: the Lord of the syzygy is strongest, the mundane Lord of the Quarter of the year is next strongest, the mundane Lord of the Year is least strongest.

[117] As found in al-Rijāl, p. 301. Al-Rijāl's Abū Ma'shar says: "If the Lord of the election were the Lord of the sign of the luminaries in the revolution of the year of the world (or the Lord of that year or the Lord of its Ascendant), and were made fortunate in the revolution and the election, it signifies height and nobility in the matter undertaken, and in all of its doings."

[118] Abū Ma'shar according to al-Rijāl, p. 301. I have changed Bonatti's somewhat puzzling syntax to match Al-Rijāl's version: "And he said that if the Lord of the Ascendant of the year of the world had no testimony in the beginnings or in the place of the luminaries, nor in the Midheaven, the matter will be of low quality and condemned."

[119] *Subtilis.*

[120] Al-Rijāl, p. 301. Al-Rijāl's al-Tabarī is slightly different: "Al-Tabarī said: If the place of the conjunction or the prevention and their Lords were in good bounds and in good places, the matter will be firm and durable. Likewise he who is born then, and he who entered some dignity in such a constellation at the hour of the inception, or if this were according to the Ascendant of the nativity of that man."

[121] Al-Rijāl's al-Tabarī adds: "in good bounds."

born in that hour, or appointed (whether to the preferment of a provost,[122] whether an office or dignity), the matter will be firm and durable. And he said that those places were praiseworthy in the hour of the undertaking of matters.

And the ancients took testimony (in the adaptation of a matter to be done) from the Lords of the triplicity of the sign in which the Moon was at the hour of the conjunction or the prevention, saying they were the guards of matters, both of the one beginning and doing a matter, and of the matter to be done or begun, and of journeys, and other things: which if they were received in the hour of the inception or election, they will signify good; if however they were to the contrary, they will signify evil. And they said that what increases good is when the Ascendant of the election is a sign made fortunate[123] in the revolution of the year; and let the benefic which makes the sign fortunate be in the 1st, or 10th, or let it be in the 11th or 5th, or at least in the 2nd; or let it be in the house which signifies the matter for which we are electing, so that it falls well from thence for the one wishing to do it. And let the significators of the matter which we are beginning, be in places agreeing with the aforesaid significators (namely the domicile of the aforesaid triplicity); and let them (namely the significators) be strong in the hour of the election or undertaking.

And al-Rijāl said[124] that of the strengths of the planets, like when they are ascending in the north (and it is sometimes necessary that if a planet is ascending in the south, and it is a strength for it, like the Moon when she is increasing her light and number, she is ascending stronger in the south, than if she were then ascending in the north), and let the Moon be in angles in increased light and number in the matters which we wish to be increased; in matters to the contrary let it be to the contrary.[125] And he said that the significators should be going under the benefics [and] over the malefics,[126] indeed the Moon and the significator of the matter asked about or to be begun, or done in every matter which we want to be made manifest, should be above the earth. And in every matter which we wish to be hidden, let the Moon and the significators be below

---

[122] *Praepositurae praepositus.*

[123] This means by having a whole-sign aspect or conjunction with a benefic, as he now clarifies.

[124] This derives from a passage (p. 300) in which al-Rijāl describes conditions of "natural" power possessed by the planets, along with being oriental or being in its own domicile (among others). The rest of these statements are either Bonatti's own ideas based on further statements in al-Rijāl, or seem to come from p. 300 (although, if so, Bonatti seems to quote incorrectly in some cases).

[125] I.e., sometimes we want a matter to be decreased or cut short.

[126] It is unclear whether this means by latitude or by elevation above the horizon in the chart. The context below suggests it means the latter

the earth; and let the Lord of the Ascendant and all the significators which we can, be oriental; and let the planet to whose conjunction the Moon goes, be a benefic (he signifies a definite end to the matter undertaken and what is going to be concerning it).

And al-Kindī said[127] if the Sun and the Moon were to aspect each other with an aspect of friendship, it signifies the strength and goodness of any matter undertaken; and more strongly so if the Moon were in the third degree of Taurus, because then it signifies the extreme goodness of the matter which we wish to begin or do, even if the other significators are not well disposed– provided that they are not besieged by the two malefics without reception.

And Māshā'allāh said[128] that the planets are said to be strong when they are occidental from the Moon, just like they are when they are oriental from the Sun: because the Moon rules in the night just like the Sun rules in the day.

However, al-Tabarī said[129] if we were not able to adapt [both] the Moon and the Ascendant, we should adapt one of them. For if it were a diurnal election, we should adapt the Ascendant (and especially if the Moon were below the earth [at that time]); if however it were a nocturnal election, we should adapt the Moon (and especially if she herself were above the earth [at that time]). And he said that if were were able to defer our election from the day to the night, or from the night to the day, it must be considered which of them is better to adapt (namely the Moon or the Ascendant), and [we ought to] do with them what will seem better to us.

And al-Rijāl said[130] the condition of the Moon in the day below the earth, and in the night above the earth, is good and increasing the strength of the Ascendant. And if it were necessary for us to elect for someone, nor could we adapt the Moon, we should put Jupiter or Venus in the 1st or in the 10th (for they will adapt the matter with a great adaptation). And a certain person[131] said that they will make [the matter][132] last a long time.

---

[127] This *may* be a reference to al-Rijāl's reference to Alazmin (p. 301), which is both different and includes an unusual notion of the Moon's "joy": "Alazmin said: If the luminaries aspect each other with a good aspect, they signify good and better success in every matter undertaken, and especially if [it were] while the Moon were in the beginning of her joy, that is, if she is in the sign in which the Head had been."

[128] According to al-Rijāl (p. 301).

[129] Al-Rijāl, p. 301.

[130] Al-Rijāl, p. 301.

[131] Unknown source, not found in al-Rijāl's text.

[132] Reading *eam* for *eum*.

However, al-Rijāl said[133] that the adaptation of the Moon is to be preferred in all matters which we want to last a long time (like buildings, both of cities and homes, and wedding celebrations, and the like). And if the Moon were weak, she should be removed from the angles; and if we could not remove her from the angles, she should not aspect the Ascendant nor its Lord, nor the domicile of the matter to be elected, nor its Lord, nor even a planet which signifies the matter to be elected.[134] And if she could not be removed from all of the aforesaid aspects, she should be removed at least from those from which she can be removed.

And al-Kindī said[135] if we were not able to adapt all the significators, and we were able to adapt the Moon, it will be good. Nevertheless he does not promise us that the matter may not be destroyed. Whence if the Lord of the house [domicile?] signifying the matter which we want to do or begin can be adapted, it is better on account of the matter, so that it may last or come to the end which we want; and the burden will be ascribed [as being] less by the astrologer, than if he had adapted the Moon and the Lord of the 1st (which signify the person of the querent or inceptor); but in order to preserve the person of the querent or the inceptor, the Lord of the 1st and the Moon must be adapted. However, men do not consider what may happen except concerning the matter, and they look to its eventuation, not taking care about the status of the person.

If however the Moon were slow in course (namely similar to the course of Saturn), that is, that she goes less than 12° in one day, it signifies difficulty and slowness; on the other hand if it were a building which we intend to make, or which one ought to begin, or [which] the inceptor intended to raise above the earth, and the Moon were slow in course, and the other significators were below the earth, the building will never be raised; and if it were raised, it would happen very slowly; but it will not be raised during the whole age in which it was begun.

And if you could not make the Moon fortunate as you wanted to in your matter, and there were one who made her unfortunate, nor could you avoid the impediment, make the one who impedes her the Lord of the 1st: because the 1st does not impede itself nor the Moon to its own detriment. And if you could put

---

[133] Al-Rijāl, p. 301.

[134] Al-Rijāl's text is slightly different. Al-Rijāl does not speak of the Moon's weakness, but of her being made malefic; nor does he treat the matter of aspecting the angle or its Lord as a third-best option: "And particularly and always act so that the Moon does not aspect the Ascendant nor its Lord, nor the Lord of the house of the matter, nor its Lord, nor the planet signifying the matter by its own nature and character."

[135] This seems to derive from a very brief passage in al-Rijāl (p. 301) wherein he takes issue with al-Tabarī, not al-Kindī.

him in the 1st it will be better, and let him be free from the impediments which are spoken of elsewhere. And if you could not put him in the 1st, put him in some other praiseworthy place, like in the 10th or 11th or 5th; and if it were possible that he should receive the Moon, all of his malice would be totally broken; for the praiseworthy condition of the Moon, and of the other significators, increases good and diminishes evil; and their evil condition increases evil and diminishes the good.

And beware of the conjunction of the malefics with the Moon or with the other significators, or their square aspect, or opposition without reception, and do not let them be impeded. For by a trine or sextile aspect they do not harm, provided that they are otherwise free; rather when they are received by a trine or sextile aspect, and free, they are turned into benefics.[136]

And always place significators as strongly as you can, and keep them and the Moon from the impediments of the malefics as best as you know how; and so that the malefics are not in places by which the matters which we intend to do or begin are signified; nor that they aspect them by a square aspect or from the opposition.

And al-Rijāl said,[137] beware of an eclipse, and especially if there were an eclipse in the sign in which a luminary was in the hour of the nativity of him for whom we elect. And he said, nor let the Moon be under the rays; and she must be removed completely from every impediment; nor let the significator be joined to the Sun, nor he to it; and[138] it must be kept from the square aspect of the Sun and his opposition; still however if there were reception between them, it will be somewhat easier. And [al-Rijāl] said[139] that the opposition gives contentions and contrarieties.

And do not let the malefics be in angles and especially in the Ascendant or in the 10th; and especially if the malefics were the Lords of the houses [domiciles?] signifying evil (and this is the 6th and the 8th and the 12th), because then they will signify that which their houses [domiciles?] will signify. And he said that the Ascendant should not be a sign in which its Lord is about to enter combustion in that year;[140] nor let the Ascendant be a sign which was impeded in the

---

136 *Efficiuntur fortunae*, lit. "they are effected as benefics."

137 I have not found this particular statement in al-Rijāl, but it could be an expansion on his discussion of the syzygies on pp. 300-01.

138 The rest of this sentence comes from al-Rijāl, p. 302.

139 Al-Rijāl, p. 299.

140 He must mean, "at the time of the revolution of the year," just like in the following passage. In one year, *every* planet will enter combustion, because the Sun will have traveled through the entire zodiac.

revolution of that same year; nor let the Moon be slow in course in any matter which we want to come to pass quickly, because she postpones and slows it, unless there are many significators.

And [al-Rijāl] said[141] that the movable signs are to be removed in every matter whose stability and durability we want; and in the same way the fixed signs [are to be removed] in every matter which we want to transpire quickly.[142] Indeed the common ones [are to be removed] from every [matter] that you want to come to be just as the matter itself occurs. For they return whatever is difficult in them.

And he said,[143] beware lest one of the fixed stars which are of the nature of the malefics be in the ascending degree itself, or that of the Midheaven, or that of the house of the matter to be elected; and I have found that all of the wise (who made mention of them) agree on this. Because they are malicious:

Of which one is in the fourteenth degree of Aries, and another in the fifteenth degree of the same;

One is in the tenth [degree] of Taurus, and another in the twentieth;

One is in the eighteenth degree of Gemini;

One of them is in the eighth degree of Cancer, another in the eighteenth;

One is in the sixteenth degree of Leo;

One is in the eighth degree of Virgo, another in the sixteenth;

One is in the twenty-sixth degree of Libra;

One is in the seventh degree of Scorpio; in the ninth degree of the same [Scorpio] are two;

One is in Sagittarius in the twentieth degree, another is in the twenty-second;

---

[141] Al-Rijāl, p. 302.

[142] This could refer to al-Rijāl, p. 302. But al-Rijāl does not speak of them being "removed," and does not mention common signs.

[143] I have not found this statement in al-Rijāl; perhaps it is al-'Imrānī.

One is in Capricorn in the twenty-eighth degree, another in another;[144]

One is in the tenth degree of Aquarius;

Another is in the fifth degree of Pisces.[145]

I recommend well that you do all the things which he told you ought to be done; and that you avoid all the things which he told you ought to be avoided, if it can be done. However to me it seems that they can hardly or never be that way. You however, just as I told you elsewhere, do what good you can do, and avoid what evil you can avoid; because it will hardly be but that it will be profitable, even if not as much as the one taking up [the matter] wishes.

And al-Kindī said[146] that it is bad for the angles to be removed. Indeed al-Rijāl recommended that the angles be removed. But al-Kindī's intention was [concerning] when the removal was by receding from the angles—that is, if one sign was the 9th house, or was the 12th house, or the 3rd or the 6th, and that same sign that was the 9th house was the 10th house, or that the one that was the 12th house, was the 1st; or the one that was the 3rd house, was the 4th; or the one that was the 6th house, was the 7th: that removal would be bad, because it would be removed toward the cadents.[147] Indeed others understood by this removal that it be toward the angles: that is, if one sign was the 10th house, and that same one

---

[144] Perhaps he means "in the next degree."

[145] These malefic fixed stars are a subset of those listed in Tr. 5 (99th Consideration). Comparison of the lists shows that Bonatti is rounding the numbers up. For example, the star listed in Tr. 5 as being in the seventh degree and fifty-fifth minute of Cancer, is listed here as being in the eighth degree.

[146] In al-Rijāl, these statements are not attributed to al-Kindī (p. 302), but the passage does have several unattributed "he said" statements. Moreover, al-Rijāl's passage introduces a word that sounds like something from Hindu astrology. It reads: "Likewise he abhors it if the angles are cadent (for example, if the tenth sign from the Ascendant comes by computation into the 11th by the equation of houses), and he calls such things 'retrograde.' However, if they were removed by going toward the previous ones, it is a complete good (like when the 10th house comes by computation into the 11th by the equation of houses), and he names this *avasamentum*." The Latinized *avasamentum* may derive from the Sanskrit *avastat* ("on this side") or *avastha* ("appearance, condition, position, dwelling"). Ken Johnson (private communication) believes that *avastha* is the origin. Thanks to him and Kenneth Miller for their help on this matter.

[147] I.e., al-Kindī did not want both an angular and a cadent cusp on the same sign, which would happen if the sign were moving far past the angle by primary motion. But (according to others) it would be all right if both an angular and a succeedent cusp were on the same sign, which would happen if the sign had only just reached the angle by primary motion.

was the 11th; or [that] it be the 1st house and the 2nd house; or [that] it be the 4th and the 5th; or [that] it be the 7th and the 8th: that removal would not be bad, because it would be toward the angles by going toward them; and al-Rijāl recommended this removal in matters whose durability we desired.

And al-Rijāl said[148] it must be watched out for lest the Lord of the Ascendant or the Lord of the house [domicile?] signifying the matter wish we elect, or even the planet signifying the matter itself, or the Lord of the sign in which the Moon is, or the planet to which she is joined (if she is joined to one)–be in the second[149] from the Sun. That is, when they are occidental, do not let them be near him so that they fall in the second domicile from him (unless it was Venus or Mercury, because they do not have the prerogative of being able to be far elongated from him). Because this signifies vileness and delay and the impurity of the matter. Indeed the three superiors, when they are far from the Sun by two whole signs, and occidental up to the completion of the third sign,[150] are said to be in decline [or old age], which is a certain impediment for them in elections and especially in matters which we intend to perfect quickly: because they delay the matter; but they do not prevent the matter from happening, even if [it does] not [happen] quickly.

And 'Ali said[151] that if it were necessary for us to elect something, and we were to have one of the praiseworthy hours which does not harm with a great harm, [then] if the Moon is then joined to Mars or Saturn, provided that the matter which we want to elect is of the matters which are signified by the benefics (like if it were a lay dignity or magistracy or the like, which are signified by the Sun; or it were for substance or the accumulation of money, which are signified by Jupiter; or it were the affairs of women, and games and other things which are signified by Venus; or writings or merchant activities or commodities which are signified by Mercury, and the like), because the malefics cannot impede the matter so that it will not come to be and be perfected, even if something of their malice (which they signify naturally) is mixed in; and especially they will impede a middling amount or not at all when they are received: because then the malicious [planets] will be made [only] a little of what

---

[148] Al-Rijāl only says this about the Lord of the Ascendant, but Bonatti wants to expand it to prevent more significators from being occidental.

[149] In this passage it is clear that Bonatti has either 30-degree increments or whole signs in mind.

[150] This suggests that by "domicile" and "sign" Bonatti means "30-degree increments."

[151] I do not find this in the material on the planetary hours in al-Rijāl (pp. 341-42).

there is from it. Indeed if they were uncivilized[152] and horrible, not received, they will impede more. However, they could not avert the matter so that it does not come to be.

If however the matter which we want to elect were concerning things which we want to be concealed, and the Sun were to aspect the Ascendant or its Lord, and the Sun were of good condition, and the Moon were to aspect Mercury, and they were to aspect each other with the Sun by a praiseworthy aspect, the matter will not be hidden or covered up, but it will be made public.[153] And if someone were to undertake a flight then, he will be captured. And if the aspect of the Sun to the Ascendant or its Lord or the Moon were evil (namely the square or the opposition), the matter will be revealed by a vile and reprehensible revelation. And if the significators of the matter were above the earth, the matter will even be revealed; and more strongly so if they were in the Midheaven. If the Ascendant or the Moon were under the rays of the Sun, or the Sun and the Moon were cadent from the Ascendant, and not aspecting each other, or the Moon and the significators of the matter which we are electing were below the earth (and especially in the 4th), it signifies that the matter will be covered up and not revealed. And if the Lord of the Ascendant were Mars or Saturn, or some other planet made unfortunate, evil that conceals will follow from that concealment, and something contrary to him;[154] and more strongly so if the luminaries were impeded; if indeed the luminaries were free, the evil will not harm him.

And al-Rijāl even said[155] that all of the praiseworthy and unpraiseworthy things which are said, are not to be considered except after the adaptation of the roots of those things named above. And he said when the benefics rule in the aforesaid roots, it must not be considered concerning those which were touched on beforehand,[156] even if they were evil. And he said if the benefics were strong, and were ruling in the election, we ought not to look except to those which we saw were to be praised. And he said if [the roots] were praiseworthy, good fortune and the good will be multiplied. If indeed the roots were bad, those things which follow, even if they are praiseworthy, do not change nor take away the malice, but they increase the evil on account of their malignity. And he said

---

[152] *Sylvestres.* I.e., feral. Recall that in Tr. 5 (5th Consideration), Bonatti says the Moon is in this condition when she is *both* void in course *and* peregrine.
[153] This refers back to the statement that the Sun and the Ascendant signify things that are revealed.
[154] *Contrarium sibi.*
[155] This is probably based on al-Rijāl, pp. 297-98.
[156] *Praetaxata.*

that if it were necessary for us to begin something, and the malefics were in charge[157] over the inception, the things that follow must be adapted, because they [would] subtract something of the evil, even if they do not abolish it completely. And he said that it is to be watched out for lest the ones following are evil: like if someone asked of the astrologer that he elect for him a good hour to do something, or it were a matter which he did not want to disclose to the astrologer: now the astrologer is in doubt about what [the client] wants to begin, because he has not revealed his intention to him; nor therefore is the astrologer certain which planet or what sign would signify the matter which he intends. Whence he must then adapt the Ascendant and its Lord, both luminaries, and the 4th and its Lord, in order that the body and mind of the inceptor, and the end of the matter, are taken care of (whether the matter which he intends to do will be completed or not).

And ['Ali][158] said that in all such things one must begin in hours in which Jupiter or Venus or the Sun rule: because by observing this every matter will be adapted, whatever kind it is.

And ['Ali] said[159] that if we were to know the nativity of the querent or inceptor, or we were to have his question, and it were necessary for us to weaken one of the significators, we ought to weaken the 7th of the nativity or the question, or its Lord, just like what happens when we wish to go off to war or out hunting, in which the 7th house and the like would be weakened. If however we did *not* know the nativity, nor did we have the question, we will adapt what was said should be adapted: namely the Ascendant of the election, and its Lord, and the Moon, *etc.*, as was said elsewhere; and we will weaken the 7th of the election, and its Lord, *etc.*, as was said elsewhere.

And it is necessary that we adapt the planet and the sign and the hour signifying the sex of the person for whom we are electing: like Venus for women in their affairs, as was said above; and we ought to adapt a feminine sign if we can, and carry out their affairs in feminine and nocturnal hours. In the affairs of men we must adapt masculine signs, and carry out their affairs likewise, if we can, in masculine and diurnal hours; and even the sign signifying the social group[160] must be adapted, and likewise the planet signifying the social group is to be

---

157 *Praefuerint.*
158 I have not found this statement in al-Rijāl.
159 I have not found this statement in al-Rijāl.
160 *Gentem.* This could mean either a national ethnic group or clan (say, "Italians"), or cities defined in terms of local custom (say, "the Genoese").

adapted, as I told you.[161] And the planet which signifies the region or province or city for whom you elect, must be adapted, [and] it is a very difficult matter to know which planet rules a city or land; nor could you know this except by conjecture, unless perhaps you have the hour of the founding[162] of that land, which can be arrived at most rarely (however you could have its signification more easily through a question). But if you did not have the hour of the founding, or the question, consider the customs of the people of that land, and their life, and consider what tends to happen to them in great and difficult dealings concerning victories, and the contrary. And you could base its signification on the planets in accordance with how you saw the planets ruling in those accidents, whether they were good or bad. You will even consider the customs of their citizens, what kind they are: which if they were good and honest, and they were people of good sustenance, and make money freely from honest profits, or at least not disgraceful ones, and who freely spend and live honorably, even if perhaps luxury overflows in them, still it is a sign that Jupiter is their significator: whence you can adapt him in their elections in case you did not have a question. However a question is an easy matter, and you easily have the significator of the city and of the citizens through it (provided that [the question] is posed by someone whose business it is, like through the leader or administrator constituted for it, and the like).

If however they were misers, thieves, miserable people, their customs dissimilar from others, from wherever they strive to gain wealth, not considering whether by licit or illicit means, it is a sign that Saturn is their significator.

If however they were stately people, affecting to rule, and desiring to be praised, however having a good and praiseworthy life, and appropriate spending, it is a sign that the Sun is their significator.

If however they were bellicose, predatory, contentious, and spirited,[163] doers of evil, raging, arrogant, wherever they make money from, and pilfering by [both] good and wicked means, and stingy, avoiding expendi-

---

[161] Bonatti must be referring to the planets having universal signification over ethnic groups, like Venus for Arabs, *etc.*

[162] *Constructionis.*

[163] *Animatus*, in the Platonic sense of being easily excited to anger and the like.

tures, and acting with disgraceful customs and vices, it is a sign that Mars is their significator.

If indeed they were ingenious men, wise, literate, profound in the sciences, with good spending, having good customs, not envious, merchants of average dealings, spurning money, not intent on acquiring wealth, it is a sign that Mercury is their significator.

If however they were men of comfort, games and dancing, feasting, drinking, users of musical instruments, and by any kind of comfort spurning avarice, it is a sign that Venus is their significatrix.

If however they were unfaithful, changeable, roaming, unstable, wanting this and wanting that, and engaging in small business transactions, it is a sign that the Moon is their significatrix.

We can even adapt any planet to diverse matters: for we can adapt Saturn to the aforesaid, and we can even adapt him to those wishing to dye in the color black, because he naturally signifies blackness; and he is to be put so that he aspects the 1st and its Lord by a praiseworthy aspect; and even let the Moon (or at least the Lord of the domicile in which she is) be in an aspect of friendship with him, or let her be in the domicile of Saturn, not cadent from the Ascendant or from the 10th (however it is better that she aspect Saturn by a good aspect).

Likewise we can adapt Jupiter to the aforesaid, and to many other things, and particularly to those wishing to dye in the color citrine: because he naturally signifies it, and he is to be placed as was said concerning Saturn.

We can even adapt Mars to the aforesaid and to many other things, and particularly to those wishing to dye in the color red: because he naturally signifies that color, and is to be adapted as was said concerning Jupiter. Mars can even be adapted to slaves on account of their falseness, because slaves often act by it.

We can thus far adapt the Sun to the aforesaid and to certain other things, and particularly to dyers wishing to dye in a mixed color which takes part in a commixture of many and diverse colors.

We can likewise adapt Venus to all the aforesaid and to many more, and particularly to those wishing [to dye] something in white, because she naturally signifies white.

We can equally adapt Mercury to all of the things named above, and likewise to certain other things, and particularly to whose wishing to dye in a color that is almost indigo, or purple, or semi-purple, and for putting together all other commingled and varied colors.

Likewise we can adapt the Moon to everything already said above, and to additional other things, and particularly to those wishing to dye in the color grey [or sparkling], or *zallo*;[164] likewise to other colors of little durability.

And just as one planet can be adapted to many and diverse things, so one house [domicile?] can be adapted to many and diverse things; and many houses [domiciles?] can sometimes be adapted to one and the same matter, just like the 2nd house is adapted to substance and likewise the 6th is adapted to substance (because it signifies slaves, which pertain to substance, and smaller animals, which pertain to substance), and the 12th signifies likewise larger animals, which pertain to substance. And understand this with all the houses, just as was said in the Treatise on the twelve houses.

And even multiple planets can be adapted to one matter, like when we wish to elect for a slave or a purchased Slav:[165] because he is reckoned to be among the slaves. We can adapt Mars or Saturn for any of them [i.e., slaves or Slavs] because each of them is a lying [planet]. Likewise we can adapt Venus to all things, and even to the adaptation of clothing and other ornaments of women. If however it were a military banner or other clothing that pertains to war, like the *zupa gaiferia*[166] or the like, Mars will have to be adapted, the Lord of the 1st, and the Moon and its Lord. And if it were other clothing, we will adapt the 1st

---

[164] *Zallo*. Unknown color, but perhaps "sallow" (weakly yellowish, like the Moon).

[165] *Slavoni*. This word is late Latin word for the Slavs, who (before their conversion to Christianity) were used as slave labor when conquered in war (and were probably still used as slaves by the medieval Turks and other invading eastern peoples). Note: slave-Slav (similar to German *Sklave-Slawe*).

[166] Both *zupa* and *gaiferia* are synonymous Italian terms for flags representing a group; it is unclear whether Bonatti means this as a special two-word phrase, or as synonyms (to be separated by a comma).

and its Lord, the Moon also, and how many of those planets we can; and we will put the Sun in the 10th, just as will be said in its own special chapter, when the wearing of new vestments is treated.

Chapter 12: On the weakening of the planets

For just as sometimes planets are to be adapted, so at times some of them are to be weakened (just as I remember I touched on above), in proportion to how it is necessary to weaken [any] in a matter which we wish to do. For if we wished to go out against an army, it is necessary to weaken the 7th and its Lord just as much as we can, and to strengthen the Lord of the 1st, *etc.* If however we wished to go out hunting, it is necessary for us to weaken the 7th and its Lord; and it is necessary for us to *weaken* the Moon, but not make her *unfortunate*,[167] unless perhaps the Lord of the 1st or the Lord of the 6th were to make her unfortunate (because it signifies the aforesaid things or the animals with which we hunt). However it is well [that] there are certain people who say she is to be made unfortunate. If for instance we want to follow a robber or other fugitive, it is necessary for us to weaken the Moon, and even make her unfortunate—and especially if we could make it so that the Lord of the 1st is he who makes her unfortunate. Because then it signifies that [the fugitive] will not escape from the hands of those pursuing him. Sometimes the Moon is weakened, but she is not then to be made unfortunate, [like] when we give drugs:[168] because she is then to be put in Scorpio, so the humors run to and fro through all parts in which the drug is adapted to work its powers and what pertains to it. And it is necessary that we stay away from the malefics, namely from Mars and Saturn: for Saturn could bind up the medicine, Mars could incite it so that it leads to the flowing of blood; and perhaps that the intestine would be wounded, and from there dysentery could be generated, which could be the reason for the death of him who took the drug. And thus the Moon should not be made unfortunate in these things, but only weakened, and the Lord of the 1st made fortunate and strengthened; and on this our ancient sages seem to agree.

---

[167] Emphasis mine.
[168] *Pharmaca.* Could this also mean "poison"? Usually Bonatti would use the Latin *medicina* for medical arts or medicine, and *venenum* for poison. The Greek-derived *pharmacus* means "poison," but it is masculine, not neuter.

Chapter 13: On particular things which pertain to elections

After a general mention was made in the matters which preceded concerning the steps pertaining to general elections, it seems fitting that we get down to particulars, as what are universally called "particulars" are better known by experience. Nor even is it necessary for us in the particulars to recall to memory the things which are discussed in the universal things for the work would be prolonged too much and would generate weariness in readers), but only to subjoin those concerning the deed or belonging to whatever chapter. Nor however could it be crossed with a dry foot[169] without some of the aforesaid occasionally being touched on. However I will proceed by as easy a path as I can; nor will I get involved in saying everything which could be contemplated by the wise in elections, even if certain ones said that the Indians always avoided the combust hours in every matter. I however [would give] praise if someone could adapt every contingency; but just as I remember having told you elsewhere, it seems somewhat impossible to adapt everything, and if we wanted to inspect everything to a fine point, the hours would grow to be so fearfully many that we would make only the most rare and fewest elections. You however [ought to] follow what I have told you.

On the hours of decrease

And the Egyptians avoided certain hours of certain days of every month, which are called days and hours of decrease; which, if someone could observe them, would be good; but if they could not be observed, it is not a dangerous matter like some people sometimes believed. And I will make a table of them for you so you may know what they are if you wished to avoid them.[170] Nor should you be surprised if mention is not made here about many things which seem appropriate to this work (namely elections), namely about the sex of a figure,[171] and on their ordering,[172] on their ascending and setting, and the like; because all of these, if you remembered them, are discussed elsewhere.[173] For here they are not discussed except solely as exceptional useful things, just as the

---

[169] I.e., we cannot treat of particular elections without getting our "feet wet" by returning to themes already covered.

[170] Bonatti does not provide the table, but the hours do not seem to be the hours of the *bust*, i.e., the "combust and incombust hours," because he elsewhere reports dire warnings of what happens to those who do not observe them.

[171] Reading *figurae* for *figura*.

[172] *Ordinatione*. I do not know whether this is a technical term or not.

[173] I am not sure what Bonatti is referring to here.

remedies of the philosophers are said to be the exceptional useful things in their books.[174]

Chapter 14: What things ought to be considered in the beginnings of the elections of those whose nativities we know

In the aforementioned elections, the things which ought to be considered universally were discussed; next we must look at those things which in particular cases are first and principally to be looked at. And the ancients said that there are principally three things in elections:

OF WHICH THEY SAID THE FIRST is that it be considered which of the planets is stronger in the root of the nativity or question, and that he is to be put in the angles or in their succeedents, if it can be done; and that he should be free from the malefics and from other impediments, and let him be strong and fortunate, and he should be above the earth joined to the benefics; and if he himself were a benefic, it will be better; but if he were malefic, he should be removed from the angle, because he will be provoked in his operations, so that he could impede the matter so that it does not come to be (and it will have seemed that he was more quickly the cause of its destruction). Nor let him be put in a cadent, because his virtue would not be so strong that he could perfect it. And so he will have to be put in a succeedent, and thus his virtue and power will be suitable for our matter. And the Lord of the sign in which the Part of Fortune was at the hour of the nativity or the question is to be adapted; likewise even the Lord of the revolution of the nativity or the question,[175] if it can be done; and the Part of Fortune of the year of the revolution, and its Lord, and the Lord of the second sign from the Ascendant of that revolution, and the Lord of the hour of the election (which is called by some the "Lord of the orb").[176]

THE SECOND is that the Ascendant of the election and its 10th be free of the malefics and their prohibited aspects; and it is recommended that there be a benefic in it, or that [the benefic] aspect it by a trine or sextile aspect; and it is even recommended that the ascending [sign] be the first [sign] of the root of the nativity or the question (or its 10th, or at least its 11th) if it were then free [in the

---

[174] Meaning unclear and translation somewhat rough: *hic enim non dicuntur nisi solum exceptae utilitates, sicut in antidotariis philosophorum dicuntur exceptae utilitates suorum librorum.*

[175] Does Bonatti mean the "Lord of the question," or the "Lord of the revolution of the question?" If the former, perhaps he means the Lord of the 1st of the question; he does speak in Tr. 6, 10th House, Ch. 9, of a solar revolution for a question, but those must be very rare.

[176] See Tr. 9, Part 3, 12th House, Ch. 13.

election], and were free in the nativity or the question. And it is a greater impediment if it was not free in the election, than [if it were not free] in the nativity. Which if it could not be so, the ascending [sign] of the election is to be made the sign in which the Part of Fortune was in the nativity or the question, or the second [sign] from the ascending [sign] of the nativity or the question, provided that it is free. Which if it could not be one of these, as often happens, adapt the ascending [sign] of the election as well as you can, and the others which I told you. And if you cannot adapt the things you want, adapt what you can for this purpose so that your election is of value to him for whom you are electing.

You could even elect in another way, which is not to be condemned: namely, that you make the ascending [sign] of the election the sign that signified the matter (for which you elect) in the nativity or the question, provided that it is free from the malefics and their aspects (unless the impeding malefic is the Lord of the sign of the Ascendant of the nativity or question, because then he does not impede himself).

And one should beware above all other avoidable things, lest the Ascendant of the election be the 6th or the 8th or the 12th of the nativity or the question. And if you can occasionally make the Ascendant of the election one of the good places which were in the nativity or the question, it will be good; and if you can, even adapt the place of the Part of Fortune of the nativity or the question in your election, and its Lord; and the sign of the profection, and its Lord; which if you could not adapt them together, remember what I have already told you many times: adapt those which you can. And whatever happens concerning the others, adapt the Ascendant [of the nativity or the question] and its Lord, and the Moon, and the Lord of the Ascendant of the election, and the planet signifying the matter for which you elect. And make them strong, as much as you can, and put them in the aspect of the benefics. And if you could not put all in the aspect of the benefics, put at least the Lord of the Ascendant [of the election] and the Moon and the planet signifying the matter, because these will remove all malice from your election. And if you could put the planet signifying the matter for which you elect in the Ascendant of the election,[177] your matter will come to be more easily, and not with great labor.

And if there were benefics which aspected the aforesaid significators, strong and free from the malefics and the other impediments, the matter for which you

---

[177] Reading *electionis* for *nativitatis*, since one cannot choose which planets are in the Ascendant of the nativity!

elect will come to any end which you wish. If however the Lord of the nativity or the election, or the question, were in the domicile signifying the matter for which you elect, and it was free, or aspected the domicile by a trine or sextile aspect, the matter will come to be, but with difficulty and obstacles and labor. If however it were impeded, it will impede the matter, and will hardly or never permit it to be perfected. And if the Lord of the matter for which it is elected, and the Lord of the Ascendant of the election (or the nativity or the question or the revolution) were to aspect each other by a trine or sextile aspect, and they were free nor impeded, it signifies that the matter will reach a praiseworthy end.[178]

INDEED THE THIRD is that it be seen whether the one whose nativity is evident or whose question we have, wishes to begin something whence he hopes for good, like great journeys, great business matters, or even great buildings, or some such work that is reputed great: for then it must be seen by his nativity or universal question, or that which was made for the occasion, [whether] something unlucky (or something horrible that is to be feared) is signified in that year in which he wishes to do the thing: for then it is to be prohibited him so that he does not begin the matter until the disposition of that planet which seems then to threaten the evil for him, passes over. Which if it could not be deferred, let the Lord of the Ascendant of the election be made fortunate and strong, and the Moon and the Lord of the house [domicile?] signifying the matter; and let the planet which threatens the horrible thing be made weak, nor let it aspect the Ascendant nor the domicile signifying, nor their Lords, nor the Moon. And if you were not able to avoid all of these, avoid it at least [to the extent] that it does not aspect the Ascendant, nor its Lord, nor the Part of Fortune (or at least its Lord); and make it (if you ever could) so that some benefic or its rays fall by a trine or sextile aspect in the place in which the impeding one was at the hour of the nativity or the question. And if you could not do this, then remove the malefic who threatens the horrible thing from the Ascendant, and from the place of the matter, as was said. Even remove, of the other malefics, as many as you can; and always, whenever you see some planet in your election that signifies impediment to the matter for which you elect, in the nativity of him for whom you elect, you will weaken it as much as you can, and may you strive in all ways to strengthen the planet signifying the matter, and the sign in which it was in the nativity or question; and if you could not

---

[178] In this sentence Bonatti seems to be making a general statement about many types of charts, and not merely for elections.

strengthen both, at least strengthen the sign. And may you strive to strengthen everything which I told you; and if you cannot do what you want, I tell you yet to do what you can in the relief of the aforesaid: namely that it is necessary for you to beware of a planet signifying fear in the nativity. If it is signified in the nativity that the matter which you or another wishes to begin, is useful, you will hardly ever be able to make a weak election without its effecting being good; nevertheless your election is to be adapted as you are able, so that it goes better for you from it. You must even beware that you make no election about a matter in the hour of the eclipse of one of the luminaries, unless perhaps it were in some matter to be hidden; and it is better to avoid an election then, if the eclipse were to take place in the sign which the Ascendant was at the hour of the nativity or the question; and it would be good if you could avoid that whole triplicity; however you must not be concerned about it as [much as] with the Ascendant.

If you can, you must even beware, like if Venus is impeded in the nativity, that you do not put the Moon in the sextile aspect of Mars or Saturn, whether they were to receive [the Moon] or not. And if Jupiter were impeded, you would not put [the Moon] in their trine aspect. And if Mars were impeded, you should not put her in the square aspect of Saturn. And if Saturn were impeded, you would not put her in the opposition of Mars. And if Mercury were impeded, you would not put her near one of them by less than 31°, if you can do it.[179]

Chapter 15: If the matter about which a question were proposed by someone ought to be perfected or not, when we elect for it

Just as was said elsewhere, very many sages (of which one was [Abu 'Ali] al-Khayyat),[180] when they wanted to elect for someone, nor did they have his nativity for this purpose so that they could know if the matter (about which the question arose) could be perfected or not, they took the *question* of whatever matter was to be begun, and if they saw that it was supposed to be perfected, they saw[181] whether it would be useful or not; and they elected according to the question just as they would elect about a nativity. Nor did they elect otherwise

---

[179] The rationale is based on the aspects archetypally related to the planets by the *Thema Mundi*–as when the sextile is said to be like Venus (see Tr. 2, Part 2, Ch. 13). The idea seems to be that if a planet is impeded, then if the Moon is related to the malefics by this archetypal aspect, she will make the planet's hindrance more obvious and communicate it to earth.

[180] Compare with Sahl, *On Elect.*, Ch. 1; al-Rijāl, p. 297.

[181] Reading *videbant* for *videbat*.

for someone, and it seemed that their opinion was sound for this purpose so their elections were perfected and secure.

But it did not seem useful to elect thus for anyone wishing to have an election about a matter which he wanted to begin. However it was good to elect [based] on the nativity or question. But sometimes agreeable elections take place, about which we could not judge questions, nor see their end according to judgments; and still it is necessary for an astrologer to elect for him who consults him; and I have already told you above that you can elect something for anyone wishing to begin [something], and your election will be useful to him, just as I showed you elsewhere, if you remember well.[182]

It is even true that through a nativity or question we can know the end of a matter undertaken or to be begun, which does not happen by every election; still we ought to hope they are useful, wherefore we elect what seems better to us; because just as I have already told you, a good election can bring profit, indeed it can harm little; nor have I found Ptolemy (who was the best astrologer) having anywhere prohibited the astrologer from electing without the aforesaid nativities or questions. And it was the intention of the philosophers that the evils which are signified by the nativity or by a question can be abolished by a good election; and if they are not abolished wholly, they can be diminished and alleviated much.

Likewise there were certain others who wanted it that we not elect except for those whose nativities we knew (and they are few): and elections would profit few people if it were so.[183] For they used to say that the nativity is a natural thing, [and] a question is not one, or rather it is non-natural thing. Still however, even if a question is not a natural thing, still it is very close to one, just like the reason for making an appeal for a judgment is close to the principal reason that he who wins afterwards by reason of making an appeal is made stronger in the judgment of the matter judged.[184]

---

[182] The purpose of the prior two paragraphs is to emphasize that the best elections have proper roots: a nativity or a horary question (either of which must show that the action will be successful). But Bonatti concedes that sometimes we must do what we can, and elect without a root (although this is not preferred).

[183] Again, Sahl, *On Elect.*, Ch. 1.

[184] This analogy rests on the meaning of *appellatio*, which can refer to making an appeal to a court. The idea seems to be this: if we lose a court case on the original merits, the appeal we make to a higher court will still have a relation to the original grounds for the case, even if we are bringing in other, technical reasons for the verdict to be reconsidered; and a favorable appeal can overcome substantive obstacles the appellant faced in the original trial. Similarly, a nativity is like an original verdict on the future of the inceptor, but we can still elect for him on the basis of a successful horary question for someone whose nativity is unknown, because

And there is another way of electing, and it can be known by it whether the matter will be perfected after the question that is posed: like if the Ascendant of the question or the Ascendant of the conjunction or prevention which was before the question, was made fortunate: it is a sign that the matter will be perfected. If indeed it were made unfortunate, it signifies an impediment so that the matter will not be perfected. If however the nativity or question were had, the ascending [sign] of the election should be made the ascending [sign] or the 10ᵗʰ of the nativity or question, or the sign signifying the matter which we wanted to begin, if it were made fortunate. If indeed one of those were not made fortunate, it must be considered what the ascending [sign] was in that year in the hour of the entrance of the Sun into Aries (or his entrance into the other quarters of the year, when the year is revolved according to quarters), if it were made fortunate; or its 10ᵗʰ, or the sign signifying the matter in that hour: and which of them you were to find more fortunate, make that one the ascending [sign] of the election of the matter for which it is elected; and [do] this both for those whose nativities are known or whose questions are had, and in the other [cases]; and likewise this will signify the effecting of the matter.

It can even be elected in another way for those whose nativities are not known, and whose questions are not had, but this way is difficult because we do not know all the things which happen to someone.¹⁸⁵ But if some great accident of someone's were made plain to you, you could know how you ought to elect for him in the inceptions of his matters; and stronger and better and more secure than this is if the accident were the first thing which happened to him, whether the accident were good or bad (good like dignities or some great magistracy or something similar to these which do not usually tend to happen); and by how much greater the dignity was, so much more will [the election's] ascending [sign] be similar to the ascending [sign] of the nativity of him for whom you wanted to elect; and so by how much greater was the evil, likewise its ascending [sign] will be harmonious with his ascending [sign].

But if the accident were evil, that Ascendant will be something to be avoided in his elections, just as it will be something to take up if the accident were good;

(assuming it is properly rooted) the horary question will still have a bearing on the inceptor's future, so that it has a good chance of overturning whatever negative verdict might have been rendered in the nativity. Bonatti will also use this legalistic metaphor in Tr. 9, when referring to conception charts and horaries on fetuses in the womb.

¹⁸⁵ From here to the end of the chapter, Bonatti is offering a last-resort option for those lacking horary charts or nativities: we adapt planets universally signifying good or bad events in the native's life–e.g., if he is very wealthy, we can assume he has a good Jupiter (which can then be adapted).

and its contrary (namely the seventh [sign]) will have to be rejected, and through the seventh [sign] from the ascending [sign] of the evil accident you could elect for him, if you did not have his nativity or question.[186] Indeed an accident is called evil when something greatly inconvenient comes to him: like adversity which is not accustomed to coming to him, like the loss of his greatest (or great) things, like illness or shipwreck or a long captivity, and the like. Whence the Ascendant of those accidents[187] is to be known and observed, just like the Ascendant of the nativity or the question, if it can be known; which if it could not, do as I told you elsewhere: adapt that which you can adapt so that your election profits him for whom you elect.

And according to this same method we can consider that when some planet is made fortunate and strong, or some sign is made fortunate, pleasing and useful things happen to someone, that it would have virtue in the root of his nativity;[188] and when some sign is made unfortunate, or some planet is made unfortunate, and adverse things fall to him, then that sign or that planet would have virtue in the root of his nativity. Likewise if one of the aforesaid accidents happens to some great man (namely from among whose who are fit for a kingdom), that there would be virtue to that planet or that sign in the root of his nativity. You can say the same about some clime or some region, when some-thing great and horrible happens to it, and even when it happens to some city or castle, or some building of great durability by some sign or some planet existing in an impeded way–it is a sign that it would have power in the beginning of the building. Whence you can put it as the ascending [sign] in his elections; or when some great and good things happen to him, you can do the same if that same sign (and that same planet) appears strong and fortunate; and likewise in all customs of the citizens of some city or region, to which sign or to which planet they are likened. And you can give it to them as a significator; and even in individual and private cases it can have a place.

Chapter 16: When that which was undertaken is to be believed that it will be perfected

---

[186] I believe this means that if the ascending sign were bad, one could substitute the opposite sign to yield a good election.

[187] I.e., a chart cast for the exact moment of an accident.

[188] I.e., we can assume something about his nativity, as a general and rough form of rectification.

When we begin something and the Lord of the first and the Moon and the Lord of the matter which we begin are in angles or in their succeedents, free from impediments, and made fortunate (or at least the planet signifying the matter which we begin), and the matter is a durable one (like the construction of a city or castle, or even the building of a house and the planting of trees, and the like); and they are in the aspect of the Sun by a trine or sextile in the day (or even in a square with reception), or of the Moon by night, or in the aspect of those whose domiciles were those in which [the luminaries] are, it is a sign that the matter will be perfected, and will come down to a good end, and its duration will be for a long time. Whence in such cases you must always put the significators in fixed signs, and in angles or in the succeedents, strong and made fortunate, just as well as you could.

However, in matters which we want to be finished quickly, nor to last for a long time (like banquets and the declarations of women and their betrothals, of which we desire a quick end and speedy durability), the significators can be put in those cadent from the angles, provided that they are not otherwise impeded. And if a movable sign were ascending, it will be better, provided that its Lord is not impeded: for the speed and slowness of matters are considered just as nature demands of any thing (like magnitude and smallness). For if one matter is supposed to be perfected in one hour,[189] and its nature demands this, and it lasts for four or five hours until its perfection, indeed with the delay being reckoned for the matter,[190] when it ought to be perfected quickly, it is perfected slowly, like this: someone who had invited certain people to lunch was supposed to prepare the food for them in the third hour, and he put off the preparations until the fifth hour: in this way the matter was delayed because it was not prepared at the required hour. Likewise someone was supposed to go to some place that day, and he put off going until the following day: in this way the journey was delayed, because he did not go on the appointed day. For this is just like magnitude. For indeed smallness is considered just as it is referred to its signification, [like] a big and and a small horse.

---

[189] I.e., the *action* is supposed to be performed in a given hour, and the inceptor does not begin or finish on time.

[190] *Relata quidem tarditate ad rem illam.* Meaning somewhat uncertain, especially since Bonatti does not finish the clause but moves right into his example. My conjecture (based on this and the following paragraphs) is this: if an action is supposed to be undertaken quickly, but we know that there will be a delay, we can put the significators in fixed signs, provided that they are cadent or the Ascendant is a movable sign. That way, the nature of the event will be geared toward its quickness, but the planets in fixed signs will allow for a delay (with subsequent success).

Likewise concerning speed, like when someone was supposed to go to someone who had promised him he was going to give him a house after one year,
and he went to him before a half-year or even prior to the year: in this way he
hastened to go to the place where he was supposed to go, wherefore he came
before the required and ordained time. And understand the same about every
hastening or speed, whether the speed or delay lasted for a year or for a
moment. And so it can be said concerning diverse matters according to diverse
considerations, and according to diverse relations [or respects]: because
according to the same year, according to the same month, according to the same
day, according to the same hour, according to whatever identical time, it can be
called slowness and quickness. And the significations of all the times are taken
from the signs and from the planets, from the places in which they are, and
from their natures. Because slow planets signify slowness, and chiefly the
retrograde ones or even the stationary ones (and especially in the first station
and when they are slow). Indeed the light ones signify speed according to the
condition of their motion, and especially the direct ones; and more strongly so
when they are increasing in number.

> From the signs we take the signification of the time, because fixed signs
> signify the slowness and delaying of time; the common ones, the average
> [or middle speed] of time; indeed the movable ones signify speed and
> ease. And even the signs of direct ascensions aid slowness; and the signs
> of crooked ascension aid speed; and the planets constituted in them [aid
> similarly].[191]

> The airy ones likewise aid speed, and the fiery ones more so than the airy
> ones. The watery ones increase slowness, and the earthy ones more so
> than the watery ones.

> The angles likewise aid speed; the cadents, slowness; the succeedents
> seem to aid speed in a moderate way.

> Whence if one of the signs were ascending, or were the house [domicile?]
> signifying the matter to be begun, or one of the aforesaid planets were in one of
> those places, whatever one of them it is will aid or impede in speed or slowness

---

[191] By "aiding" slowness, he means "makes it slower." By "aiding" speed, he means "makes it
faster." See below.

according to the nature, sign, or place in which it is: like if it were a fast planet in a place or sign or house signifying speed, it will help that speed and the matter will come to pass quickly. If however it were in a sign or house signifying slowness, it will subtract somewhat from the slowness. And if it were a planet signifying slowness in a house or sign signifying slowness, it will aid the slowness and the matter will come to be slowly. And if it were in a house or sign signifying speed, it will subtract somewhat from the speed. And if the significators were oriental from the Sun, they aid the speed and subtract something from the slowness. And if they were occidental from him, they aid the slowness and decrease the speed.

And al-Rijāl said[192] that the signification is taken from the places of the signs, according to how they are from the houses. For he said that the Ascendant and the tenth [sign] signify speed, namely days and hours; the seventh [sign] slowness, that is less speed, like a month or a week; the fourth [sign] less speed again, because instead of months it could signify years. Indeed the succeedents signify that which their angles do, but they delay the matter somewhat more. Indeed the cadents signify slowness. And he said however, those which are above the earth, universally signify a more certain speed than those located below the earth. And he said that the eastern quarter which is from the Midheaven to the Ascendant, signifies speed; the southern one which is from the tenth to the seventh, middling speed; the western one which is from the seventh[193] to the fourth designates middling slowness. The northern one which is from the fourth to the first, slowness. And he said: and if it were to happen that a sign signifying speed is in a quarter signifying speed, but if a movable sign were the Ascendant or the tenth, this will be the faster speed from signs that we could have.

Chapter 17: From which planets the signification of times is taken

Indeed of the planets from which we take the faster signification, they are: the Lord of the matter, and the planet which is joined to one of them, or who transfers the disposition of one of them to another, and the luminaries, and the planet to which the Moon is joined. And whichever of the aforesaid planets had

---

[192] This may be based on a lengthy chapter on predictive techniques (many of which are completely unknown today) at the end of al-Rijāl's treatise on elections, pp. 346-51.
[193] Reading *septimo* for *decimo*.

more dignities or strengths in the Ascendant, and in the 10th of the matter,[194] or at least in the house of the matter, we take from that one the signification of the time of the coming of the matter which we want to know.

And al-Rijāl said[195] that a faster speed and a slower delay of any matter in its own kind, and in its own nature [or condition], is signified by the planets according to their speed.[196] And he said that the planets signifying the time in which the matter undertaken is supposed to be perfected (whether the thing signified were good or not), will give their own signification when their condition will be changed from strength into weakness or *vice versa*. And he said that the weaker change which a planet can make is when it is in some quarter of the circle and it is changed from that one to another: like from the rising to the setting one, or [if] it were below the earth and is changed to above the earth, or it descends from the superiors to the inferiors.[197] And he said that their change is strong, like if it were oriental [and] it became occidental, or *vice versa*; or it is changed from one sign to another, and especially if it were a change from a sign in which it has dignity to another in which it does not have any dignity, and *vice versa*.

Moreover, in order to know the time of a matter undertaken or to be begun—when it will come to be or when it will be ended—it is necessary for you to take the number of degrees which there are between the planetary *al-mubtazz* over the place signifying the matter, and between another which has likewise a signification over the same matter: and by how many degrees there were (if the planet were of those which signified hours), the hours until the end or duration or perfection of the matter will be that many; and if it were to signify days, they will be so many days; and if it were to signify months, they will be so many months; and if it were to signify years, they will be so many years according to the nature of the place, and according to the nature of the significator, and according to the nature of the matter, just as it can come to be or be ended in hours or days or months or years.

For example, let it be put that Mercury is the significator of the time, and let him be in the ninth degree of Pisces; and let Jupiter be in the sixteenth degree of Cancer, to whose conjunction Mercury now goes. And there are 7° between them up to the completion of their conjunction. In this way, since Mercury is of

---

[194] Does Bonatti must mean by derived houses, or the 10th from the Ascendant?
[195] Probably based on al-Rijāl, p. 351.
[196] I.e., Saturn indicates a slower time than Jupiter does.
[197] I am unsure what "from the superiors to the inferiors" refers to, but perhaps it means from above (in latitude) to below (in latitude).

the lighter planets, which signify the hastening of matters, he now signifies hours (or in a matter that is not very fast, days). Whence if it were concerning matters of hastening, the matter will come to be in up to seven hours, namely they ought to come to be that same day. If it were concerning less speedy matters, which transpire over in a week, it will come to be in up to seven days, or up to the hour in which Mercury is [actually] in the sixteenth degree of Pisces, so that he directly aspects the degree in which Jupiter was when the matter was undertaken (or the question proposed about it), if its arrival to that degree were after seven days. And if it were a matter which one could expect in months, it would come to be up to so many months [later]. And if it were of those [matters] expecting [to take] years, it would come to be in up to so many years [later].

Understand the same about everything according to the quantity of the distances in degrees existing between the significators: and that will be the hour of the perfection or eventuating of the matter quaesited or undertaken. And if there were a greater quantity of degrees between the significators, it would likewise come to be according to so many hours or days or months or years, according to its nature and the relation to the matter.[198] And if it were such a quantity that signs could be made from it, the matter would come to be in up to so many hours or days or months or years, by how many signs resulted from those degrees, and up to fractions according the quantity of degrees of an incomplete sign. For example, between a planetary significator (of whatever sort the significator was), and a heavier one to which he was joined, there were 180°, which yielded six signs; in this way the effecting or durability or full amount of this matter is signified by six hours, if it were concerning matters which would come to be in hours as nature requires of them. And if it were of those things which come to be in days, it will come to be in up to six days; and if it were of those things which come to be in weeks, it would come to be in up to six weeks; and if it were of those which come to be in months, it will come to be in up to six months; and if it were of those things which come to be in years, it will come to be in six years; and perhaps that some fraction[199] could fall between them, but not one which would lead into error.

And understand the same about all the distances of the numbers of all degrees or signs, by comparing all proportions just as they happen for you. Moreover, if the planetary significator of a matter were joined to some planet,

---

[198] *Secundum…relationem ad eam rem.*
[199] Reading *fractio* for *factio.*

or another were joined to it, and there comes to be mutual reception between them, their years are to be considered: like if they were in angles, and there were a significator with authority (namely who had greater virtue or power in the matter), you will consider the greater years of the significator from those heavy planets who signify years, and say that the matter will last up to so many years. And if it were then the beginning of his inception, and the significators were below the earth, the matter will be completed in up to so many years as there are greater years of the planet signifying it. And if the significator were in the succeedents, put the number of years according to its middle years. And if it were in the cadents, make the number of years its lesser ones. And if the significator were among the planets signifying months or days or hours, make their number according to the number of aforesaid years, and in the aforesaid way, in proportion as the significators were strong or weak, light or heavy.

And al-Rijāl said[200] that in every matter the Moon signifies hours, and especially in speedy ones; and likewise the Sun. However the Sun can signify days where the Moon signifies hours, and months where she could signify days. And he said when [some planet] arrives who carries away the disposition between between significators to him to whom he carries [it] away (whether by body or by rays),[201] that the degrees which are between them will be taken, and for every degree months or days will be put. And he said that the Lord of the Ascendant and the Lord of the house [domicile?] of the matter, if they were conjoined, will signify the speed of the effecting of the matter, if it were testified to (and especially if the Lord of the Ascendant were heavier). And he said that if the Moon were to descend in the Ascendant[202] or in the house [domicile?] of the matter, or were to aspect one of them by a square aspect or opposition, it will be an hour. And he said that the Sun signifies the same as the Moon does in the same places. And he said that the Sun is stronger than the Moon in this business. And he said that when the Moon has reached the place of the significator, that will be the hour. He said the same thing about the *al-mubtazz* concerning the beginning of the matter.

And he said[203] that he has found certain people who extracted the *hīlāj*[204] of the matter just as it would be in nativities, and they used to direct the degree of

---

[200] This seems to recall the discussion in al-Rijāl, p. 351.
[201] This could refer to the transfer of light.
[202] What could it mean to "descend in the Ascendant"?
[203] This could be based on al-Rijāl, p. 349, but there al-Rijāl is speaking of the direction of the *hīlāj* itself.

the *hīlāj* to the place of the benefics and the malefics; and they put a year or a month or a day (according to the nature of the matter) for every degree by [oblique] ascensions. If the direction were to reach a benefic first before a malefic, they said that the matter would be perfected with success. If however it were to reach a malefic first before a benefic, they said that the matter would be perfected with adversity. (And he said that Mars signifies speed, but he admixes something of martial matters.)[205] And they used to work in the same way with the degree of the Ascendant and the degree of the house of the matter. To me however, it seems that even if it could be so, that it would be a great complication, and that the above opinion should suffice for you, and because it would take a long time to expound to a fine point all the things that occur to us, and the sayings of the philosophers, and it would be something practically abominable, and tedious for the reader. May you understand the aforesaid from your own industry, and may you see and perceive what ought to be perceived (namely, whether the significators are of the light or heavy planets, or are in angles or the succeedents or the cadents, or are in fixed signs or movable ones, or direct or crooked ones, or in places signifying years or months or days), all of which you could perceive what you intend from the aforesaid if you were to consider well and were perspicuous.

Chapter 18: On the fixed, common, and movable signs

Indeed Sahl put great power in the signs, and he put great significations in them, [and] not without reason. And they are to be referred to the significators when they are in them, and to the Moon; and to her before all other significators, because she is the significatrix of all matters, as is said elsewhere.

Even if all the other significators were abandoned, she must always be considered, except that the Lord of the hour is to be observed beforehand in the place which I told you. For the said wise man stated[206] [that] the fixed signs are congruent to every work whose stability and prolongation of time is sought, and that which its author wants to be durable and good and useful, is in them: building, and celebrating a marriage, the betrothal having been made in the

---

[204] The use of *hīlāj* here refers to a more general significator in horary and electional figures. Al-Rijāl also speaks of a *hīlāj* in this sense on occasion.

[205] Bonatti inexplicably inserts this sentence into his material from al-Rijāl.

[206] Al-Rijāl, pp. 302-3. See also Sahl, *On Elect.*, "The Ascendant and what is in it concerning elections, in the knowledge of the natures of the signs, of which the first are the movable ones."

movable ones.[207] And if, in them, the wife were sent away by the husband, she would not return to him in a short time; understand this unless the testimonies of the benefics were multiplied in them. And he who had been conquered in them, his imprisonment will be prolonged; and he who grows angry in them, would not be able to be soothed quickly; indeed farming and renting are useful in them; and it will be good to build and lay foundations. And he said, however, Scorpio is lighter than the other fixed ones; and Leo is more fixed; Aquarius is slower and worse; indeed Taurus is more easy.

Chapter 19: On the common signs

And [Sahl] said[208] the common signs are useful in partnerships and taking part in things; "and whatever is done under them will often be repeated: indeed to buy" (understand, things which we want to remain in the possession of the buyers), "and to celebrate a wedding…will not be useful…and there will be cleverness and deception under them. And he who is accused of something under [the common signs] will escape and be relieved of that which he is accused of; and he who is incarcerated [under them] will not be stuck [there], except that he will have fear on account of his small retinue and his exits;[209] and he who goes out from a prison will return to [his own place]; and if he is caught under them, the fugitive will return to his flight a second time; and he who goes forth to a judge under them, the sentence will not be made firm for him, nor the judgment; nor should someone go out by boat under them, because he will be changed completely from that one to another" (for no good reason). And if something is permitted under them, it will be dissolved, and it will not be completed for him; and a sick person would be healed under them, then incur a renewal [of the illness]. Therefore everything that happens to a man under them, [both] of the good and the bad, is duplicated upon him; and if someone were to die under them, then someone else will die after him in that place, nearby. And

---

[207] As Bonatti has already said, one should celebrate betrothals using cardinal (movable) signs, because periods of betrothal should be short; now he is recommending the wedding be celebrated by using fixed signs, since marriage is supposed to last a long time.

[208] Al-Rijāl, *ibid.*; Sahl, *ibid.*

[209] *Nisi in timore proprie propter parvitatem suae apparitionis et exitus eius.* I take this to mean that he will not have many people to help him and visit him (e.g., to bring him clothing and such), and he will not be let out much. So the idea seems to be that while he will not remain there, he will still suffer.

exchanges [or barters], and the washing of the head and beard, and the cleansing of gold and silver are appropriate under them; and sending boys to learn.

And the same author [al-Rijāl] said,[210] if however under them you wished to begin one of those things which I have told you, then put the Moon in the domicile signifying the matter which you intend to do, and conjoin her with a benefic receiving her in that sign. And he said, indeed the signs of the day [diurnal signs], are stronger in operations during the day; and make the Ascendant a diurnal sign or the sign signifying your matter.[211] And he said the airy signs (which are Gemini, Libra and Aquarius) are suited to hunting by land and sea; and the signs of kings (which are Aries and Leo)[212] are suited to kings; and signs having voices are suited to singers and those wanting to play musical instruments; and the fiery signs are suited to every thing which you might wish to do with fire; and the equinoctial signs are suited to all equality and every measure, and every matter in which truth is esteemed, and pole bars (which are balances), and measures and weighty justice. And the movable signs (and they are those in which night and day begin to change) are suited to those who wish to be turned around from a matter to a matter, or from a place to a place. And he said,[213] consider, for every work which you wish to begin, what is the nature of that sign in the circles;[214] and conjoin the Moon and the Lord of the Ascendant with that substance; and the root of that nature and its virtue is in that hour, namely in the hour of the inception.

And consider the Sun in the affairs of lords, magnates, princes, and the chief overseers of cities, and officers, as is said elsewhere. And in the affairs of those making abundant and great expenses, consider Jupiter. And in the affairs of farmers and low-class people, consider Saturn. And in the affairs of generals and the masters of armies and fighters, consider Mars. And in the affairs of writers, painters, bankers or moneychangers, tradesmen,[215] and even merchants, consider Mercury. And in the affairs of queens and other excellent women, consider the Moon (and even in the affairs of mothers and stepmothers). And

---

[210] This paragraph is a further paraphrase of al-Rijāl (p. 303), except for the sentences about equinoctial and movable signs.

[211] Al-Rijāl adds that we ought to put the Moon in diurnal signs, too.

[212] 1491 also omits Sagittarius.

[213] Al-Rijāl actually says, "Afterwards, see of what nature is the matter which you want to begin, and which of the signs of heaven agrees with that nature, and make the Moon and the Lord of the Ascendant apply to that nature, and make that nature better, and strengthen it as much as you can in the hour of the inception."

[214] *Ex orbibus.* He means, "in the circle of the signs."

[215] *Merzariorum.*

in the affairs of other women, consider Venus, and chiefly [those] of young girls and those who gladly decorate their faces so as to please men. And in all of these, make effort to consider those things you must consider, just as is said to you.

Chapter 20: On the movable signs

And [Sahl] said[216] the movable signs signify the hasty mobility of matters; and nothing durable comes to be under them; nor is the time of deeds done prolonged while the Moon and the significators are in them. However, they are suited for those who wish to sow seed, and to secure a woman and become betrothed (all these are successful under them); likewise buying and selling merchandise, and those things which change quickly from the hands of one to the hands of another; and if someone were then sick, he will be liberated (his illness will be ended quickly); and if some lawsuit were undertaken them, it will not be prolonged; and if someone were to flee then, he will be returned quickly; and if someone were to promise something to someone, he will not observe his promise to him; it will even be good and useful to go on a pilgrimage under them; rumors which were spread then, will be false; and dreams under them will not have a signification;[217] nor is it good to begin to cure some sick person then, if the illness were such that it could be put off until the Moon appeared in a movable sign; nor should a tree whose durability we want be planted; nor plugging a fig tree,[218] nor a building, nor to lay some foundation; and to do or start nothing whose durability or prolongation we desire. But should you desire the speed of any matter, begin [it] under them; and those will be faster which are more crooked, and of greater mobility (like Aries and Cancer); indeed Libra and Capricorn are stronger and more temperate.

And Sahl said,[219] adapt the Moon according to [your] ability. You should not ever put her in the Ascendant of any beginning, and particularly [in that of] any journey; because it signifies that some infirmity (or something equivalent to an infirmity) will happen to the traveler in his body, unless the Lord of the Ascendant or a benefic aspects the ascending degree: because when a planet aspects the Ascendant and its Lord, it is like a man who guards his own house:

---

[216] Much of this paragraph is a paraphrase of Sahl (On Elect., Ch. 2), with slightly different endings on several words in the direct quotations.
[217] See also Tr. 6, Part 2, 9th House, Ch. 9.
[218] See 4th House, Ch. 9.
[219] The rest of this paragraph is a paraphrase of Sahl, On Elect., Ch. 3.

because anyone which is in it, fears him; and he who is outside it, fears to go there. If indeed it did not aspect, it will be to the contrary. And if the Lord of the first were malefic, make him [aspect it] by a trine or sextile aspect; and beware lest you put the Moon (or the Lord of the Ascendant) in an angle if the malefics were to aspect her, unless by chance she were to receive it by a trine or sextile aspect. Nor should you even put the Moon in an angle unless she is free. But put the benefics and the Part of Fortune in angles; and in every way, if you ever can, make it so that the Moon aspects the Part of Fortune or is joined to it corporally (even though this rarely can happen). And if you could not make it so that the Part of Fortune were not cadent from the Ascendant, make it so that the Lord of the Ascendant aspects [the Part of Fortune], or is joined to [the Part of Fortune] just like I told you about the Moon. And make the effort, if you can, to put the Lord of the Ascendant with the Part [of Fortune]; because this signifies greater wealth on a journey, and greater usefulness. And[220] beware lest you put the Moon in the second or the sixth or the eighth or the twelfth,[221] because this is horrible and is something to fear.

Sahl said,[222] if you can do it, make effort to put the Ascendant and its Lord and the Moon in signs of direct ascension (namely because it signifies ease and progress); and you should not put them in crooked signs. For he said, because [the crooked signs] signify complications and duress and delay; for the Ascendant and the fourth [sign] signify what happens concerning the election. Therefore look to the benefics and the malefics with regard to their places, and at their strength and weakness, and speak according to what you were to find with regards to the strength or weakness of the beginning or end of the matter.

And Dorotheus said[223] if you were to find the Moon impeded, and it were a matter which could not be put off, you should not give the Moon a portion[224] in the Ascendant; and make her decline from it,[225] and put a benefic in it; and greatly strengthen [the Ascendant] and its Lord.

---

[220] In this sentence I have used Sahl's whole sign houses, since Bonatti is trying to stick so closely to Sahl's text. 1491 and 1550 use the feminine, but without clarifying whether quadrant houses or domiciles are meant.
[221] Sahl adds: "from the Part."
[222] This paragraph is a paraphrase of Sahl, *On Elect.*, Ch. 3.
[223] This is Dorotheus according to Sahl, *On Elect.*, Ch. 3. I cannot seem to find this statement in Dorotheus himself.
[224] This is the word Sahl uses to indicate having a dignity.
[225] I.e., make her cadent from the Ascendant.

And[226] by no means should you put the Moon in the Ascendant in [cases of] journeys, whether she is impeded[227] or not.

---

[226] Al-Rijāl, p. 300.
[227] Reading *impedita* for *impedimenta*.

[PART 2]: On those Things which Seem to Pertain to Particular Elections

Chapter 1: Preamble to particular elections of the houses

Even if it was discussed sufficiently above concerning those things which generally pertain to elections, still the things that were said do not seem to suffice perfectly for those who wish to use elections, unless we arrive at those things which pertain to particular elections. And these will be the ones which are stated in a manner as though [they were] a standard or a collection of the aforesaid. Nor does it seem possible to descend[228] to particular elections so that some of those set out in advance are not touched on;[229] and it was said above that we must adapt certain things which are rooted in elections, as much as it seems possible, even though it is impossible to [adapt them] all when we want to be able to adapt [them].

And they are the first [sign] and its Lord, likewise the fourth [sign], and its Lord; the Moon and the Lord of the sign in which she then is; the Sun and the Lord of the sign in which he is; also the Part of Fortune and the Lord of the domicile in which it falls in the election; also the house [domicile?] signifying the matter for which it is elected, and its Lord; and the planet which naturally signifies the matter; and the Lord of the sign in which [the planet] is. All of these are to adapted according to the sayings of the wise in the beginning of each election, so that the election is secure in every way. But this (just as I have told you) will hardly or never be possible. And I have already told you often: if you cannot adapt whatever you want, adapt that which you can.

And al-Rijāl said[230] that none of the significators which we must weaken ought to be put in the beginning of any matter which we want to begin, and especially if it were strong in the nativity (if the nativity for which you elect is evident) or in the question (if the question is had), or in the revolution of that year.[231] And [he said] that perhaps it will be necessary for us sometimes to weaken one of the said significators in some [cases], just as it is [necessary] to

---

228 This is an implicit reference to the traditional philosophical view that one must descend from more general principles to more particular ones.
229 Bonatti is notifying the reader that some of the general principles will be reviewed again in what follows, since particular elections are special applications of them. This is a repetition of his statement earlier about not being able to cross a stream or road with a "dry foot."
230 I cannot find this statement in al-Rijāl.
231 Bonatti means the mundane ingress, as stated earlier.

weaken the Moon in going out to hunt or in the investigation of a thief or another fugitive; and even [to weaken] the planet to which she is joined; and to strengthen him from whom she is being separated.

And twelve headings will be contained in this Treatise, following the number of the twelve houses, to which the other chapters will be subordinated. And it will not be surprising if some of those things which are listed above are going to be listed in them: because certain ones have a univocal meaning, which are of equivocal signification;[232] and sometimes it is put in one place for one signification, and it is put in another for another.

The first chapter, on the 1st house and its significations; the second on the 2nd and its significations; the third on the 3rd and its significations; the fourth on the 4th and its significations; the fifth on the 5th and its significations; the sixth on the 6th and its significations; the seventh on the 7th and its significations; the eighth on the 8th and its significations; the ninth on the 9th and its significations; the tenth on the 10th and its significations; the eleventh on the 11th and its significations; the twelfth on the 12th and its significations.

---

[232] By this medieval logical terminology Bonatti simply means that we might list the same instructions (e.g., "put a benefic in trine aspect to the Sun") under different houses for different reasons, depending on our purposes.

ON THE FIRST HOUSE

Chapter 1: On nursing boys

If someone wanted to hand a boy over to a wet-nurse so she may nurse him, it is necessary that when the wet-nurse begins to nurse him, [that], first, the Moon be joined to Venus corporally; which if this could not be, let her be joined to her by a trine or sextile aspect with reception (namely from Taurus or Libra); and if Venus were descending in her eccentric or epicycle, it will be better.

And al-Rijāl said[233] that it is necessary that the rooted matters be adapted from the beginning; you however, adapt those of the rooted things you can adapt; and if you cannot adapt all of the rooted things, still adapt what I told you above (namely Venus and the Moon).

Chapter 2: On the weaning of boys from milk

If you wanted to take a boy away from milk, put the Moon as far from the Sun as you can, namely from the ninetieth degree to the one hundred sixty-seventh. And al-Rijāl said that it seemed to certain people that the Moon should not be in one of the domiciles of Venus in this work, because they feared that the mother of the child would not take the child[234] away from the breasts.[235] And a certain person said that if we were to separate a nursing child from the wet-nurse, if the Moon were in *Marchafa*, which is the twelfth mansion of the Moon (and it is in Libra), the child will not care about the milk any more.[236] And certain others said that the Moon and the Lord of the Ascendant should be in signs of seeds, namely Taurus, Virgo and Capricorn: because this signifies that the boy will incline to the eating of seeds and herbs.[237] And if she were in Leo, he will incline to the eating of meats. And if she were in Cancer or Scorpio or Pisces, he will incline to the eating of fishes. And if she were in the other signs, he will eat generally those things which are given to him for eating.

---

[233] Al-Rijāl, p. 313.

[234] Reading *filium* for *alium*.

[235] Al-Rijāl (p. 313) does report that others wanted to avoid the domiciles of Venus, but he does not give the reason.

[236] This is an error. Al-Rijāl's text (p. 313) clearly says the mansion is *Azarfa*, which Bonatti lists as the eleventh mansion in Tr. 10. There is no mansion called *Marchafa*, but without the leading *M*, *Archafa* does look like *Azarfa*.

[237] Al-Rijāl (p. 313).

Chapter 3: On the cutting of fingernails and toenails

If you wanted to cut off the fingernails or toenails, let the Moon be in a succeedent to an angle; and if she cannot be put in a succeedent, let her be put in an angle (for the cadents are to be avoided); and let the Moon be increasing in light and number; nor let her be in Gemini, and especially if one of the malefics (namely Mars or Saturn) were to aspect her by a square aspect or from the opposition. For if Saturn were to aspect her, it is to be feared that they will not grow back (and if they were to grow back, so that they will not grow back wormy).[238] If however Mars were to aspect her from one of those aspects, it will be feared that the inner flesh of the fingers will be cut off, whence will follow discomfort and pain; and perhaps that the pain could be so increased that from thence an abscess (or some such thing) will result.

And al-Rijāl said that she should not be in Gemini nor in Sagittarius,[239] nor let her be joined to their Lords; but let her be in Aries or in Taurus, Cancer, Leo, Libra (but put her outside the *via combusta*, understand), nor let her be impeded in those signs. However in the cutting of toenails, one must beware of Gemini and Pisces and the *via combusta*, and the impediments of the malefics.[240]

Chapter 4: On the cutting of hair and the shaving of the beard

If you wanted to cut hair [on the head] or shave the beard,[241] let the Moon be in common signs (except for Gemini). And al-Rijāl said[242] that there was a certain man who did not recommend Virgo, nor did he condemn Libra nor Aries nor Taurus nor Capricorn; nor did he offer a reason why. I however do not condemn Aries in the *trimming* of the hair or the beard; but in *shaving* the head and beard I do. And he said that when the Moon and the Ascendant were in signs of seeds, [and] safe, that the hair and whiskers would grow back and

---

[238] Reading *tineosi* for *tiniosi*. Bonatti may be referring to something like *tinea*, i.e., ringworm.
[239] Al-Rijāl says to avoid Gemini and *Pisces*.
[240] Bonatti is selectively quoting or misquoting al-Rijāl. Al-Rijāl (pp. 305-6) says to avoid Gemini and Pisces and the aspects of Mercury and Jupiter. He says nothing about Sagittarius and does not distinguish fingernails from toenails. He also says the Moon may be put in the domiciles of Venus or Mars (or Cancer or Leo)–but Bonatti omits the domiciles of Mars.
[241] Al-Rijāl, a Muslim, does not make recommendations on shaving the beard.
[242] I do not know where Bonatti is getting this quote.

increase quickly. And he said that one must beware of the impediment of Saturn and Mars, lest an infection[243] should come to be in the hair then and there.[244]

Chapter 5: On the circumcision of boys[245]

To certain people it seemed that this chapter should be included under the 6th house, because it seemed to them that it was a certain infirmity.[246] However it seems to me that it must be included under the 1st house because it is practically among the first accidents of the body. For much of the time it takes place on the seventh day after the nativity, in the body of the native; however under whatever place it is included, there is no power in the hour of its election.[247]

Whence if you wanted to elect for someone that some boy be circumcised, make the Moon joined to Jupiter by a trine or sextile aspect, or by a square (but with reception); and let her be north of Venus; and beware lest Saturn aspect the Lord of the first or the Moon or Venus by a square aspect or the opposition, or even the Ascendant itself–because it signifies the putrefaction of the incision.[248] And let the Lord of the sign in which the Moon is, be northern, if it can be done, and the Moon going to an angle. And beware of Mars, lest he be in one of the angles; but let him be in a cadent. If you do not want to put him in a cadent, beware lest the Ascendant be Scorpio, nor let the Moon or the Lord of the Ascendant be in [Scorpio].

---

243 *Furfures*, a scaly infection of the skin.

244 *Tunc et hoc.*

245 Al-Rijāl treats circumcision and infant baptism in the same way (p. 313), presumably since they are each rites of passage for boys.

246 This is an interesting point, since medieval Latins did not circumcise, and viewed it negatively. I am surprised that Bonatti includes it, but in his career he undoubtedly mixed with Muslims and and Jews. Al-Rijāl includes it in a chapter on the 5th house, since it pertains to children– and presumably the inceptor is an adult wanting to circumcise his *own* child.

247 *Vis non existit in hora electionis eius.* I am unsure what Bonatti means by this–perhaps that circumcision does not have any intrinsic value? This could be why his main concern seems to be the infant's safety.

248 Al-Rijāl says Saturn indicates the infant would have to be cut again, and that poison [infection?] would overcome him.

ON THE SECOND HOUSE

Chapter 1: On lending and taking

In the significations of the 2nd house, we cannot descend to particulars in the beginning, without some things which seem to be universal being set out in advance on them (namely what pertains to substance or wealth or anything whence wealth may be expected). For instance, it is necessary for us in this matter to adapt the Lord of the 2nd house, and the planet in whose domicile it itself is; and even Jupiter is always to be adapted in every election which pertains naturally to substance, just as was said elsewhere.

And Sahl said[249] if you want to elect the hour for the taking and lending of money, let the Moon be in Leo (except for in its first bound, you understand), or Scorpio, or Sagittarius.[250] And do not let the Moon be in the first degree of any of them; nor let her be in Gemini, nor let the Ascendant be the first bound of any of them; because they signify the good of the one accepting, and the contrary to the one giving.[251]

However, in making restitution,[252] let the Moon be in Aquarius or Pisces; and let the Moon be decreasing in light. Even let Jupiter and Venus (or either of them) be ascending to the longer longitude, and let them aspect the Ascendant or the Moon (or her Lord),[253] or at least let one of them aspect them; nor let one of them be impeded, if it can be done. However, at least save the one of them that you can.

And [Sahl said],[254] let Mercury (who naturally signifies coins) be cleansed of the impediments of the malefics; and likewise the Moon, and particularly from the impediments of Mars: because if the Moon were impeded by Mars in such a matter, it signifies contention and quarrels and distress, and denials in the recovering or restitution of the money or commodities. If however she were

---

[249] Sahl, *On Elect.*, Ch. 4.

[250] Sahl adds Pisces and Aquarius, so Bonatti is selectively paraphrasing.

[251] See Sahl's Dorotheus, *On Elect.*, Ch. 4: "And Dorotheus said you should not begin a loan, nor should you loan something to someone while the Moon is in the first degree of Leo or Gemini or Sagittarius, or [if] these signs were ascending, because it is hateful for the loan especially." It seems to be a version of Dorotheus, *Carmen*, V.20. But Dorotheus himself says Capricorn, not Sagittarius.

[252] This is based on Dorotheus, *Carmen*, V.20 (who moreover uses different signs). Note that Bonatti only uses Aquarius and Pisces here (see above).

[253] This statement seems to be Bonatti's own. Although Bonatti's language could say "its Lord" (i.e., the Ascendant's Lord), his placement of it after the Moon suggests the Moon's Lord.

[254] This paragraph is a paraphrase of Sahl, *On Elect.*, Ch. 4.

impeded by Saturn, it signifies complications and prolongation and fatigue, and much destruction in its recovery or restitution.

Chapter 2: On wealth, that it may remain always in the possession of him for whom you elect

If indeed the intention of him for whom you elect were to make money, so that it would always remain in his possession, indeed so that it is not given over in the end to someone else, let the Ascendant at the hour of the election be a fixed sign; and [let] the Lord of the Ascendant and the Moon and the Lord of the second be in fixed signs, free from impediments, and do not let them be removed from the angles.[255]

If indeed the election were for the wealth of a thing that must be sold, or given away in another way, or repeated,[256] let the Ascendant be a movable or common sign (however a movable one is of more value in this). And let the Lord of the Ascendant and the Moon be in movable or common signs; and let them be free from impediments; and let the angles be removed, if it can be done; and in any of these cases always adapt whatever you can of the rooted things. If indeed it were the intention of him who gained wealth to observe the matter acquired so when he wished he could use it,[257] adapt the first and its Lord in his taking and storing up of it, and Jupiter, and make Mars be cadent from the aspect of the Moon, and of the Ascendant, and of the Part of Fortune, and of the Part of Substance and from its domicile, and from all the Lords of these domiciles, or at least from the Moon and from the Ascendant and its Lord. They even recommend the common signs in the taking of money, from wherever it is acquired.

If indeed the matter which someone wanted to repay were of those things which are chewed, like grain, meats, and the like, which men commonly use, we must beware that the Ascendant not be one of the signs of much eating (and those are Aries, Taurus, Leo, the last part of Sagittarius, Capricorn, and Pisces); nor let the Lord of the first or the Moon be in them; nor let Saturn be aspecting the Ascendant, or its Lord, or the Moon; or [do not] let one of them be in his corporal conjunction. For these [places or signs] signify that it will be eaten

---

[255] This seems to be based on al-Rijāl, p. 306; al-Rijāl wants all of the angles to be fixed signs, "and that they not be of removed angles."

[256] *Reiteranda.* Perhaps Bonatti is referring to the ongoing activity of buying and selling, which he attributed elsewhere to common signs.

[257] *Ut cum voluerit utatur,* reading *cum* for *eum.*

beyond measure, and under the pretense of eating it will be laid waste in this matter more than it ought to be.

Chapter 3: When the taker does not wish that the loan be known

If[258] indeed you were to accept a loan, [and] you did not want that someone know it, but you wanted that it be concealed so that it is not perceived by anyone, let the Moon (when you accept it or when you ask for it) be under the rays of the Sun, going toward the conjunction of some benefic, so that she is joined by aspect to one of the unimpeded benefics, immediately when she goes out from under the rays: for this is easy for the one elected for, and keeps him safe, so that in no way will the matter be made public, even if it is something deposited for safekeeping[259] or another matter of whatever sort it may be which someone wants to be hidden. And beware at that time lest the Moon be joined to the malefics: because if she were to go toward Mars when she was separated from the Sun, the matter (of whatever sort it was) will be made public and will be divulged, and it will fall into the mouths of men who gladly speak evil things. One must even beware lest in addition the Moon be with the Head of the Dragon or its Tail, or in the *via combusta*, because this is evil and horrible.

And Dorotheus said[260] you should neither lend nor accept a loan while the Moon is in the first degree of Leo or Gemini or Sagittarius, nor let one of those signs be ascending: because this is horrible loan.

Chapter 4: On buying for the purpose of making money

If someone wanted to buy some thing for the purpose of making money, as men often are wont to do, and it is his intention only that he make money from it, adapt the Moon in all of this (because she participates above all the other planets in those things which men do); and even adapt Mercury, who naturally signifies things of this sort; and adapt the Lord of the 2nd house, and even adapt the Lord of the Ascendant if you can adapt it (there should not be great emphasis on this),[261] and let the Moon be joined to Mercury; and let them both

---

[258] This paragraph is a more verbose paraphrase of Sahl, *On Elect.*, Ch. 4.
[259] *Depositum.*
[260] This is a paraphrase of Sahl's Dorotheus (*On Elect.*, Ch. 4), and slightly more faithful than its earlier version above.
[261] *Non sit in eo magna vis.*

be free from the impediments of Mars as much as you can. If however you could not adapt Mercury, adapt the Moon and the 11th and its Lord; nor however should you neglect to make it so that Mercury is free from Mars and his rays; however, if you can, make him be joined to Venus by body or by rays; or with the Lord of the 11th. And always let it be your concern, because however much better you were able to adapt Mercury in these matters after the adaptation of the Moon, by that much more would you be able to rely on the wealth of the thing which someone seeks: because he and the Moon and the 2nd and the 11th rule in these, and wealth is to be sought from them. And always keep them from Mars and his rays as best you can.

Chapter 5: In other common purchases and things commonly done

However, in other purchases which daily [and] ordinarily come to be from everyone indifferently, adapt the Part of Fortune as well as you can; and make it fall in one of the domiciles of Jupiter; and so that Jupiter or some other benefic would aspect it; because this will be better for him who buys than for him who sells. Likewise if the Moon were in crooked signs in little light–and it will never be better for the buyer.[262]

If however the Moon were in signs of direct ascension, in increasing light and number, and joined to the benefics, it will be better for the seller than for the buyer. And it will hardly ever happen that the buyer will make money from the purchase which happens then (or that he will not lose from it). And in all of these [cases], always make Mars be cadent from the Moon and from Mercury: because Mars always is contrary to the buyer and seller, and always introduces labor and contention. And beware of the Tail of the Dragon lest the Moon or Mercury or the Part of Fortune be with it, because Mars is not particularly worse than it.

There is even another method in buying and selling: because al-Tabarī[263] seemed to say that the Ascendant and its Lord are of the seller, the 7th and its Lord are of the buyer–which *seems* contrary to the sayings of the wise, when they [really] are not. For al-Tabarī considered when the sale takes its motion or beginning from the seller: that is, when the seller incites the buyer (for others understood that the buyer incites the seller); whence he said the Ascendant and

---

[262] Comparing this statement with the following one, it seems to mean that having the Moon in crooked signs, *etc.*, is very good for the buyer.
[263] Source unknown.

its Lord is the seller's [and] the 7th and its Lord is the buyer's. Indeed the Midheaven and its Lord belongs to the price, the fourth [sign] and its Lord belongs to the thing to be sold; even the planet from which the Moon is being separated is the seller's, and the Moon herself belongs to the thing to be sold; and the planet to which she is joined is the buyer's.

Al-Khayyat said[264] it is not evil if the Moon were in the Ascendant in buying and in selling, even though she is to be hated [there] in journeys.

Chapter 6: If someone wanted to sell some thing in order to make money with its price

If someone wanted to sell some thing and it was his intention that he make money on the price that he accepted for the thing, put the Moon in Taurus or Cancer or Virgo or Pisces, not impeded, and make it so that she is being separated from the benefics (or at least from one), whether by body or by aspect; and that she be joined to the malefics by aspect, not by body: for these signify good for him from whom the thing is separated, and who sells it.[265]

Chapter 7: If someone wanted to practice alchemy

At one time people applied themselves, and even today certain people (who often reprimand others for avarice) apply themselves to the art of alchemy; and often they lost their work, time, and expenses; nor does this happen to them because of one error, but from many: for it sometimes happens because they do not know how to come to the conclusion of what they have practiced; sometimes because they do not know how to proportion the bodies with the spirits; sometimes because they do not know how to elect an hour nor an Ascendant, nor how to place the Moon where she ought to be placed in order to perfect the work; and this is one of the greater errors which there can be for an alchemist. Nor do they even know how to adapt the planet signifying the matter which they intend to work on.[266]

Whence if someone wanted to practice something concerning these things, and he wished that you would elect the hour of its inception for him, put the

---

[264] Source unknown, but al-Rijāl says the Moon can be helpful in the Ascendant (p. 307).
[265] And that the Moon will give a worse deal to the buyer because she applied to a malefic.
[266] This speaks against the astrological and other occult sophistication that moderns usually attribute to medieval alchemists.

Moon in common signs,[267] cleansed of all impediments, and from all defects, and every bad condition; and let the Ascendant be a common sign, and let its Lord be adapted [or fit] and free from impediments. And adapt and strengthen the planet signifying the kind [of material] which he intends to work: like if it were lead, adapt Saturn; if it were crude ore[268] or yellow copper [or brass],[269] adapt Jupiter; if it were copper, adapt Mars; if it were gold, adapt the Sun; if it were *stagnum*,[270] adapt Venus; if it were electrum, adapt Mercury; if it were silver, adapt the Moon; and strengthen whichever one [it is] in the beginning of his working, according to the kind and according to the condition of each. If however it were a matter which ought to be repeated, may you do the same.

Chapter 8: On another way of lending money

Moreover, [here is] another chapter on lending according to al-Rijāl: for he said[271] that the Ascendant and its Lord belong to the debtor, the 7th and its Lord belong to him to whom it it owed (namely, he who loans). Mercury and the Moon signify what is owed. Therefore if there were concord between the Lord of the Ascendant and the Lord of the seventh, and Mercury [were] in the Ascendant or with his Lord, made fortunate, it will be perfected with ease. If indeed the Moon were under the rays of the Sun, it will be the Sun signifying the substance itself instead of the Moon. And he said if she were in the *via combusta*, or descending into the south[ern ecliptical latitudes],[272] or she were in the first degrees of Leo or Gemini or Sagittarius, or if those degrees themselves were ascending, they do not signify good for the one giving, but they confer usefulness to the one taking. And he said that certain people said it is never useful in loaning when it is in the hour of Saturn or the Sun.

---

[267] The source of these instructions is Sahl (*On. Elect.*, Ch. 8). The reason to use common signs seems to be that alchemists put their material through repeated heatings, coolings, and other processes (see al-Rijāl, p. 308). But it is strange that the paragraph ends, "*If* however it were a matter that ought to be repeated...".

[268] *Aes*, especially copper ore and alloys made with copper.

[269] *Aurichalcum* (var. *orichalcum*).

[270] *Stagnum* (var. *stannum*) is an alloy of silver and lead; also tin.

[271] Al-Rijāl, p. 307.

[272] Al-Rijāl (p. 307) says: "or were she toward the south in latitude."

Chapter 9: On the entrance into a house or inn in order to live in it

If you wanted to elect for someone about this matter, see whether the house is his own or rented. For it the house were his own, let the Ascendant be a fixed sign, and the Moon [be] in a fixed sign. And if the house were rented, let the Ascendant be a common sign and the Moon [be] likewise in a common sign. Whence the Ascendant and its Lord are to be adapted; the Moon also, and the Lord of the sign in which she herself is; the second [sign] and its Lord, the fourth [sign] also and its Lord; and the Part of Fortune is to be adapted, and its Lord. For the Ascendant and its Lord and the Moon and her Lord [are] for the person of the one lodging; the second [sign] and its Lord, and the Part of Fortune [are] for money and the conserving of substance already acquired; and it will happen if you could put Jupiter, fortunate, in the second [sign] in that hour (whatever kind of condition[273] he was [in]). However, Jupiter has value in this case. You will adapt the fourth [sign] to the end of the whole matter.

And al-Rijāl said,[274] let Taurus or Leo be the 4th house: for these signify that the place will be good, and the house will be cleansed, and few impeding or poisonous animals will be staying in it; for Scorpio signifies poisonous reptiles, and more strongly so if there were an aspect from Saturn [or Mars].[275] May you protect all of the aforesaid places from the malefics and their aspects as best you can, and make the benefics blessed, and their aspects according to [your] ability. And if you cannot make them all blessed, make at least the first and second (or at least either one) [blessed]; for after men make money, they do not care much about other things.[276]

---

[273] Reading *esse* for *esset*.
[274] This paragraph is a paraphrase of al-Rijāl, p. 308. For al-Rijāl, the topic of the chapter is, "On migrating from one house to another."
[275] Adding *et Marte* with al-Rijāl, p. 308.
[276] This last phrase is Bonatti's own comment.

ON THE THIRD HOUSE

Chapter 1: On short journeys

If someone wanted to make a short journey (which is of one day or less) which did not pertain to war, and you wanted to elect the hour for him to make the journey, adapt the Ascendant and its Lord; also the Moon and the Lord of the sign in which she is; and the Part of Fortune and its Lord; even the third and its Lord; likewise the planet to which the Moon is joined, and likewise the Lord of the hour; and the house [domicile?] signifying the matter for which the traveler goes (if he had specified it to you) and its Lord. And again I tell you, if you cannot adapt all the things which you ought to and want to, adapt whose which you can; among which let it be at least the Moon and the Lord of the hour. Which if you were not able to adapt the Moon, nor could you defer the journey, at least adapt the Lord of the hour, and make the Moon cadent from the Ascendant; [and] even from her Lord, if you can, and your election would be useful,[277] even if weakly so. These things will be said more extensively in the treatment of the 9th house [below], however.

Chapter 2: On the reconciliation of brothers and other blood-relatives, and neighbors and fellow citizens

Sometimes brothers disagree with each other, or even someone with his lesser blood-relatives, or even with his equals, both rich and powerful, at any age;[278] and they sometimes want to be reconciled together. And they want that you should elect for them the hour for doing this, so their reconciliation may be strong and lasting. Whence if some one of them were to come to you, that you may adapt the hour for them to this [purpose], adapt the Ascendant and its Lord, the Moon also and the Lord of the sign in which she is; likewise the third and its Lord (which signifies brothers and blood-relatives). And let the Lord of the third be in the conjunction of the Lord of the first or in its trine or sextile aspect, and this with perfect reception (namely by domicile or exaltation) or two

---

[277] Reading *proderit* for *perderit*.
[278] *Quam aetate.*

other lesser dignities;[279] and let the Lord of the third aspect the Ascendant by a praiseworthy aspect; and let the Lord of the first aspect the third in the same way, if it can be done; or let the Lord of the first be in the 10th or 11th, and let the Moon aspect both significators (or at least one of them). And it is necessary for you even to consider whether the reconciliation may be with older brothers or with middle ones or with younger ones. For if it were with older ones, it is necessary for you to adapt Saturn after the adaptation of the aforesaid. If however it were with middle ones, it is necessary for you to adapt Mars. If however with younger ones, it is necessary for you to adapt Mercury. Understand all of these in masculine [cases]. If however it were with sisters, it is necessary for you to adapt Venus just as was said about Saturn in masculine [cases] for older brothers. Understand the same about blood-relatives, neighbors, fellow citizens, according to the condition of each one in its own kind.

Chapter 3: On those things which pertain to a divine cult and the knowledge[280] of them

Certain of the ancients said that the 3rd house signifies religion, just like the 9th—which is true in lesser religions, not in the great ones which are called clerical or famous dignities (like the Papacy, cardinalship, archbishopric, bishopric, abbacy; and the religions of great voices or great fame): like those are which are under the above-written by name and fame, and which are of a strict life, and who labor in the divine cult.

Whence if you wanted to elect for someone wishing to adhere to one of those religions, or to exert himself in those things which pertain to the worship of God, adapt the Ascendent and its Lord, the Moon also and the Lord of the sign in which she is; and adapt the 3rd house and its Lord; adapt even Jupiter (who naturally signifies this); and adapt the Sun. Even make it so that the Ascendant is Sagittarius or Pisces, if ever you can. If if you wanted to give exact attention to those things which pertain to religion itself, adapt Mercury and make it so that the aforesaid significators aspect each other with a praiseworthy aspect, and that each one aspects the domicile of the other or the planet in

---

[279] I have placed the parentheses so as to exclude the "two lesser dignities" option from the definition of "perfect reception," because the only other place where it is defined confines it to domicile and exaltation only.

[280] *Eruditionem.* This word can also mean "instruction."

whose domicile it itself is;[281] and if you cannot adapt all of these, adapt those which you can adapt.

---

[281] I.e., so that it is received by domicile.

ON THE FOURTH HOUSE

Chapter 1: On the buying of houses or inheritances, and the like

To certain sages it seemed that a chapter on building should be set out before this [one], because building a house or castle (and the like) is more noble and of more renown than buying land or other possessions–with whom I can agree well enough. However, to me it seems to be more fitting first to have land upon which we build than that we begin to build, even though there is no great import in it.[282]

Whence if you wanted to elect the hour for someone wishing to buy some inheritance or a house or land or other estate, adapt the first and its Lord, even the Moon and the Lord of the sign in which she is; the fourth also and its Lord; adapt even the Part of Fortune and its Lord; and if you cannot adapt all of these, adapt the Moon and the fourth, and add to them the Part of Fortune if you can. And if not, at least do not let the adaptation of those two be lacking. You will even see if the place were fit or should be adapted so that it may be inhabited: let the Moon be in Cancer or in Taurus, or let her be in the 10th or at least in the 11th [domiciles?] and let her aspect the Lord of the first by a praiseworthy aspect. And beware lest she should aspect Mars from any aspect: and if you cannot free her from his aspect, make it so that he receives her by a trine or sextile aspect, and let him not be impeded then. And let the 4th house [domicile?], as was said, be Taurus or Leo or at least Aquarius; even let the Lords of the angles be oriental in the world and from the Sun (or from one of them); and let them be ascending northern.[283]

And al-Rijāl said,[284] in the buying of any inheritance let there be benefics having dignity in the angles; and if they could not have dignity in all the angles, let them have them in the first or in the fourth, or at least in one of them; let even the luminaries be aspecting the ascending [sign] and the fourth (or one of them) by an aspect of love; nor let the Lords of the angles be retrograde; nor let there be a retrograde planet in [the angles].

And al-Kindī said,[285] do not let a malefic be in the 9th or first or 11th, nor let the 4th house [domicile?] be a fiery one, nor let a fiery planet be in it, and

---

[282] I.e., it is not of great import which chapter comes first.
[283] I believe this means they should be in northern ecliptical latitude, moving further north.
[284] Al-Rijāl, p. 311.
[285] Al-Rijāl, p. 311.

especially if it were cadent from the benefics. And if the 4th house [domicile?] were a watery sign, beware lest Saturn aspect it. And you must beware lest the Lord of the 10th be a malefic. For the Ascendant and its Lord signify the land itself which someone buys, and its possession and the usefulness of it. The 10th or 11th and its Lord signify whatever is erected from it above the earth and from its surface, like trees and other things born of the earth which grow old in it. Indeed the 7th and its Lord signify its cultivators.

And al-Rijāl said[286] that it seemed to certain people that the 7th signifies herbs; indeed the 4th and its Lord are said to signify the goodness of the matter and whatever is had in it in terms of seeds. And he said whichever one of them were to be found good, judge good in the things which it signifies. If you were to find the benefics in the 1st, judge the goodness of the trees and of those things which are elevated from the surface of the earth. If however [they were] in the 7th, judge the goodness of the farmers. If however you were to find a benefic in the 4th, judge the goodness of the matter and the goodness of the seeds located in it. And if you were to find one of the malefics in one of those places, judge malice according to what is signified by that house [domicile?], and particularly in the 7th (which signifies the deceit and malice of the cultivators according to the nature of that malefic which signifies them): Saturn signifies their deceit and dishonesty, Mars signifies their inconstancy and thievery.

And al-Tabarī said[287] Jupiter and the planet from which the Moon is being separated belong to the buyer; he to whom the Moon is joined signifies the end of the matter and into what it will devolve. If however you intended to buy land or a vineyard, or something else similar without building, not considering at all to build on it but only that you might use it and have it and keep its fruit (and the returns from the laborers or renters, or even others), [then] adapt the aforesaid–namely the Ascendant and its Lord, and the Moon and her Lord; the Part of Fortune also and its Lord; even adapt Saturn (because he signifies these things on account of his severity, and because from severe work put into [the land], they will be acquired).

Therefore put [Saturn] in Libra; or if the purchase were made in the day, put him in Capricorn or Aquarius; and if it were made at night, put him in Aries or Leo or Sagittarius (Aries however, is less useful). And even in diurnal purchases you can put him in them. But he is not as strong in [diurnal purchases] as he is

---

[286] This refers in part to al-Rijāl, p. 311.
[287] In al-Rijāl, p. 311.

in nocturnal ones.[288] Or let him be in one of his own bounds; and let him be made fortunate and strong; let even Jupiter be aspecting him by a trine or sextile aspect, or a square from an angle; and make Mars cadent from [the angles]; and let the Moon be in the beginning of the increase of her light (namely in her first quarter), increasing in number, aspecting Saturn (or the planet who aspects him) with an aspect of friendship. And if Jupiter were to aspect her, it will be good, because he signifies the population[289] of the land, and that it will be planted around with many fruitful trees, and even other small ones; and that it can give good and useful returns.

And Sahl said[290] if you could not have an aspect of Jupiter with Saturn, make it so that you have the aspect of Venus with him instead of the aspect of Jupiter; and you will make the watery signs fortunate, because when you make them fortunate with the benefics, they will be better than the airy signs. And he said, let the Moon be in her own exaltation, or in the Midheaven, and the Lord of the Ascendant aspecting her. And he said, let the Moon also and the Ascendant be cleansed of the malefics and from defects.

Chapter 2: On the reconciliation of a father with a son

Just[291] as brothers sometimes debate amongst themselves, so it happens that a father might disagree with his son, and *vice versa*. And if they want to be reconciled together, and a son were to come to you so that you could elect for him the suitable hour for it, adapt the Ascendant and its Lord, the Moon too and the Lord of the sign in which she is; adapt even the fourth and its Lord (which signifies the father and the uncle, and a father-in-law, and all older blood-relatives—naturally the ancestors—even though, however, any of them could be signified through the proper house [domicile?]). And let the Lord of the fourth be joined to the Lord of the first by a trine or sextile aspect and with reception, if it can be done; and let it aspect the Ascendant by the same aspect, and let the Lord of the first be in the first or the 10th or the 11th; let the Moon

---

[288] The rationale here seems to be this: Saturn is a diurnal planet, so it is best (in a diurnal chart) to put him in the sign of his exaltation or domiciles, so that he will act strongly and favorably for the inceptor. But if nocturnal, he is disposed to act unfavorably toward the native, so he should be made less effective by putting him in one of his triplicities.

[289] "Population" here means the populating of the land with things that are sown or planted.

[290] *On Elect.*, Ch. 12.

[291] See the 5th House, Ch. 1. Bonatti places this chapter here because he assumes the *son* wants to reconcile, hence we adapt the house of *his father*. Later, the father will want to reconcile with the *son*, and we will adapt the 5th.

be aspecting the Lord of the first and the Lord of the fourth (or at least one of them): for these signify a useful and good and durable reconciliation.

Chapter 3: In the building of cities or castles or houses and the like, and on the populations of lands or of the plugging of fig-trees[292]

Men tend to build according to diverse methods of building, and according to the diversity of the condition of the men, and even to plant trees and plug fig-trees, and to populate[293] lands in diverse ways, according to the diverse customs of men.

For, even though all of these ways would seem to be directed to one end, still it is it necessary that it be elected for those wishing [to build] in diverse ways belonging to the diverse kinds of buildings. For in a certain manner it must be elected one way for one wishing to build a city or castle; and another for one wishing to build another building, like holy buildings and profane buildings (about which will be spoken in its own proper place and time); another for one wishing to plant trees or plug fig-trees; another for one wanting to sow seed.

Whence, if you wished to elect the hour for someone so he might build a city or castle, adapt the Ascendant and its Lord; the Moon also, and the Lord of the sign in which she is; and likewise the Part of Fortune and its Lord; and in the Ascendant of the building of the city or castle, put one of those fixed stars which are of the nature of Jupiter or the Sun or Venus or Mercury or Saturn (if Saturn were of good condition), or of the Moon, or at least of the nature of the Lord of the Ascendant of that hour. For these [fixed stars] signify the prolongation of the city or the castle and its perpetual durability on account of their most slow motion, and their most slow changeability. For a city and a castle ought to be things of perpetual durability; and it is necessary that this happen by the succession of their own individual parts, which are houses–which, even if they last a long time, still they are not continued perpetually except by succession.[294]

And it seemed to al-Rijāl[295] that Saturn is to be adapted in the building of cities. Indeed Sahl[296] seemed not to want us to give Saturn a role in the building;

---

292 *Ficulnearum fixionibus.* Fig trees (like some other plants) are propagated by cutting branches from an existing tree and planting the stems directly into the soil, hence they are "fixed" or "plugged" into the ground.

293 Again, this is meant in an agricultural sense.

294 This means that cities and castles, due to successive repairs and changes, last a long while even though not every feature of their structure remains the same. Bonatti's comment relates directly to Tr. 5, the 141st Consideration.

295 Al-Rijāl, p. 309.

still however they do not contradict each other. Because al-Rijāl understood [this] in terms of the building of cities. Indeed Sahl understood [this] in terms of the building of houses.

And al-Rijāl said[297] that the Ascendant should be an earthy sign, fixed, in buildings; and the Lord of the Ascendant likewise, and the Moon, [should be] in earthy, fixed signs.[298] And he said that the Moon should be in increased light and number, going toward her exaltation; and that she should be joined to a benefic which should be in its own exaltation or in the exaltation of the Moon, and she should be received. And al-Rijāl even said that it seems[299] fitting to him that the Moon be in a watery sign, and that it is useful if she is otherwise ascending,[300] and she should be more in the middle of her light.

And Sahl (with whom it seems to me to be fitting enough to agree) said,[301] make Mars cadent from all of the significators of the building, and never should you give any role in the building to him. And he said that if you cannot make it so without giving him a role in it, put Venus strong in her own place;[302] and [do not] give her strength[303] over Mars, and join her to him from a trine or sextile aspect: because Mars will not impede the matter of Venus if reception or even some benefic aspect (namely a trine or sextile) intervenes, on account of the greatness of their friendship. And he said, make Saturn cadent from Venus according to your ability, on account of her enmity with him.

Chapter 4: On the building of houses

However, in the building of houses you will not consider the fixed stars, but only the planets, whence the Ascendant and its Lord are to be adapted; the Moon also and the Lord of the domicile in which she is, and the planet to which she is joined; the fourth [sign] also and its Lord; even the second [sign] and its Lord; likewise the tenth [sign] and its Lord (and more strongly so if it were a

---

[296] *On Elect.*, Ch. 10.

[297] Al-Rijāl, p. 310.

[298] Perhaps this should read, "earthy *or* fixed."

[299] Omitting *non* ("not"). Al-Rijāl is reporting with approval the view of a "Harzet" or "Hazet."

[300] I.e., by latitude and declination, according to al-Rijāl's report.

[301] *On Elect.*, Ch. 10.

[302] I.e., in one of her own dignities.

[303] This almost sounds like the Hellenistic doctrine of "overcoming," i.e. being in the tenth sign from another planet. If so, Sahl is saying not to put Venus in the tenth sign from Mars. Otherwise he could be saying not to let Venus dispose Mars by domicile, exaltation, or term.

building that ought to be elevated far above the ground). And beware lest you put the significators of the building below the earth, because they will not permit the building to be elevated unless perhaps after a great time, just like it happened with the tower of the Viviani, which is at St. Guglielmo's in Forlì. Still however, if the Moon were below the earth (namely in the 5ᵗʰ or the 3ʳᵈ), joined to a planet (not impeded) above the earth, it will not be horrible.

And al-Tabarī said,[304] let the Moon be in crooked signs (which signify increase). Indeed al-Kindī said,[305] let the Part of Fortune be in an angle, and do not let the angles be removed; and let the Tail be in the 12ᵗʰ, and the Lord of the conjunction [prior to the election] be in one of its own dignities, fast in course (the which opinion al-Rijāl praised). And he[306] likewise recommended that Saturn aspect the significators from a trine aspect with reception, and he recommended this very much. But whereas on the other hand it seems somewhat impossible always to be able to adapt all the things which are necessary for us in buildings, and the elections of buildings occur for us every day, we must adapt what can be adapted, namely by rendering individual [elections] in each case. That is, if someone wanted to build a city of castle, adapt the Ascendant and the other things which were said above; and if you cannot adapt them all, adapt the Lord of the exaltation of the Ascendant, and use him more in this than the Lord of the domicile or of the other dignities. And if again you cannot do this, adapt the Ascendant with one of the aforesaid fixed stars. And beware lest one of the fixed stars which are of the nature of the malefics should fall in the ascending degree or near it by 2°. I tell you likewise concerning the 4ᵗʰ house (namely for which the stars are listed in the Treatise on revolutions, in an appropriate place). And when you have done this, you have already adapted the beginning of the building of the city or castle, if even if you could adapt nothing else.

Indeed in building houses, if you cannot adapt all the aforesaid, adapt the Ascendant and its Lord; likewise the Moon and the second and the fourth and their Lords (or at least the second); and make the Moon to be joined with Jupiter from any aspect except for the opposition; and if you can, put Jupiter in the second: in this way you have already adapted the greater part of the building

---

[304] Source unknown.
[305] *Book of the Nine Judges*, 4ᵗʰ House, "On the building of the houses of cities."
[306] Al-Rijāl, or al-Kindī? Both al-Rijāl's and al-Kindī's statements (from the *Book of the Nine Judges*), say that Saturn is bad.

of the house by thus sojourning in the house.[307] And even the Lord of the exaltation of the sign in which the Moon is, should be adapted more strongly than the Lord of the domicile, if it can be done. For in every building and planting he is to be preferred to the Lord of the domicile; and of the aforesaid, adapt whatever you can adapt; but these which I have told you now are to be preferred—since indeed, the conjunction of Jupiter with the Moon signifies the comeliness and beauty and goodness of the house.

And beware in the building of houses lest you give Saturn or Mars some role in them, even though Saturn may be given a role in the building of cities; indeed in no building should Mars be given a role. And beware lest you put the Tail in the first or the 2nd or the 4th (and especially in the 2nd), because it diminishes substance. However, put the Head in them with confidence, because it increases it. And beware of the Moon in the conjunction of Saturn or Mars or with the Tail (or any of them) in the first, even the 2nd or in the 4th (except perhaps Mars, if you could not avoid him in the adaptation of Venus, however, just as was said). For Saturn in the first or in the 4th signifies deformity and its slowness, and that the house will hardly or never be raised up; and if it were raised up, it will hardly or never be inhabited (and especially by its builder). And if it were inhabited, its inhabitants will suffer many inconveniences (like fears, horrible dreams, and diverse tribulations); and it signifies[308] that the building will be shattered and broken, and perhaps that it will fall down from the shattering. Indeed in the 2nd he signifies the diminution of substance. Mars however, when he is in one of those places, signifies the burning of the house or of the building, and its fall and destruction, and the loss of money through fires and thievery; and all the more so if he were ascending to his *awj* or to the further longitude, or were otherwise ascending.[309]

And Sahl said,[310] let the Moon be increased in light and number then, because it signifies the usefulness of the Lord of [her] domicile, and let the Lord of her domicile be aspecting [it].[311] And he said that the Lord of the Ascendant should be aspecting the Ascendant, and be cleansed of the malefics. And he said if the Lord of the Ascendant did not aspect the Ascendant, the master of the

---

[307] *Sic in hospitando domum.* This seems like an odd construction, and perhaps Bonatti is making a pun: that by lodging Jupiter in the (2nd) house, we will be adapting the future, *physical* house. But I do not feel very confident about this.

[308] Reading *significat* for *significati.* I.e., having Saturn in the 4th.

[309] "Ascending" is meant in the sense of his own movement in his Ptolemaic circles.

[310] Sahl, *On Elect.*, Ch. 10.

[311] I.e., let him be aspecting his own domicile (in which the Moon is). Bonatti reads "her," but Sahl reads "it."

house will not stay long in it. (If however the building were of a low-class or ignoble or humble person, adapt all that you can of the aforesaid; moreover because many adapted significators will make up for the weakness of the root of that nativity).[312]

Chapter 5: On the building of churches

If however it were the building belonging to a religion, you will consider in two ways concerning it. For if it were a humble building, nor very expensive, as are common churches, small hermitages (like those of the Order of Saint Augustine of Brother Zanniboni),[313] and abbacies similar to hermitages and those of common people[314] and chapels and monasteries, and the like (which are not of great fame): in such cases you will adapt the Ascendant and its Lord; likewise the Moon and her Lord; the 9th and its Lord.

If however it were famous or stately, as are great monasteries (as are Claraevalentia,[315] as is the Church of St. Mark in Venice; the Archbishopric of the Pisans; St. Vitalis of Ravenna, and many other churches of the Minor Brothers of Bologna, the Campanile[316] in Forlì, the Baptistry of Florence, and the like), going beyond the way of religion, you will not elect for them as you do for spiritual buildings, but as for temporal ones.[317] Whence, for *them* you will adapt the Ascendant and its Lord, and the Lord of the exaltation of the Ascendant; chiefly the Moon and her Lord; and likewise the tenth[318] instead of the ninth.[319] And if it were the building of a house of study, adapt Mercury, and make him of

---

312 I have placed this sentence in parentheses since it is not Sahl's and seems to be a remark by Bonatti. The statement is another indication of the debate over whether it is worth electing for low-class people, since by definition their weak nativities will be arguments against success.

313 This must be the Order of Hermits of St. Augustine (i.e., the Augustinians), transformed into a mendicant Order in 1256 under Pope Alexander IV. I am not sure *fratris Zanniboni* is correct: it may be a garbled reference to the Bonites, a branch of the Augustinians named after John Buoni (d. 1249).

314 *Plebes.*

315 Clairvaux?

316 Lit., "bell" or "bell tower." This bell tower is part of the Church of San Mercuriale in Forlì (1180 AD).

317 In other words, buildings such as that verge on secular grandeur, pomposity, and civic pride, as opposed to the truly spiritual requirements of religion. In the High Middle Ages these places were often schools and universities teaching Aristotle and other secular learning.

318 The Latin reads *10.*, but it must be the tenth sign or place to match the "ninth" that follows.

319 Again, because such buildings go beyond religious functions.

good condition, fortunate and strong; and put him in a good place, so that he aspects the Ascendant by a trine or sextile aspect. If however it were a building of delights, as is one of drinking, games, and the like, adapt Venus, and make her fortunate and strong and of good condition, and let her aspect the Ascendant from an aspect of friendship. If however it were a building in which victuals ought to be served (like grains, wine, olive oil, honey, and other edibles and potables), adapt Jupiter, make him fortunate and strong, and so that he aspects the Ascendant with a praiseworthy aspect. If however it were a building in which some people ought to be put in prison, adapt Saturn, and make him strong in his own place,[320] and so that he aspects the Ascendant by any aspect except for the opposition.

Chapter 6: On the destruction of constructed buildings

It seemed that this chapter was to be put among the chapters on the 7th house, but to al-Rijāl it seemed[321] that it ought to be set out in advance among the chapters on the 4th house. For he said that since destruction is the contrary of building, the chapter on it should be put next to the chapter on building (though there is little significance in this), saying if you wanted to destroy some building, make the Ascendant one of the fiery or airy signs; and let the Lord of the Ascendant and the Moon be in fiery or airy signs.

And al-Tabarī said,[322] let the Ascendant be a sign of direct ascension, and let the Lord of the Ascendant be occidental, decreasing in number, going toward a sign in which it is cadent;[323] nor however should it be retrograde, but let it be cadent from the angle. Also, let the Moon be decreasing in light and number, cadent from the angle, even joined to a planet cadent from the angle and going to its own fall; or let her be in Scorpio or Capricorn, and let her be below the earth or joined to a planet located below the earth; and let her be descending southern, or let her be joined to a retrograde planet; even let her be in the last quarter of the lunation,[324] and let the Moon be cadent from the Sun (nor let her be received); and let the Lord of the 4th house [domicile?] be weak, and the

---

[320] I.e., in one of his own dignities.
[321] This is not really true. Al-Rijāl includes this in the 7th House, under the topic of destroying the buildings of *enemies* (p. 323). He says we should adapt the significators to do the opposite of building.
[322] Al-Rijāl, p. 323.
[323] *Iens ad signum in quo cadat.* Literally, "going toward a/the sign in which it falls."
[324] I.e., in her last quarter.

planet to whom the Moon is joined, and even the other significators of the building. And above all else you will weaken Mars, even if you cannot weaken all the others; nor however should you forget to weaken him, because just as he is contrary to someone building, so in the contrary of destruction he strives to rebuild the building. For those things which I told you above do not permit the torn-down building to be remade, nor rebuilt. If however [the inceptor] did not care whether the building would be rebuilt or not, let the Moon be separated from a malefic, and joined to an oriental benefic, or let her be received, and the building will be torn down more easily.

Chapter 7: On the renting or leasing of houses or lands or vineyards or their fruits, or of other things which are leased and rented

If you wanted to elect the hour for someone so that he might rent some thing, or lease it out for a certain price, and a certain return, or for a certain portion of the fruits of what are to be gathered or received from the thing, adapt the Ascendant and its Lord; also the Moon and the Lord of the sign in which she is. For the Ascendant and its Lord signify him who rents the thing, indeed the seventh [sign] and its Lord signify him who leases it out. Indeed the tenth [sign] signifies that which is given for the rental. However the fourth [sign] signifies the end of the matter, and what the rental results in; and what follows from thence for each.[325]

Therefore, see which of the aforesaid places are made fortunate, and which unfortunate. For if the Ascendant and its Lord were made fortunate, it signifies good for the renter, and the renter will be truthful, and lawful, and will observe for the lessor those things which he promised him. If however it were unfortunate and evil, it will be to the contrary. If indeed the 7th and its Lord were fortunate, it signifies that the lessor will observe those things which he promised to the renter, and he will be lawful and of good faith. If however it were evil and unfortunate, he will lie to his partner, and will not observe what was promised, and he will be fraudulent to him.

If indeed both significators were fortunate and good, each will observe the faith of the other, and they will both be lawful. If both were evil and unfortunate, each of them will strive to deceive the other, and will be fraudulent to him.

---

[325] Note that Bonatti assumes the querent is the renter, not the lessor. In either event, the querent should get the 1st and its Lord (*etc.*), as usual.

And al-Rijāl said,[326] he to whom the Moon is joined signifies him who leases out, and he from whom she separates, signifies him who rents; [al-Rijāl], however, as I believe, considered it if the leasing were motivated first from the lessor; [but] if the renter were motivated first, it will be to the contrary. The Lord of the sign in which the Moon is, signifies the end of the matter.

And al-Ṭabarī[327] said we should adapt Jupiter and Saturn, and put them aspecting each other from a praiseworthy aspect. And he said, for this purpose, that the promises of the one leasing out and of the renter would be observed and would be firm.

And al-Rijāl said[328] that in leasing [something] out, let the Ascendant be adapted, and its Lord, and let him be going toward the angle in an earthy sign (and likewise the Moon); or let him be in the angle of the earth. Indeed let the planet from which the Moon is being separated be free, and let it be in one of its own dignities (because it signifies the land).[329] And he said that the Lord of the seventh should be made fortunate, harmonizing with the Lord of the Ascendant; and [do] this just as well as you can. Indeed let the planet whose conjunction the Moon seeks, harmonize with the planet from which she is being separated. And he said that the seventh [sign] and its Lord, and the planet to which the Moon is joined, signify the [one leasing the land from the owner];[330] and the Ascendant and its Lord, and the planet from which the Moon is being separated, signify the [owner who rents out the land],[331] and it[332] signifies the Lord of each. And wherefore the fourth [sign] and its Lord signify the land. And he said that in the inception of an election of the land you are to use the same election.[333]

---

[326] Al-Rijāl, p. 312.

[327] Al-Rijāl, p. 312.

[328] Al-Rijāl, p. 312.

[329] Al-Rijāl actually says "because it is the significator of the lord [or master] whose land it is."

[330] Al-Rijāl actually says "And the seventh and its Lord and the planet to whom the Moon goes, are significators of him who takes up the land for a pension." Here and in the next sentence, Bonatti has it backwards.

[331] Al-Rijāl actually says "The Ascendant and its Lord, and the planet from which the Moon is being separated, are the significators of the lord whose land or field it is."

[332] I do not know who Bonatti means, and I am not sure where he is getting this in al-Rijāl.

[333] I do not find this in al-Rijāl. Bonatti may mean we are to use the same principles when setting out to choose *the land we are interested in*, not just when we make the agreement with the owner.

Chapter 8: On the extending of rivers or canals and the like

If someone wished to extend a river or canal, or other waters, and you wanted to elect for him the hour fit for this, adapt the Ascendant and its Lord; the Moon also, and the Lord of the sign in which she is; even adapt Saturn so that he is oriental; and let even the Lord of the Ascendant be oriental, free from impediments in an angle, in one of its own dignities; and let the Moon be below the earth, in the 3rd or the 5th, in an earthy sign. And if she were above the earth, let her be in the 10th or 11th.

And al-Rijāl said[334] that it is good for Saturn to be in the 11th, provided that the Moon is not joined to him by body. You will even adapt Jupiter. Nor let any malefic be in the 10th.

And al-Kindī said,[335] let the Moon be in the 1st, square from the Sun, made fortunate, in increased light and number; and let her be in an angle (namely of the first or the tenth or the fourth); and do not let the angles be removed; and let the Ascendant be a watery sign, made fortunate with a strong benefic.

Even the Part of Fortune is to be adapted, and the Lord of the conjunction or the prevention which was before the election, and the rest of the things which were said in the renting of land; which if you cannot adapt all of these, adapt those which you can—of which one is chiefly the adaptation of the Moon. You will even adapt the Lord of the Ascendant and the Part of Fortune.

Chapter 9: On the planting of trees and fig-trees

The methods of planting trees or orchards are many: for either they are planted or plugged. Again, of trees, some are planted with roots or stakes (as are figs, olives, apples, almonds, nuts, and the like). Others are planted without roots, and are called plugs (like poplar, willow, and the like). Others are called orchards (like vine branches, wild olivetree [oleaster], [and] the like). And of those to be planted, certain ones are sometimes plugged, and of those to be plugged certain ones are sometimes planted; and every one of these methods can be said to be "planting."

Whence if you wanted to elect the hour for someone in order to plant trees or orchards or plug fig-trees, begin from the Moon and put her in Taurus joined

---

[334] Al-Rijāl, p. 311.
[335] Al-Rijāl, p. 311. Al-Rijāl says, "Nor let the angles be removed by means of the number of the figure, as we have stated above," but he does not mention al-Kindī.

to Venus by whatever method, if you can. And if you could not put the Moon in Taurus, put her in Aquarius (though Aquarius is below Taurus [in effectiveness]). Which if you could not do this, put her in Leo (however Leo is below Aquarius [in effectiveness]). Which again if you could not do this, put her in Pisces or in Virgo (but they are below Leo [in effectiveness]), provided that she is aspected by some planet from a watery sign, if she were in Leo. But Taurus is to be preferred before all the others.

And let Saturn be in the first ([and] direct), or in the eleventh, or the fifth, or the second, in any one of his own dignities or strengths, or let him occupy one of the aforesaid signs there. And if you could not put him in the first, put Jupiter there aspecting Saturn (or wherever Jupiter is); make him aspecting Saturn by an aspect of friendship, and let him be in a place in which he would have some testimony. And if neither of them could be put in the first, put the Moon there, or put her in the tenth or in the eleventh,[336] or at least in the fifth or third. And you should never make her impeded in plantings and seedings. And beware lest you give Mars a role in planting or seedings, except in buildings; and make the Moon (and the Lord of the sign in which she is) cadent from him, and likewise the Part of Fortune; and adapt the Lord of the exaltation of the Ascendant if you can do it, because it is not evil if it is preferred to the Lord of the domicile in this.

And al-Khayyat said,[337] let the Lord of the domicile of the Moon be aspecting her from a watery sign; and if the Ascendant were not a fixed sign,[338] let the Lord of the Ascendant and the Moon (or at least one of them) be oriental, ascending.[339] For if the Lord of the Ascendant were oriental, and were ascending to its own *awj*, or the farther longitude [or distance], it signifies that a tree which is planted then will grow quickly. Indeed if it were ascending and it were not oriental, it signifies that the tree will grow quickly, but it will delay the bearing of its fruit. And this does not bring harm in trees that are not fruit-bearing. And if it were oriental, descending from its *awj*, or toward its nearer longitude, it will grow slowly, but it will hasten to bear fruit. And if it were occidental, descending, it will delay the growing and bearing of its fruit. And if

---

[336] In earlier chapters, when Bonatti groups the tenth and eleventh together, he makes them feminine and without expressly designating whole signs.

[337] In al-Rijāl, p. 312.

[338] According to al-Rijāl, al-Khayyat says "Even if the Ascendant were not a fixed sign, *let it be a common one*, and [let] its Lord be oriental, ascending in its own latitude." This adds a bit more to the clauses above, and differs slightly from Bonatti's subsequent instructions.

[339] "Ascending" here means "ascending to its own *awj*." See the following sentence.

you cannot make the Ascendant a fixed sign, make the Ascendant a common sign, and [put] the significators in common signs. But since it is difficult to adapt all things which can be considered in elections, as I have already told you many times, if you cannot adapt all things which you want, adapt the ones which you can. For in the planting of trees, if you cannot adapt something else, adapt at least the Moon and put her in Taurus, free, not impeded, or in the last part of Sagittarius joined to Jupiter by any sort of aspect (except for the opposition). Nor let Jupiter be impeded, and put him in the Ascendant, if you can, free, or in the 10th, or the 11th, or the 5th, or the 4th. And I tell you the same concerning the Part of Fortune, if it can be done.

Chapter 10: On the sowing of seeds which we intend to bear fruit in the same year or in the following one

If you wanted to elect the hour of sowing seeds for someone, it is necessary in every sowing that the Ascendant be a movable or common sign, and the Lord of the Ascendant be in a movable sign (if it can be done). However, just as I told you in plantings, start from the Moon, and work through her: because her virtue in plantings is to be preferred to the virtues of all the other planets.

And al-Rijāl said,[340] let the Moon be in movable signs; whence she is to be put in a movable or common sign, earthy (or of sowing). But if she were in Aries, it is necessary that a planet aspect her from a watery sign, lest a portion of the seed dry out. And al-Rijāl praised Cancer and Capricorn; indeed he praised Virgo before all the other earthy signs or those of sowing, both in seeds which bear fruit in the same year, and in those which bear fruit in the following year (like those which are seeded when they are planted, like leeks, cabbages, and the like). And sometimes they bear fruit in the same year in which they are planted.

Indeed Sahl said[341] that the Ascendant should be a common sign, and its Lord in a movable sign, aspecting the Lord of its own domicile; and let [the Lord of the Ascendant] be free from the malefics: because if the malefics were to aspect him, the seed will be found impeded. And let the Moon be increased in light and number: because if she were under the rays, or were decreasing in number, it signifies that the seed will be decreased, and [nothing] will emerge out of it except for a middling amount.

---

[340] See al-Rijāl, p. 312. But he does not mention Aries–this must be Bonatti's interpretation based both on the lack of fire signs in al-Rijāl's account, and his admonition to avoid Mars.
[341] *On Elect.*, Ch. 15.

And of the fixed signs, Taurus is recommended, but it thins[342] the seed according to the quantity that is sowed. Whence it is necessary that something more be cast forth[343] of the seed than is usual; nor however should it exceed the proper limit. And even the last half of Sagittarius is of value in sowings, and even Pisces is recommended. If indeed it were the seed of trees (just as on occasion some are seeded in order that the trees which emerge from the seeds might be planted again and arranged),[344] let the Moon be in Taurus. You however, if you cannot adapt all of the aforesaid, put the Moon in Virgo free from impediments, and you have adapted the hour of sowing.

Chapter 11: On beginning to cultivate inheritances

If you wanted to elect the hour for someone wanting to begin to cultivate an inheritance which he had obtained, or which another is searching out for him, adapt the Ascendant and its Lord, and the Moon, and the planet in whose domicile she is, so that all are received; and let the planet which receives any one of them be in an angle or a succeedent, free from impediments; and if not all of this can be done, let at least the Moon be received by a strong and fortunate planet, and [let her be] in a good place. And make it (if you ever can) so that a benefic, free from impediments, is in the second.

And al-Kindī said,[345] let the Lord of the Part of Fortune and the Lord of the conjunction or the prevention be in any angle, or going toward it, and let the Lord of the sign in which the Moon is, be a benefic; which if all of these were absent, at least make it so that the Moon is in the Ascendant, or in a good place from it, received.

---

[342] Reading *rarefacit* for *rarificat*.

[343] Bonatti is assuming that the farmer sows by throwing seeds by hand out of a bag or basket directly onto the soil.

[344] The last part of this clause is difficult to express simply: *ut iterato & ordinatius plantentur*. The verb *itero* can mean "to plow again," and has the connotations of repetition; *ordinatius* is a comparative adjective from the verb *ordino*, "to arrange, dispose," etc. The idea seems to be either that the trees are discarded after a year and the field plowed again, or else they are transplanted elsewhere, or their seeds are used for further planting. There might be a technical meaning here which escapes me.

[345] See al-Rijāl, p. 311. But al-Rijāl's account says "Part of Substance."

Chapter 12: On putting together ships or galleys[346]

The methods of putting together ships are three, to which all others are subordinated. For either it is the putting together of a galley or of something equal for overcoming enemies; or it is the putting together of a great ship for transport; or it is a ship for other common navigations, like small merchant trips, and the like.

Whence if someone wanted to put together a galley or other ship of passage, either for overcoming enemies, or for sailing the sea by another method of speed,[347] adapt the Ascendant and its Lord; even the Moon and the planet in whose domicile she is in; and put them in the Ascendant or in the 10th or in the 11th; and let the Ascendant be a fixed sign; and if it can happen, let the other angles likewise be fixed signs.[348] And adapt the 4th and its Lord, because it naturally signifies ships. And make it, if you can, so that [the 4th] is a watery sign; or at least put its Lord in a watery sign, free from impediments, and joined to some benefic. And let the planet from which the Moon is being separated, be strong and fast. And if you cannot put the Lord of the Ascendant or the Moon in the 10th, put a benefic there, strong and made fortunate, having a strong testimony there, and let it be oriental and fast in course; however, [let] the Lord of the seventh be weak and slow in course.

If however it were a boat for transport, let the Moon be in her own average course with the other things above being adapted, as was said, so that she does not run more than her average course in one day; and if she were to travel less [than that] by three or four minutes, it will not be bad on account of the fear that it would be harmed by excess speed.[349]

If indeed it were of the other aforesaid [kinds of] ships, you will adapt the aforesaid, but it does not matter whether the Moon is fast in course or not, provided she is not very slow so that she does not go less than her own [average] course by more than by 31' in one day. And strive to adapt the Lord of the conjunction or the prevention according to your ability, because this is good; and if the Moon were separated from another planet, make her to be

---

[346] *Galearum.* The word *galea* means a "helmet." Galleys were used for war, rather than cargo; so perhaps they were called "helmets" due to their structural and armored defenses.

[347] *Velocitatis.* I am not quite sure what Bonatti means, but perhaps he wants to include both rowed ships and those powered mainly by sails.

[348] An indication of the use of quadrant houses.

[349] That is to say, making the Moon of average course will *prevent* the excess speed that would lead to fears of harm.

joined to some benefic; and if the Lord of the Ascendant were not in an angle, make it so that he goes toward it.

And al-Rijāl said[350] that certain people affirmed it was good if the Moon were in Taurus or in Gemini. And he said we must beware of the aspect of Mars with the Moon or with the Lord of the Ascendant, or with the Lord of the fourth in the putting together of a ship. And al-Rijāl said that it is useful if the Moon were above the earth. And he said these same things are to be adapted in the launching of ships into the water, and in their purchase; you, however, adapt all that you can adapt; but always let it be your concern to adapt the Moon. And when a mast is raised higher in the ship,[351] then the tenth [sign] is to be adapted, and its Lord; likewise the Moon is to be put in it.

Chapter 13: On the building of mills

Mills are built in many ways: for one kind is built on ships,[352] another is built on pole-bars, so that it is raised up and pressed down as the puller wishes (and that is said to be a hanging mill). Another is built [to be] immovable, so that it is neither pressed down nor elevated, but rather remains stable; and this is called a transverse mill. Another is built in a house to be inhabited, which is turned by some animal or with some fashioned instrument, and it is called a *posternum*.[353] Another is built in high places, which is turned by the wind, and it is called a windmill. And according to their diverse modes of building, their elections are to be diversified. Whence if someone wanted to build one of the aforesaid mills, and came to you so you would elect for him the hour fit for it, and it were a mill on ships, let the Ascendant be the last half of Pisces or the last of Virgo. If however it were a mill that is called "hanging," suspended from a pole-bar or on ships, let the Ascendant be the first half of Aries or the last half of Libra; because the one and the other signify equality. If indeed it were a fixed mill that is neither raised up nor pressed down, which is called a transverse one, or[354] it is a mill in a house which is turned by beasts or fashioned instruments, which is

---

[350] See al-Rijāl, pp. 331-32.

[351] Literally, "when a tree is raised more on the ship."

[352] Bonatti seems to refer to mills floating on rivers: one boat held the gears and millstones and another the other end of the mill-axle, with the wheel dipping into the water between them. See Mantello 1996 (p. 498).

[353] This must refer to the kind of harness (around the protruding breastbone or *posternum*) used on draft animals.

[354] Reading *aut* for *et*.

called a *posternum*, let the Ascendant be a fixed sign, either a watery one or an earthy one. If indeed it were a mill that is turned by the wind, like customarily happens in certain places, let the Ascendant be an airy sign, and the Moon in the aforesaid signs or in the Ascendant or in the tenth or the eleventh.

And al-Rijāl said, beware lest the Moon be in Cancer or Capricorn;[355] likewise to be avoided are Gemini and Sagittarius on account of the great inequality of the days and nights when the Sun is in them; and let the Moon, in any building of a mill, always be in her average course, or a little faster, if it can be so. If however you could not put the Moon in the aforesaid signs, nor could you make them the ascending [signs], but the Moon and the Ascendant were in other signs, al-Rijāl said that if it were with the aspect of a malefic it will be good; nevertheless if it were with the aspect of a benefic it will be better.

The beginning of a ship-mill is when its renter begins to build the first ship. Indeed the beginnings of the other mills are when it begins to be built by the professionals which are of the substance of the mill.[356] And if it were a mill that needs a watermill, make the watermill begin to be dug[357] when the other aforesaid beginning comes to be.

Lest perhaps you might believe or fear some contrary or unnecessary or broken thing in the judgments or in the elections of astronomy, it may always be found (concerning any heading) according to how you would find it stated by the wise. Judge thus, nor will you care what is stated elsewhere, nor would you be able to go astray–but you will always judge and elect aright.

---

[355] Al-Rijāl, p. 312.
[356] I am not sure what this means–perhaps when the engineers who specialize in that type of mill begin the actual construction.
[357] This must refer to the trench that must be dug in order to let water power the wheel of the mill.

ON THE FIFTH HOUSE

Chapter 1: On the reconciliation of a son with his father

Just as a father may disagree with his son, so a son sometimes is moved on his own to disagree with his father. Whence, if a father wishing to be reconciled with his son were to come to you so that an hour fit for this might be elected, you will adapt the Ascendant and its Lord; even the Moon and the Lord of the sign in which she is; adapt even the fifth and its Lord (which signifies the son), and make it so that the Lord of the fifth is joined with the Lord of the first by an aspect of friendship. And if it were with reception, it will be better; even let the Lord of the first be in the first, or in the tenth or in the eleventh; and then let the Moon aspect the Lord of the first and the Lord of the fifth (or either of them) for this purpose so their reconciliation may be lasting.

Chapter 2: On the sending of legates or heralds

If someone wanted to send a herald or a legate to some person, you will consider in this action the Moon before all other significators; and make her joined by a trine or sextile aspect to the planet signifying the person to whom [the herald or legate] is sent. And if you can, make it so that he receives the Moon or at least the Lord of the first. So if he were to send [him] to a king, make it so that she is joined to the Sun or to the Lord of the tenth; and let the Sun or the Lord of the tenth (the one of them to whom the Moon is joined) be in the first or in the tenth or in the eleventh. And if you cannot put him in one of those places, put him in the ninth or in the fifth or in the third, but this will be of middling usefulness.

And beware, when you are sending [someone] (or going off to) a king, lest the Moon be in Aquarius or Pisces. And if he were to send [him] to other nobles or magnates or judges, or to the Pope or cardinals or bishops or other religious figures, let the Moon be joined to Jupiter from the aforesaid aspects, in an angle, or in a good place from the Ascendant. And if he were to send him to bellicose men, let her be joined to Mars—nor let the conjunction be from the angles nor let [Mars] be in an angle, but let [Mars] be in the ones following an angle. And if he were to send him to old men or Jews or farmers and the like, let her be joined to Saturn from the said aspects, and let Saturn be of good condition in a succeedent to an angle. And if he were to send him to a woman, let her be joined to Venus. And if he were to send him to a wise man or to writers or merchants or to young men (from age 14 to age 20), let her be joined to Mercury–and beware lest Mercury is then impeded (or any one of the planets to which the Moon is joined).

Chapter 3: On the donning of new vestments or their cutting[358]

To certain sages it seemed that this chapter pertained to the 1st house, because it seemed to be of the matters which pertain to the 1st; however to me it seems fitting (if there is not great significance in it), that it could pertain to the 5th house, because the 5th house signifies delights and gladness, and men delight in new vestments, and rejoice in them, just as in other delightful things. Whence, if you wished to elect the hour for someone so he might buy, or cut, or make, or wear a new vestment, adapt the Ascendant and its Lord, and the Moon, and put them in movable signs; and let the Ascendant be a movable sign; therefore let the Moon be in Aries except for its first 6°[359] ([the acceptable degrees of] which are after the eighth up to the end of the fifteenth degree of Aries), and except for the twenty-third and twenty-fourth degree of it; or let her be in Cancer except for its first 6° and the last 3°; or let her be in the first half of Libra, or let her be in the first 18° of Virgo; or in the first 19° of Sagittarius, or in the first 20° of Pisces.

And the ancient sages said the fixed signs are not to be recommended, except for vestments pertaining to war. I, however, was not in the habit of avoiding the first 20° of Taurus, because it is the domicile of Venus, who signifies delights, and because the Moon is exalted in it. And all condemned Leo unanimously. Whence Ptolemy, in his *Centiloquy*, [said] it is dangerous to make new vestments or to consider the Moon in Leo.[360] And I do not dissent from them, unless perhaps the Sun were to aspect the Moon by a trine or sextile aspect. And wherever you were to find her received by perfect reception, you will not condemn her. If however you can, adapt her well indeed, as was said; and if not, put her outside of Leo and outside Capricorn and outside the *via combusta*; nor should you ever make her anywhere impeded, but [rather] free.

---

[358] I.e., having new clothes made.

[359] I do not know what is wrong with this bound of Aries, since it is ruled by Jupiter. Likewise with the other degrees he mentions–some are bounds of malefics, some of benefics, some I am not sure why he forbids them.

[360] Aph. 22.

And al-Rijāl said,[361] adapt the second and its Lord, and especially in the purchasing of vestments; and that the Moon should be in increased light. If indeed you could not adapt all of these, adapt the Moon in the donning of new vestments, and in making them, and put the Sun in the Midheaven: for these things signify that the vestment will be noticeable and beautiful. And if you cannot adapt anything else, make it so the Moon is not impeded, nor should she be in Leo without reception, as was said; and [make it so] that the Sun is in the Midheaven.

Sometimes certain fools were sophistically in the habit of asking why food does not harm, nor is it prohibited when the Moon is located in Leo (since [food] enters the body), and vestments are prohibited (which do not enter the body). To which it may be responded in this way, namely that food is potentially of the nature of the body: it having been received through the mouth and transmitted to the stomach, its power devolves into action by the mediating movements of the supercelestial bodies and the guiding[362] virtue of the body, and it is effected by the substance of the body. For from nutriment and what nourishes, becomes one thing, just like from food and eating. Whence it must defend it and watch over it and maintain it naturally by the aforesaid virtue, nor contradict it, nor could it impede it. Indeed clothes are accidental, and do not defend the body (nor even its nature) naturally; for they have what they have accidentally: wherefore without clothes someone can live, indeed without food he cannot. And even though they make clothes for the good condition of the body, still they do not make for the condition [itself], nor are they of its substance. Indeed the superior bodies operate in the donning of new vestments solely from their own motions; however in food it is not so, because even if they operate in the taking up of foods from their motions, they do not operate without the agency of the intrinsic nature of the one acting, by transmutating food into the nature of the body by nourishing it. Whence it does not impede on account of that reason; for it is not the business of nature to impede itself. And even because nature is the first factor of the generation and corruption for something growing, and of the destruction of perishable bodies by a moving,

---

[361] This is clearly based on al-Rijāl (pp. 313-14), but he does not say specifically to adapt the second. However, he does say to put the Sun in the Midheaven and the Moon in increasing light, which in the second whole-sign house would put her in a whole-sign trine.
[362] Regitiva.

regulating planet, and since it is in the intention of nature to serve, it does not impede it.[363]

Chapter 4: On the generation or conceiving of a son or daughter

Sahl said[364] if you wanted to elect the hour of conjoining with your wife to generate a male child, let the Ascendant and its Lord, and the Moon [and] the Lord of the house [domicile?] of children be in masculine signs, or in the masculine part of the circle (which is the right-hand side) at the hour of the conjoining; and you should not put [any planet] in the Ascendant in the same hour, nor in the sign of children, unless it is a masculine planet. And if you want it to be a female, let these significators be in feminine signs, and in the feminine part of the circle (which is the left-hand side). And if you could not do this, and the significators were diverse (namely so that certain ones of them would be in masculine signs, and certain ones of them would be in feminine signs), let the Lord of the hour participate with the planet which receives the Moon's disposition. And judge from those which have more testimonies in masculine or feminine signs, and the conceived child will be according to that.

Indeed al-Rijāl made a longer statement on this than Sahl did. For he said[365] it is necessary in this election that the Ascendant be a masculine sign and of direct ascension; let the angles be fixed [signs][366] and not removed; [let] the Lord of the Ascendant be in the Ascendant or in the Midheaven, or in the eleventh; and let the planet which first comes to the degree of the Ascendant by its own motion be a benefic. And he said it is known necessarily by the things which are set out in advance; both luminaries are to be adapted likewise in these

---

[363] The point here is that elections are made for things that are not either directly part of, or immediately susceptible to, human nature. We do not elect for breathing (which belongs directly to human nature) nor for eating a meal (since food is immediately susceptible to absorption by the body and is essential to our nature). Rather, we elect for matters which are accidental and which pertain to external goals (however much these are distinguished from what is natural, internal, and essential). Having money is accidental to being a human being, so we elect for merchant transactions so as to have wealth accidentally; likewise, wearing fine clothing is accidental to us (insofar as wanting to have a good social status is not "natural" to us), so we elect for fine clothing so as to have status and influence accidentally.

[364] *On Elect.*, Ch. 16.

[365] Al-Rijāl, p. 313. But al-Rijāl does not specifically say anything about the angles not being removed.

[366] According to al-Rijāl.

things,[367] and especially [that] it is very necessary to adapt the lord of the time;[368] do not even let a malefic be in an angle, but a benefic, free and strong. And he said it is also necessary that we turn ourselves to the Lord of the Ascendant;[369] and that we seek to prevent from the start that the Lord of the Ascendant be the planet who is impeded in the ninth month; for we often see births come to pass in it. The same is even recommended, and if it were possible, to seek to prevent it in the seventh [month], and in the tenth [month], for birth sometimes tends to happen in them. And the Lord of the Ascendant must be in these places, made fortunate and strong; and even the luminaries. And one must guard beforehand lest the Lord of the sixth or the eighth–if it were a malefic–be commingled with any significator in any way. And those things are universally to be avoided which are said to be unpraiseworthy in books of nativities; and we must observe those things that are approved in them with the roots of elections.

And al-Khayyat said[370] that what we said is best, that the Moon be in the Ascendant in the trine aspect of the Sun. He even said, beware of the *via combusta*, and we ought to adapt Venus; for if Venus were impeded, the *aliara*[371] is corrupted (that is the woman or the womb). Indeed if the Moon [were impeded], the seed is corrupted. Also, adapt the 5th house [domicile?] and its Lord. Certain people even approve of this to be in the odd-numbered hours, that is in the first, third, or fifth [hours], or the like. Which if it were to happen that the Ascendant and the Moon were in Libra (which is a rational sign), it will be good, *if* however [Libra] and its Lord were free: for then Cancer (which is a sign of many children) will be in the Midheaven; and let the rest of the significators be in masculine signs, for she will be impregnated and will conceive a male child. And we ought to apply our work in matters which pertain to it: that is, we will judge so that the *aliara* or her womb is not distorted nor in any natural illness.[372] For the circular significators perfect according to how the material

---

[367] I take this to mean that the luminaries ought to be in a masculine or feminine sign, depending on the desired sex of the child.

[368] That is, the sect light (the Sun by day, the Moon by night): see al-Rijāl (p. 313), "*luminare*." Bonatti's use of *dominum* makes it sound as though he might mean something like the planetary Lord of the hour, but he undoubtedly knew what al-Rijāl meant.

[369] That is, that we look at it in order to adapt it. Al-Rijāl simply says, "look at."

[370] Al-Rijāl, p. 313.

[371] Unknown word, but perhaps a medieval variant on Gr. *hule* or "matter." Al-Rijāl (p. 313) reads: "it brings harm upon the mother."

[372] *In aliquo infirma ad physicam.*

subjects can receive them.[373] This is the opinion of al-Rijāl on generation and corruption.

But since it would be most difficult to adapt so precisely, and to observe the sayings of the philosophers just as they professed them, it seems to me that you should adapt the Ascendant, the Moon and [her or its][374] Lord in the conjoining of the man with the woman; and you should put Jupiter in the degree of the 10th house, if you can do it: because this signifies that the woman will conceive in the first coitus which she were to have then, unless perhaps it were Virgo ([in which case] she would not be able to conceive in the first copulation; however she can conceive at the second one). And if you could not put him in the degree of the 10th house, put him in the 10th or the 11th in such a degree that he would aspect the Ascendant degree by degree; or put him in the 5th, so that he aspects the Ascendant or the Moon or the Lord of the 5th by a praiseworthy aspect; or put the Lord of the 1st and the Moon (or one of them) in the 5th, so that [they or one of them] is above the line of the 5th house by 2°, or at the most by 3° or by 15° at the most below it.[375] For these signify that the woman will conceive then. If the majority of the significators were masculine or in masculine places, it signifies masculinity; and in feminine ones, femininity. And if the same number of significators were masculine as there are feminine ones, they can signify either of the two, namely either one or more masculine children, and the same number of feminine ones, or a hermaphrodite.

Chapter 5: On taking out aborted children from a woman

As[376] often tends to happen, if the conceived child were dead in the maternal uterus, and you wanted to elect the hour for taking it out (whether by surgery or by drugs, or by an *industricum* method,[377] or by whatever means it was), let the Ascendant be a feminine sign of direct ascension, and likewise even let the Moon be defective in light (if it can be done), and let her be beyond the line of the 10th house by 6° or more, descending towards the 7th house; let there even be some benefic aspecting the Moon by a trine or sextile aspect, or a square

---

[373] Following al-Rijāl, p. 313. Bonatti's construal is ungrammatical: *significatores etenim circulares perficiunt secundum quod eas recipere possunt ipsi subiectae materiae.*

[374] Bonatti says *eius*, which could mean "her" or "its."

[375] By "above," Bonatti means "in an earlier zodiacal degree"; by "below," he means "in a later zodiacal degree."

[376] Based on Sahl, *On Elect.*, Ch. 17.

[377] Unclear meaning. *Industrius* means "diligent, active." This phrase is not in Sahl.

(whether the Moon is received or not). And if Mars were then to aspect her by the said aspects, with reception, it will be good; if however without reception, it will not be evil, provided the Moon is in a feminine sign; and let the Ascendant be a feminine sign of direct ascension, as was said. And one must beware lest the Ascendant be a crooked sign, or [lest] the Lord of the Ascendant or the Moon be in one of them.

Chapter 6: On handing over a son to instruction

This chapter seems like it should be contained under the house of mastery;[378] but because [the 10th] does not make mention of anything concerning the instruction of a son, it is rather to be put under the 5th house, which signifies sons. Whence if you wanted to elect the hour for someone wishing to turn his son over to some instructor, or to some teaching, or to some lesson or profession to be learned, whether it is of numbers, or measuring, or singing, or astronomy, or some practical art, let the Ascendant be one of the domiciles of Mercury (of which the better one is Gemini); let the Moon be free from impediments, joined to Mercury by a trine or sextile aspect; and let Mercury be sound and free from impediments, and let him be oriental, ascending direct, made fortunate, and strong; [and let] the Lord of the domicile in which Mercury is in, be free and sound; let even the Moon be in increased light and number, because this signifies the quickness of his learning; and if she is slow or defective [in light], it will signify the slowness of his learning.

And Sahl said,[379] let the Lord of [their] domiciles be aspecting them. Which if you were not able to do all of these, adapt the Moon according to your ability; and adapt Mercury so that he is not retrograde, nor under the rays of the Sun, nor in his first station; and let him be occidental from the Sun, or even oriental (provided he is direct).

Chapter 7: On giving and taking gifts

In this matter (namely gifts to guests), two things are considered: namely the giving and taking: just as men take gifts, so they sometimes give them. And all of this is called a gift, just as he who takes in strangers, and likewise he who is

---

[378] The 10th house.
[379] *On Elect.*, Ch. 18.

taken in is called a *hospes*.[380] Whence if someone wanted to take a gift from someone, then the first [sign] is to be adapted, and its Lord, and the Moon, and the Lord of the sign in which she is; even the second [sign] is to be adapted, and its Lord, in order to turn the gift to the usefulness of the taker. Even the Part of Fortune is to be adapted, and its Lord, in order to amplify the usefulness. Likewise Jupiter is to be adapted (who signifies substance acquired naturally through moral means), in order that amplified utility might be conserved, and that it may pass over to the substance of him who receives the gift, and it may happen regularly.

If however someone were to give a gift that was already acquired, or were to send it to someone, we must adapt the fifth and its Lord, and Jupiter, and let Mars be in either case cadent from the Ascendant and its Lord; [let him be cadent] from the Moon, too, and from the planet in whose domicile she is. Likewise [let him be cadent] from the 2nd and its Lord; also from the Part of Fortune, from the Part of Substance, from the fifth, and their Lords. And if it can be done, let the 2nd and the 5th houses be common signs, of which the better ones are Sagittarius and Pisces; and Virgo is below these [in effectiveness], and Gemini is below Virgo. And it is even to be watched out lest Saturn aspect the Moon or the Ascendant or its Lord, or the Part of Fortune or [the Part of] Substance without reception; and let the Lord of the Ascendant be elevated above the Lord of the seventh.[381] Which if you could not do all of this, adapt the Moon and the Lord of the 2nd house, and Jupiter in the receiving of the gifts; indeed in giving [them, adapt] the Moon and the Lord of the 5th house and Jupiter or the Part of Fortune.

---

[380] *Hospes* can mean both "host" and "stranger/guest," depending on the context.
[381] This could refer to it being in a more northerly ecliptical latitude, but this could also refer to the Hellenistic "overcoming." See Introduction and footnote to Tr. 3, Part 2, Ch. 20.

ON THE SIXTH HOUSE

Chapter 1: On the healing of the sick

If you wished to elect the hour for someone wishing to heal a sick person, look to see if it is a general sickness in the whole body, or if it were particular to something (namely to a particular member, like in the eye or in the ear, or any other official member, like an arm, hand, and the like).

For if it were a sickness in the whole body, let the Ascendant be one of the human signs, out of all of which Libra is to be recommended: for the Ascendant signifies the whole body unless a member is specified. If indeed it were a sickness in a certain member of the twelve parts of the human listed above (which are the head, neck, arms, shoulder, breast, back, the belly, the private parts, the hips, the upper thighs, the knees, the legs, and the feet),[382] Arthephius said the Ascendant should be the sign to which is assigned the member of the one who is sick; let even the Lord of the first be free from impediments, and let the planet signifying the member be sound and free; even the Moon is to be adapted.

And 'Ali said[383] one must beware lest the Moon then be in the opposition of the Lord of the 6th or the 8th, even if it were a benefic. However, in a trine or sextile (if it were a benefic), it is not to be feared. If however the Lord of the 6th or the 8th were a malefic, the Moon is not to be in any aspect with it. If indeed you could not avoid her being in the aspect of one of [the malefics], let her be in a trine or sextile, and not from any other [aspect]; nor from the corporal conjunction; nor let the Moon be descending.[384]

And Māshā'allāh said[385] that the Moon should be in the sign assigned to the member that is diseased when someone heals it. You may understand this by the method of drugs, or by ointment, or by plasters; but not by the method of surgery (so that the member is touched by iron or fire or the like). According to Ptolemy in the *Centiloquy*,[386] "To touch a member with iron when the Moon is located in the sign assigned to that member, is dangerous."

---

[382] In the text, this is the end of the sentence; but the next part about Arthephius finishes the "then" clause that ought to follow.

[383] I do not find this in al-Rijāl.

[384] This could mean either "descending in her epicycle" or "descending from her *awj*." Again, I do not find this in al-Rijāl.

[385] Sahl, *On Elect.*, Ch. 22. See also al-Rijāl, p. 315.

[386] Aph. 20.

Chapter 2: On taking medical treatment on the occasion of some sickness

If you wanted to elect the hour for someone sick to take some medical treatment for the purpose of expelling the sickness (like a headache, toothache, cramps, stomachache, and the like), which are performed through ointments and plasters or through the application of cupping glasses or a sponge, and the like.

Sahl said[387] the Ascendant should be Libra[388] [or] the Moon in it, joined to benefics. And none of the malefics should be put in the angle of the Moon— which if she could not be prevented from [suffering] the aspects of the malefics, let it be by their trine or sextile aspect. And let her not be besieged nor impeded by the rays of the two malefics; nor let her be combust nor going toward combustion, but let her be free and not impeded; because if she were not free, the medical treatment will induce pain and impediment to the sick person.

Chapter 3: On a general cure to be used for the head

If for example you wanted to elect the hour for some medicine generally to be used for the head, or for some humor coming down [or out] from the head, like vomiting and gargling, and the like, let the Ascendant be Aries, and the Moon in it or in Taurus; and let her be joined to any one of the benefics, in little light.

And Sahl said,[389] beware of the square aspect of the Sun, or his opposition in Aries, on account of the peculiar heat of the Sun.

Chapter 4: If you wanted to apply a cure to the nostrils

If you wanted to elect the hour for someone wishing to heal by means of the nostrils (with some ointments or other things, like sneezing or inhaling fumes and the like), make the Ascendant Cancer or Leo or Virgo, and let the Moon be in the Ascendant joined with one of the benefics. And beware of the conjunction of some malefic with her, and that she is not joined to some planet impeded by retrogradation or combustion or fall or in some other way.

---

387 *On Elect.*, Ch. 22.
388 Omitting Bonatti's "or Scorpio," which does not appear in Sahl.
389 *On Elect.*, Ch. 22.

Chapter 5: If someone wished to heal the eyes

If you wished to elect the hour for someone wishing to heal the eyes, like if there were a blot[390] in them, or a blister,[391] or something stuck,[392] or a thorn,[393] or an inflammation, or something which must be removed by surgical means, or by any other means by instruments or medical arts, let this be when the Moon is in increased light and number, joined to a benefic.

And Sahl said,[394] beware of her conjunction with Mars when she is in increased light and number. And let Jupiter be above the earth in the Ascendant, or namely in the eleventh or the ninth. And if you cannot put him in these places, let him be aspecting the Ascendant by a trine or sextile aspect, or at least by a square, provided he is not impeded.

And beware lest [the Moon] or the Ascendant be in earthy signs. And if you can avoid the conjunction of the Moon with Mars, your work will be put off while she is being separated from him;[395] and you will abandon him in every curing of the eye; however at the end of the month[396] he harms less.

However, Sahl said[397] the sages agreed on the impediments of Mars in the head, and, they said, [with the case of] everything that is cured by iron or fire[398] the Moon is not to be put in a sign signifying the member which is cured; nor even in a movable or common sign. And they said that when she is badly disposed with Mars or with Saturn, that if some part of the body were cut off or punctured, it will putrify. They even said in all of these things that we must beware during the conjunction of the Moon [with the Sun], and in her prevention, while she transits the Sun by 12° or less.

---

[390] *Macula.*

[391] *Vesica.*

[392] *Proiecta*, lit. "things that are thrown/projected."

[393] *Ungula.* Literally, "claw." Perhaps some other ailment is meant?

[394] *On Elect.*, Ch. 22.

[395] That is, if the Moon is conjoined to Mars and you have enough time to wait until she is separated, do so.

[396] Probably at the end of the *lunar* month.

[397] Based on *On Elect.*, Ch. 22.

[398] Sahl, *On Elect.*, Ch. 22.

Chapter 6: On the particular cure of any other official member

If you wanted to elect the hour for someone wishing to heal some other part of the body. And if the sickness were in the neck, let the Ascendant be Taurus and the Moon in it; if it were in the shoulders or arms or hands, let the Ascendant be Gemini and the Moon in it; if it were in the breast, let the Ascendant be Cancer and the Moon in it; if it were in the back or in the ridge of the spine, let the Ascendant be Leo and the Moon in it; if it were in the belly or in the navel or in the parts adjacent to them, let the Ascendant be Virgo and the Moon in it; if it were in the hips,[399] let the Ascendant be Libra and the Moon in it; if it were in the private parts, let the Ascendant be Scorpio and the Moon in it; if it were in the upper thighs, let the Ascendant be Sagittarius and the Moon in it; if it were in the knees, let the Ascendant be Capricorn and the Moon in it; if it were in the legs, let the Ascendant be Aquarius and the Moon in it; and if it were in the feet, let the Ascendant be Pisces and the Moon in it.

And may you always understand that the Lord of the Ascendant is [to be] sound and free from impediments, if in any way it could be [so]; and if it could not be [so], always put Jupiter in the sixth, nor will this be less than if you had adapted the aforesaid.

And Māshā'allāh said,[400] look in every cure at the place of a body's infirmity: which if it were in the head or throat or shoulders or arms or hands, cure it when the Moon is in Aries or Taurus or Gemini, which is the upper part. And if it were in the breast or back or belly or navel, cure it when the Moon is in Cancer or Leo or Virgo, which is the part in the middle. And if it were in the hips or private parts or upper thighs, cure it when the Moon is in Libra or Scorpio or Sagittarius, which is the part sloping downwards. And if it were in the knees or legs or feet, cure it when the Moon is in Capricorn or Aquarius or Pisces, which is the lower part.

And in every one of these cases, let the Moon be in increased light and number, if it can be done, [and] joined to the benefics; which if it could not be done, at least adapt Jupiter just as I told you. And [Māshā'allāh] said[401] that every pain and all illness which is from the head to the pubic hair ought to be cured when the Moon is from the angle of earth up to the Midheaven, since this part of the circle is ascending (which is called the high part of the circle). And if it were from the pubic hair up to the lower part of the feet, it ought to be cured when

---

[399] I have corrected the attributions for Libra and Scorpio, which are switched here.
[400] As cited in Sahl, *On Elect.*, Ch. 22. See also al-Rijāl, pp. 313.
[401] As cited in Sahl, *On Elect.*, Ch. 22.

the Moon is from the angle of the Midheaven up to the angle of the earth, which is the submerging part or the lowest part of the circle. And let there be some benefic in the Ascendant.

For these signify that the medical art will likewise bring benefit, and that the sick person will get well. And may you know that the places adapted for speed are from the 1st up to the 10th, and from the 7th up to the 4th; indeed the other places are made for slowness. However, always have this in your memory: that you should not touch a member [of the body] with iron or fire when the Moon is located in the sign deputed over that member; but in other remedies and other cures, like drugs, ointments, poultices and the like, cure with confidence.

Chapter 7: On remedies which come about through surgery

If you wished to elect the hour for someone wanting to be cured by surgical means, let the Moon be in increased light and number; even let her be made fortunate by Jupiter or by Venus.

And al-Khayyat said[402] one must beware of every impediment of Mars; for he said that the Moon is more impeded by Mars when she is in the increase of her light, and less when she is in its decrease. And when she is in its decrease she is impeded more by Saturn, and less when she is in its increase. And he said that the Moon should be in a fixed sign, nor should she aspect the sign signifying the member which is being healed by iron by any aspect, nor should the Lord of the Ascendant be in [that sign]; nor should that sign be the Ascendant, nor should the Lord of the Ascendant nor the Moon be cadent. It is even good if the Lord of the Ascendant is in the Ascendant or in the Midheaven, and let it be in the same way if it is in the treating of the eyes, on account of an abscess or blemish or whiteness.[403] And adapt the sign and the planet signifying the member. And I recommend this opinion, if it can be observed (but if it could not be observed wholly, let it be observed to the extent that it can be observed, and especially so that the Moon is adapted, and the Lord of the Ascendant, or at least the Moon, so that she is not in the sign deputed over that member, nor in the conjunction or in the aspect of one of the malefics.

---

[402] This may originally be from al-Khayyat, but it is a virtually verbatim quote from Sahl, *On Elect.*, Ch. 22.

[403] *Albedinem.* Could this mean a cataract?

Chapter 8: On electing the hour for one wanting to practice bloodletting

If you wished to elect the hour for someone wanting to perform a useful bloodletting, adapt the Ascendant and its Lord, nor let the Ascendant be Gemini, nor the Moon in [Gemini]. And beware lest Mars or Saturn be in the Ascendant; nor should the Moon be in the opposition of one of them; however, let her be joined to Mars by a trine or sextile aspect in this working, provided that her aspect is not to him from Taurus, indeed so that she is not in one of them,[404] nor should Mars be ascending in the north or in the circle of his *awj*.

And 'Ali said,[405] let the Lord of the domicile of the Moon be aspecting it[406] with a praiseworthy aspect. And he said that a certain person had said one must beware of Taurus and of Leo in this working, and it will testify [that] the signs of the two of them[407] should not be feared, and especially if a benefic were in them; however, I have found the corporal conjunction of the Moon with Jupiter to be prohibited in the draining of blood by bloodletting; and I do find the rest of the other sages who speak of the bloodletting of the arm [to agree with me]. And certain ones said, if it were necessary to drain a moderate amount of blood, let the Moon be in Libra or in Scorpio (I however recommend the first half of Libra; and if the Mars were to aspect the Moon by a praiseworthy aspect, I recommend the last half of Scorpio). And the sages used to hate the movable signs, and they forbade the conjunction of the Moon with Mercury or with Saturn; and they hated Virgo and Capricorn and Pisces; and they put the Moon in the defect of her light. And the same sages said that the 2nd domicile from the house of the Moon was not unfortunate; all of these things are to be avoided, they said, unless the aspect of the benefics were present. However, to me it seems that all of Aries and the first half of Libra (as I said) are to be recommended, even though they are movable [signs].

And Abū Ma'shar said[408] Mars is in [this] work (except in those which pertain to blood and the opening of veins and the draining of blood by cupping

---

[404] *Ita quod non sit in aliquo ipsorum.* I am unsure what this means, or if Bonatti actually means the Moon and not Mars.

[405] I do not find this in al-Rijāl, although some of the comments seem to echo p. 316. Perhaps Bonatti is referring to 'Ali ibn Ridwān?

[406] I.e., "aspecting its own domicile."

[407] *Testatum fore signa duorum eorum.* This is phrased awkwardly; perhaps Bonatti is paraphrasing from 'Ali ibn Ridwān.

[408] Source unknown.

glasses or in the medicating of the sick). This is true, if the Moon were in the defect of her light, joined to him by an aspect of friendship.

And al-Kindī said[409] it is necessary that the Moon be in airy or fiery signs, and their Lords [too]. Nor is any member [of the body] to be touched while the Moon and the Lord of the Ascendant are in the sign to which that member belonged.

They even recommended that the Lord of the Midheaven be a benefic aspecting the Moon or the Lord of the Ascendant; and the Lord of the Ascendant and the Moon should be in the 4th house; and airy [signs] are better after the prevention [prior to the election].

And they said, draining is also more to be recommended in the beginning of the month,[410] which I say has a role in those who require bloodletting from the forty-fifth year onwards. One must even beware of the conjunction of the Lord of the 8th house with the Moon. And one must beware lest the Moon be under the rays of the Sun or in the combust degrees.

Chapter 9: On giving purgative medicines by defecation

If you wished to elect the hour for someone wanting to take medicine by mouth (going out by defecation), adapt the Ascendant and its Lord, if you can adapt [them]; and whether it can be adapted or not, put the Moon in the last half of Libra, or in the first half of Scorpio,[411] and let the one in whose domicile she is (whether it were Venus or Mars), be free from impediments, fortunate and strong. And if you can make the Ascendant one of those two signs, it will be good. Lacking this, however, make the Ascendant one of the southern signs, and let its Lord be sound. Likewise if the Moon cannot be put in Libra or Scorpio as I said, let her be at least in one of the southern signs.

And if the purgation were because of the illness of some particular member, let the Moon be in the sign signifying that member.

And if it were your intention to heat [the body] with this medicine, let the Moon or the Ascendant be in a fiery sign. And if you wanted to cool, let the Moon or the Ascendant be in a watery sign. And if you wanted to dry, let the Moon or the Ascendant be in an earthy sign. And if you wanted to moisten, let the Moon or the Ascendant be in an airy sign.

---

[409] Source unknown. The last sentence is from pseudo-Ptolemy's *Cent.*, Aph. 20.
[410] Presumably Bonatti means the *lunar* month.
[411] I.e., in the *via combusta*.

And one must beware lest the Moon or the Ascendant (and particularly the Moon) be in the cud-chewing signs, which are Aries, Taurus, the last half of Sagittarius, and Capricorn: because they signify nausea and vomit. And Capricorn is worse than the others, but Aries less so than him, Taurus less so than Aries, and the last part of Sagittarius less so than Taurus.

Even let the Moon be ascending southern.[412]

And 'Ali said[413] a certain person had said [that] of the cud-chewing [signs], only Capricorn is hateful. And the ancient sages forbade the Moon every aspect of Mars and Saturn: for Saturn presses together and constricts the medicine; indeed Mars excites it and makes it lead to the emission of blood. May you understand[414] this about any laxative medicine, whether it is one that melts in the mouth, or it is a decoction,[415] so long as it does not harm, whatever kind of Ascendant it was,[416] provided that it and its Lord and the place of the Moon are made fortunate. And one must beware lest the Lord of the Ascendant or the Moon is in the 8th house or joined to its Lord.

Chapter 10: On giving medicines producing vomiting

And if you wish to elect the hour for someone wishing to take a medicine producing vomiting, you must then use the cud-chewing signs. Whence the Moon and the Ascendant are to be put in one of them, if it can be done; out of all of which Taurus is more to be elected on account of the dignity of the Moon in it; more strongly so if she were then in its first 3°, where her degree of exaltation is. And if the vomiting were necessary for the particular illness of some member, let the Moon be in the sign deputed over that member, namely made fortunate and strong, and let the sign be adapted just as well as it can be adapted.

And al-Rijāl said[417] that if the Lord of the Ascendant were going to its own exaltation, it will be good.

---

[412] This may mean, "Let the Moon be northerly in ecliptical latitude and in a southern sign."
[413] I do not find this in al-Rijāl, perhaps it is al-'Imrānī.
[414] Reading *intellegas* for *intellegat* (with 1491).
[415] A medicine made by boiling the herb or other substance.
[416] This could also be read, "so long as whatever kind of Ascendant it were, it does not harm," i.e., referring to the potential harmfulness of the ascending sign.
[417] Al-Rijāl, p. 317.

Chapter 11: On sneezing, gargling, vomiting, and like things by the method of giving potions

If you wanted the elect the hour for someone wishing to cause sneezing or gargles or to vomit, or something like them, al-Rijāl said[418] it is necessary for him to wants to use one of these, to put the Ascendant and the Moon and the place of the significators (from among the cud-chewing signs) with all of those things which were said concerning the purgative medicines.

And al-Tabarī said[419] the Moon should be in decreased light and course, ascending in the circle of [her] *awj*.

Indeed al-Khayyat said[420] the Moon and the Lord of the Ascendant should be in Cancer or Leo or Virgo.

Chapter 12: On entering baths or the anointing of *annora* or *psilotrum*[421]

If[422] you wanted to elect the hour for someone to enter into the baths, or the anointing of *annora*, which is a certain ointment removing hairs,[423] which by some is called *psilotrum* (and certain others call it *sconapilos*), put the Moon in Aries or Scorpio, joined to Jupiter or the Sun or Venus by a trine or sextile or square aspect, but not by corporal conjunction; nor even should you make her joined to one by body; nor let her be in the aspect of Saturn; which if she were not in those signs, let her be in Cancer or Leo. However, one must beware lest she be in Taurus or Gemini or Virgo or Libra or Capricorn or Aquarius.[424] If indeed the one who enters the bath or hot water[425] does not anoint himself with *annora*, let her be in whatever sign she wants; nor even should it be condemned in the use of baths or in the anointing of *annora*, if the Moon were under the rays of the Sun.[426]

---

[418] Al-Rijāl, p. 317.

[419] According to al-Rijāl, al-Tabarī says "It is good if the Moon is in diminished light and in Taurus, and descending in latitude."

[420] Al-Rijāl, p. 317.

[421] According to Tr. 5 (62nd Consideration), *psilotrum* is a dilapitory cream or oil.

[422] See Sahl, *On Elect.*, Ch. 23.

[423] Body hair removal was a Muslim practice, but not (to my knowledge) a medieval European one; perhaps the international culture of places like Spain and Sicily introduced it.

[424] I.e., she should not be in the airy or earthy signs.

[425] *Stupha*, undoubtedly one of the rooms in a bathhouse.

[426] This is confusing, since he earlier stated that the Moon should *not* be in corporal conjunction with the Sun.

And Sahl said[427] [that] in the anointing of *annora*, the Moon was not to be put in hairy signs (which are Aries, Taurus, Leo, the last part of Sagittarius, and Capricorn).[428]

Chapter 13: On the buying of captives, slaves, and the like

If someone wanted to buy a captive or slave or Slavs, as is wont to happen in some places, and he wanted that you should elect the hour fit for this for him, you will adapt for him the Ascendant and its Lord, not to mention the Moon; and you will put her in fixed signs (except for in Scorpio) of right ascension, or the domestic [signs]: because these will signify that the slave or other bought person will be enduring[429] and supportive and [one] honoring his master. And adapt the 6th and its Lord, and make him to be joined to the Lord of the Ascendant by a trine or sextile aspect if you can, with reception, or with the Moon or with the Lord of the domicile in which she is. And if you can make him to be joined with all of the aforesaid, or with two of them, it will be better than [if it were] with only one.

For indeed the sages recommended that the Moon be in Taurus or in the last half of Sagittarius. And they likewise recommended that the Moon and the Ascendant be in signs formed in the image of a human or even in others, but not without the conjunction of the benefics–except for of Aries, Leo, Scorpio, Capricorn, and Pisces.[430] And beware lest the Lord of the Ascendant or the Moon or the Lord of the 6th house [domicile?] be in one of the aforesaid signs which are prohibited.

For Aries signifies that the slave or bought person will be negligent, and that he will not care about what things are useful to his master;[431] but he will rejoice in his harm. Leo signifies that the slave or bought person will be proud and gluttonous and a thief and lustful and greedy, but not for what is useful to his master.[432] Scorpio signifies him to be wrathful and an evildoer and an accuser. Capricorn signifies him to be a destroyer and injurer of his master. Pisces signifies the slave or bought person to be impetuous, and that he will reproach his master and will think about betraying him; and that he will disparage him in

---

[427] *On Elect.*, Ch. 23.

[428] Sahl says, "as is Aries and Leo and the rest of the bestial signs."

[429] *Patiens*, "supportive, enduring, suffering."

[430] I.e., one should avoid all of these signs no matter what. See below.

[431] Lit., "he will not care about the usefulness of his own master."

[432] I.e., he will only care about what is useful to himself.

all the ways in which he can; and he will speak evil about him. Nor will these slaves be ones obeying their masters.

And if one of the malefics were in the 6th, or elsewhere under the earth so that it aspects the 6th, it signifies that the bought person or slave is unfaithful and malevolent. If indeed the Lord of the 6th were in Sagittarius, it signifies that he who is sold is not a slave, nor of a servile condition, but is free.

Chapter 14: On the freeing of incarcerated people or of captives or the manumission of slaves

If it were your intention to elect the hour for the freeing of captives or the incarcerated[433] or manumission of slaves, adapt the Ascendant and its Lord and the Moon: because the Ascendant and its Lord and the planet from which the Moon is being separated, signifies him who frees or is manumitting. Indeed the 7th and its Lord and the planet to which the Moon is joined, signifies him who is being freed or manumitted. However, the 10th and its Lord signifies him who makes the liberation or manumission to come about, or through whose involvement they come about. Also, the 4th signifies what any one of them comes to as a result of the liberation or manumission.

For you will then consider whether the Moon is made fortunate or unfortunate. For if she were made fortunate, see in which domicile she is: because if she were in the 1st, it signifies good for the manumittor from the liberation. If however she were in the tenth, it will be good for the one interposing himself so that it happens. If by chance she were in the seventh, it will be good for the one liberated or manumitted. If indeed she were in the fourth, the end of the matter will be good for every one of them.

But if she were unfortunate and were in the first, it signifies that it will be bad for the one manumitting. If indeed she were in the 10th, it signifies that it will be bad for him who makes [the slave] be manumitted or freed. If however she were in the 7th, it signifies that it will be bad for the one freed or manumitted (for it signifies his return to prison or servitude). If by chance she were in the 4th, it signifies that it will be bad for all of the aforesaid as a result of the liberation or manumission.

And Sahl said,[434] let the Moon be increased in light and number, joined to benefics; and let the benefic to which she is joined, be likewise oriental [and]

---

[433] Reading *incarceratorum* for *incarceratione*.
[434] *On Elect.*, Ch. 25.

increased [in light and number] . If it were so, it signifies that good will happen to him, and he will be safe. Indeed, in the defect of light it signifies that evil things will happen to him, and pains, whence it will [not]⁴³⁵ cease to be so while he remains. And he said that in the increase of number it signifies the discovery of substance. And he said the Sun and the 10ᵗʰ should be cleansed of the malefics: because if they were impeded, he who liberates and manumits will find some impediment. And he said, beware lest the Moon be in the 12ᵗʰ (following Dorotheus). And he said, let the hour of liberation be when the luminaries aspect each other by a trine or sextile aspect, so there will be love between slave and master, and one will find good from the other; while the square aspect is in the middle; indeed the opposition signifies that [the slave will contend with his master. And he who would manumit a slave while]⁴³⁶ the Moon is impeded, servitude will be better for the slave than freedom. Therefore put the Moon in fixed signs (as was said above, you understand).

Chapter 15: On the buying of animals, both of those which are ridden and of others

If you wished to elect the hour for someone wanting to buy some animal, let the Ascendant and the Moon be in a sign signifying that animal (or that which is more close to the species); and let the Moon be made fortunate by one of the planets; and if it could happen that the Lord of that sign makes her fortunate, it will be better. And if she is not received, still it will be good, provided that she is in the praiseworthy aspect of some unimpeded benefic. And if she were received, it does not matter whether it is a benefic or malefic who receives her; nor even should it be feared in any of them, then.⁴³⁷ Whence, if it were a cow or horse or other large animal (whether it is rideable or not), put the Moon in Taurus or in the last half of Sagittarius. If indeed it were a sheep or pig or goat or the like, put her in Aries or Capricorn (or Taurus itself, if you cannot do otherwise).

And al-Rijāl said⁴³⁸ if the animal were male, make more of the places of the significators masculine, and in masculine places and signs. If however it were female, put them in feminine signs and places. And he said, if it were necessary

---

⁴³⁵ Adding *non*, following Sahl.
⁴³⁶ This line from Sahl is missing from Bonatti's text.
⁴³⁷ *Nec etiam tunc in aliquod timendum.*
⁴³⁸ Al-Rijāl, p. 318.

to adapt some [bodily] member of the animal, let the Moon be made fortunate [and] in signs signifying that member; and if it were a dog with which men hunt forest animals (like hares, foxes, boars, deer, and the like), let the Ascendant be made the last half of Leo, and the Moon in it or in Sagittarius; and in no way should you forget to adapt the 6th and its Lord.

And al-Ṭabarī said[439] a certain most excellent thing is when the Moon is in the last part of Gemini or in Leo or Sagittarius, because Lepus is there,[440] and these [signs] will make a daring and impetuous and biting dog.

And ʿAlī said[441] a certain man had said the Moon was to be put in Cancer because Cancer is the domicile of the Moon; and the Moon has a faster speed than the other planets, which signifies the speed of the dog. He seems to say the same in their training and instruction for hunting.

Chapter 16: On the buying of birds with which we hunt other birds

And if you wished to elect the hour for someone wanting to buy a falcon or Asturian hawk or common hawk (or similar birds with which men hunt other birds), adapt the Ascendant and its Lord, and put the Moon in Gemini or Libra or Aquarius or in the first half of Capricorn (because the philosophers said that the Hawk is there).[442] To be adapted are even the sixth [sign] and its Lord in every purchase of any hunting [animal] that flies, and even of any other birds, both domesticated and wild. You will adapt them in the instruction or training of these birds so they are trained to hunt, and in the training of dogs that hunt birds (like *brachi, sensii*,[443] and the like).

Chapter 17: On the doctor's approaching the patient

If a doctor were called to some sick person, you will consider whether there could be a delay in it or not. If indeed a delay were not able to interfere on his part, so that he could be expected, let the name of the Highest be the beginning

---

[439] Source unknown.

[440] I.e., the constellation "the Hare." It is located near Gemini at the feet of Orion, near Canis Major (signifying hunting symbols). Sagittarius is roughly opposite it, thereby continuing the metaphor of attack.

[441] I do not find this in al-Rijāl.

[442] I.e., the constellation Aquila, above the first half of Capricorn.

[443] *Brachium* means "leg" and a *braconarius* is someone in charge of hounds; my guess is that *brachi* are pointing dogs, while *sensi* (from *sentio*, "to sense") are bloodhounds.

of his journey to him.[444] If however the election could be expected,[445] make the Ascendant and the tenth one of the rational signs, if it can be done; and if this cannot be done, let at least the Ascendant be a rational sign; and let there be one of the benefics in it, and another in the 10th and another in the 7th, another in the 4th, if it can be done. Or at least let the said angles be aspected by benefics; and if it cannot be done, let the said angles be free of the malefics and their aspects—unless it were Mars in the business[446] of wounds and by the opening of veins or another useful shedding of blood.

For a benefic in the first signifies that the doctor will be useful to the sick person. In the 10th it signifies that the sick person will be obedient to the doctor. In the seventh it signifies that the illness will be alleviated, even from the presence of the doctor, not so much from the medicine. Indeed in the fourth it signifies that the medicine will profit him (and say the contrary about the malefics in the aforesaid places). Even put a benefic and especially Jupiter, if you can do it, or the Part of Fortune, unimpeded in the second (because this signifies the doctor's money), or joined to the Lord of the eighth or the eleventh (and likewise this signifies the doctor's money). And if the Lord of the second or the Lord of the first did not receive any one of them, beware lest it be joined by opposition or a square aspect; and even see lest one of the malefics who does not have testimony in the 9th, be impeded there (because it signifies that the doctor does not acquire honor from the illness, but rather acquires infamy or disgrace from it, [both] with reason and without reason). If however a benefic were there, it signifies that he will acquire praise from it, both with reason and without reason—and more strongly so if the benefic were to have testimony there, provided it is not impeded.

However, in surgical treatments Mars is of less impediment. And in any treatment which you make, may you strive to put Jupiter in the sixth or at least in the 7th—but the 6th heals better, because he who were then to provide treatment to one suffering an illness, it will profit him.

---

[444] *Sit initium itineris eius ad ipsum nomen altissimi.* Perhaps this means the doctor should pray before he comes. I am uncertain of Bonatti's precise meaning here.

[445] Bonatti must mean that there is no need for an election if the doctor can come promptly; but if we have to count on a delay of some sort, we need to make an election.

[446] Reading *negotione* for *negotio*.

ON THE SEVENTH HOUSE

And on those matters which pertain to it

Chapter 1: On marriage

If someone wished to perfect a marriage union, whether to celebrate the marriage or the nuptials,[447] and you wished to elect a fitting hour for him to do this, the sages said, adapt the Ascendant and its Lord, also the Moon and the Lord of the sign in which she is, and let the Ascendant be likewise a fixed sign, and the Moon in a fixed sign (of which the sages said that Taurus and Leo were better). [This is true], even though Sahl did not recommend Leo absolutely: for he said[448] the marriage would be favorable, and that there will be a constancy of love and agreement between them, but they will not be concerned to increase [their] substance, but rather on the other hand they will take care to destroy it (unless the Moon is joined to the Sun when she is in Leo by a trine or sextile aspect, because it breaks all malice; indeed the square aspect decreases [the substance] much). Indeed Scorpio and Aquarius are to be avoided, and especially for the man (because they are malicious and the domiciles of the malefics; whence they harm the man). Indeed for the woman they are not so malicious.

For the Ascendant and its Lord, and the Sun, and the planet from which the Moon is being separated (if the man asks), signify the condition of the man. The seventh [sign] and its Lord, and Venus, and the planet to which the Moon is joined, signify the condition of the woman. The tenth [sign] and its Lord signify what is going to happen between them. The fourth [sign] and its Lord signify the end of both (namely of the man and the woman).[449]

And Sahl said[450] that it seemed to certain people that the fourth [sign] signified the dowry.

And al-Rijāl said[451] if the significators of the man and woman were in a masculine sign, it will be good for the man from the woman, better than for her

---

[447] Coniugium, matrimonium, and nuptiae, respectively. Coniugium denotes physical union especially, matrimonium the institution of marriage, and nuptiae either one of these.

[448] On Elect., Ch. 26. But the material in parentheses is Bonatti's own comment (or else from another source).

[449] Assuming that this arrangement is the same as that for marriage delineations in nativities, then if a woman were asking, she would undoubtedly get the Ascendant and its Lord, and the man the 7th, its Lord, Venus, and the planet to which the Sun is joined.

[450] I have not found this in either Sahl or al-Rijāl.

[451] This seems to be based on some brief comments in al-Rijāl, p. 319.

from him. And if they were in a feminine sign, it will be good for the woman from the man, better than for him from her. And if the significator of the man were in a masculine sign and the woman's in a feminine sign, it will be good for both. If however the significator of the man were in a feminine sign, and the woman's in a masculine sign, it signifies that the marriage will not be suitable, nor will they rejoice together, and they will be grave and hateful to each other.

Al-Rijāl (from whom it does not seem to me one should differ) said[452] certain people take the significator of the inceptor from the planet from which the Moon is being separated, and the other's from the planet to which she is joined. And [they give] the Moon [as] significator of both, and they give Mercury to the children. And they said the Moon was not to be put in a rational sign,[453] for it signifies the talkativeness of the woman.

And al-Rijāl said,[454] if someone wished to buy a female captive, the election will be the same; and if he wanted to do it[455] with her, it is likewise. And al-Rijāl said, in the purchasing of other female captives, this is not to be considered, but [rather] what was said in the first chapter on slaves.[456]

And Sahl said[457] that Scorpio and Aquarius are useful for women, and less malicious than for the man, and that the first half of Taurus is better than the last; and that the first half of Gemini is worse than the last; and that Aries and Cancer are bad. And he said that Virgo is not useful for a virgin–indeed [it *is*] thus for a corrupted [woman].[458] Libra is bad, and the end of Scorpio, for it signifies that their partnership will be of little duration (indeed the beginning of it is less bad for the woman). Sagittarius is bad and the first half of Capricorn (the last [half] less bad). And he said, Aquarius and Pisces are bad; nor is there any usefulness in them, nor even if Venus were to aspect the malefics. If however you want to improve the election for marriage, put Venus in one of the domiciles of some received benefic (or at least in their bounds), joined to them. And if she were in the domicile of some malefic, let her be separated from it,

---

[452] What follows is based on several statements in al-Rijāl, p. 319.

[453] Al-Rijāl only says this regarding Pisces, not the rational signs.

[454] I have not found these direct statements in al-Rijāl, but perhaps Bonatti is inferring this similarity especially from p. 317, "Moreover, if you wanted a slave-concubine so that you might have a child from her..."

[455] I.e., have sex.

[456] I.e., since by hypothesis the purchaser wishes the slave to be more like a concubine than merely one of many servants.

[457] *On Elect.*, Ch. 26.

[458] Sahl simply says, "for a woman who was already married."

and let Jupiter be elevated above her,[459] or Venus joined to him by a trine or sextile aspect (but the trine is better), and especially if it were from the watery triplicity. Even let[460] the Moon [be] free from the impediments of the malefics, in increased light and number; let even Venus always be in one of her own dignities, or in a place in which she rejoices (or at least in her own *haym*)[461] or let her be joined to Jupiter or Mercury, and let Mercury be made fortunate and strong.

And always beware of the conjunction of the malefics with the Moon by [corporal] conjunction or aspect, unless perhaps there were a reception there. And if the woman were corrupted, put the Moon in a common sign, and let the Ascendant be one of the signs discussed above in a marriage, and [let] the Moon [be] in it. And do not put one of the malefics in the Ascendant, nor let it aspect it by a square aspect or from the opposition.

Indeed if you could observe all of these, it is good; however, if not, observe those which you can. At least protect the Moon by making her free from the impediments of the malefics, so that she is not joined to them. And if you cannot help but make her joined to them, make it so they receive her by a trine or sextile aspect (namely by domicile or exaltation, or at least by two lesser dignities). And if you cannot adapt her thus, at least put her in Taurus, unimpeded, or in Leo, received by the Sun, as was said, and especially if it were by the man's initiative.[462] If however it were by the woman's initiative, put [the Moon] in the said signs, or in the first half of Scorpio, received. And if you can do it so that you put a benefic in the degree of the 10th house, it signifies that the woman will conceive in the first copulation, if she were corrupted. If however she were a virgin, she will conceive in that same night. Whence sometimes women are accused, because they conceive in the first night when they are innocent; and they are often accused by women who ought to defend them. For the accusers do not consider that there is copulation on those nights.[463]

---

[459] This could refer to it being in a more northerly ecliptical latitude, but this could also refer to the Hellenistic "overcoming." See Introduction and footnote to Tr. 3, Part 2, Ch. 20.
[460] Reading *sit* for *sic*.
[461] This parenthetical comment is not Sahl's own, but Bonatti's.
[462] Lit., "if it were the man's motion" that the event takes place.
[463] This may be a combination of misreading and interpretation on Bonatti's part. Sahl (from whom this chapter is drawn) says "And let there be one of the benefics in the Midheaven. And Dorotheus said, wherefore then a child will be granted to them in that same year in which they are joined; which if there were a benefic in the degree of the Midheaven, the woman will be made pregnant in the first conjoining [of coitus]." I myself do not find this in Dorotheus.

Chapter 2: On partnership and participation in a useful cause, and contracting monies

If some people wished to contract a partnership and cooperation amongst themselves for reasons of their usefulness, and so they could make money from it, and they wanted you to elect the hour fit for this. Adapt the Ascendant and its Lord, also the Moon and the Lord of the domicile in which she is, if it can be done; or at least let the Ascendant be a common sign, and the Moon in a common sign (other than Gemini); let even the Lord of the sign in which the Moon is, be in a common sign, or let him be in Leo (for Leo, on account of the goodness of the Sun; and the Sun agrees with partnerships; and for them because there is an intention of making money because of it);[464] and make the Moon cleansed from all the impediments of the malefics, and particularly from their conjunction or opposition, or their square aspect; and let her be joined to benefics.

And if she were in Virgo or Sagittarius, or Pisces, with reception, it will be good. If indeed without reception, Sagittarius or Pisces is not recommended; for reception signifies their wealth. And if you could not put her in the aforesaid signs, put her in Taurus, and beware of the southern signs[465] except for the aforesaid ones; and let it be with reception in them. And Libra is judged worse than all of them on account of the *via combusta* located in her. And Aquarius is judged evil in these things. And let the Moon be in increased light and number; and let her be received by a trine or sextile aspect, for this signifies that their separation will be good and with good will. For the square aspect and the opposition signify litigation and a quarrel in their separation. You however, if you cannot adapt all of these, still adapt those which you can. For after the adaptation of the Lord of the Ascendant and the Moon, [adapt] the second, the fourth, the eleventh, and their Lords; and the Part of Fortune (even though the sages did not make mention of them). If you cannot adapt all of these, adapt the Moon and the Part of Fortune, because they are necessary in this matter. Or at least adapt the Moon.

---

[464] I have rearranged some words in this clause, which appears in the text after "and make [the Moon]..." It originally reads, "*et pone eis ex quo est intentio lucrari illa de causa Lunam mundam....*"

[465] I.e., the signs of southern declination: Libra through Pisces.

Chapter 3: On the electing of the hours for going to war or for conquering enemies

If you wished to elect the hour for someone wanting to go to war or to conquer his enemies, adapt the Ascendant and its Lord, the second also and its Lord, and weaken the seventh and its Lord; even the eighth and its Lord; and make it so the Ascendant is one of the domiciles of Mars or Jupiter or Saturn (out of all of which the stronger ones are the domiciles of Mars, and Scorpio is stronger than Aries). Whence if you could make Scorpio ascending, make Mars strong and fortunate. And even though certain people seem to dissent [from this], put him in the Ascendant if he is the Lord of the Ascendant; however it will be very good if you could put some benefic in the Ascendant with him. And you will adapt Jupiter by putting him in the second or the first or the 11th for the soldiers or helpers of the inceptor. And weaken Venus, the Lady of the seventh for the enemy, and Mercury for his helpers.[466] Put [Venus and Mercury] in the first or in the second, or make them retrograde or combust or cadent from the angles and [away] from an aspect of friendship from the 7th or 8th. If indeed the Ascendant were Aries, let Mars (likewise the Lord of the Ascendant) be strong and fortunate. And weaken Venus, the Lady of the 7th, as was said.

If however you could not put one of the domiciles of Mars in the Ascendant, put one of the other domiciles [there] (namely of Jupiter or Saturn), and make him whose domicile was ascending, fortunate and strong (namely in the Ascendant or the 10th or the 11th), and strengthen the Lord of the second for his helpers by putting him likewise in the Ascendant or the 10th or 11th or in the 12th,[467] fortunate and strong, and weaken the 7th and its Lord (also the 8th and its Lord) by all the methods you can, and make them unfortunate according to your ability, make it so that he who makes them (or at least one of them) unfortunate[468]–and it is better that he by whom the Lord of the Lord of the 7th is made unfortunate–is the Lord of the Ascendant or at least the Lord of the 2nd, because it will be good.

And beware lest you put Mars in the Ascendant if he is not the Lord of the Ascendant, but make it so that he aspects the Ascendant or its Lord by a trine or sextile aspect, because it will be good; nor let him be impeded. And if he

---

[466] I.e., if Scorpio were the rising sign, the enemy would be ruled by Taurus, and Gemini would be the second sign from the seventh.

[467] Then the Lord of the 2nd would be in the 11th from his own house.

[468] Bonatti seems to interrupt his clause only to repeat it. The idea seems to be that the Lord of the 7th should be made unfortunate by the Lord of the Ascendant or of the 2nd.

were impeded, put against him a benefic who prohibits the Ascendant.[469] And beware lest you ever make the Lord of the Ascendant or the Lord of the second impeded, nor should you put one of them in the 7th or 8th, because it would be the worst thing: for it signifies they will be conquered. And likewise you should beware of the 4th and that the Lord of the Ascendant is not joined to a planet [who is] cadent or located in his own fall, unless perhaps the cadent one were to receive him.[470] And if you could not put the Lord of the seventh in the Ascendant or in the second, make him be joined to the Lord of the Ascendant, and so that he goes toward him, and the Lord of the Ascendant toward him; and let their conjunction be such that the Lord of the 7th does not receive the Lord of the Ascendant, whether [the Lord of the Ascendant] receives [the Lord of the 7th] or not.

And 'Ali said,[471] put Mars aspecting the Ascendant by a trine after you had adapted him and he had the greatest dignity in it; and it is better that he be its Lord, or that he aspect the Lord of the Ascendant by a praiseworthy aspect. And let the Lord of the seventh be made unfortunate and weak and cadent; and what is better, let the Lord of the Ascendant be the one when [the Lord of the seventh] is made unfortunate (if it can be done).[472] And let the Lord of the Ascendant be going toward an angle in one of his own dignities, elevated above the Lord of the 7th and the 10th.[473] And it is even good when the Lord of the Ascendant is transiting above the Lord of the 7th (whether he were a benefic or malefic), and so that the Lord of the Ascendant is above the earth and the Lord of the 7th is below the earth. For if the Lord of the Ascendant were to make the Lord of the 7th unfortunate, it signifies that the king or captain of the enemies will be captured. And let the Lord of the 10th be aspecting the Ascendant (or at least its Lord) by a praiseworthy aspect, and that he have dignity in it (if it can be done). And he said, nor should he be aspecting the 7th nor its Lord, nor should he have any dignity in it; which if it cannot be done, let him have greater dignity in the Ascendant than in the 7th. And he said that the Moon should be handled in the same way as with the Lord of the Ascendant.

---

[469] I believe this means that we ought to make a benefic aspect the rising sign, so that it ameliorates the bad effects of the rising sign caused by Mars's impediment.

[470] Here we have a case where Bonatti allows a cadent planet to receive another. Perhaps this is a least-best scenario.

[471] I have not found this in al-Rijāl.

[472] That is, let the Lord of the Ascendant be the one making him unfortunate.

[473] This could refer to it being in a more northerly ecliptical latitude, but this could also refer to the Hellenistic "overcoming." See Introduction and footnote to Tr. 3, Part 2, Ch. 20.

And Sahl said,[474] if you were to make them to be joined in the angles, war will take place between them. And he said, you should not go to war unless Mars is the Lord of the Ascendant or were to aspect the Lord of the Ascendant from friendship; and let him be made fortunate in a good place, not impeded. And he said, let him be in signs of right ascension, and in the *haym* of the Ascendant,[475] so that there is help for him who goes to war. And put the Part of Fortune and its Lord in the Ascendant, or in the second, joined with their Lords, or at least with one of them. And you should never put them[476] in the 7th or 8th, nor joined to their Lords. And he said, beware that you do not make the Ascendant or its Lord impeded in the beginning of the war (namely for him who wished to begin the war); and observe the *duodena*[477] of the Moon, because it is necessary in the matter of war.

And al-Kindī said[478] it is necessary that the prince against whom the armies go out, never begin to do battle with them until the Moon is made fortunate–but if it requires battle, [then go] when she is not made fortunate.

And al-Rijāl said:[479] and it ought to be hateful to those fighting to begin the war in hours which are called combust, about which I have made you adapt[480] the [planets] of war (namely Mars and Mercury; also the Moon and the Lord of her domicile): therefore look in the adaption of the hour, and may you not be negligent in this, nor be given to forgetfulness. And he said, know that when either army were more wisely readied for war, just as I have told you, he of them who was born at night, and in whose nativity Mars had a role, will achieve victory.[481] Because Mars is the master of wars, and wars are committed to him.

---

[474] *On Elect.*, Ch. 27.

[475] Based on al-Rijāl's use of this phrase, this means "on the eastern side of the chart," i.e., in the area of the chart where the Ascendant is.

[476] Reading *eos* with Sahl for *eum*.

[477] The *duodena* are divisions of the hours of the lunar month (see Tr. 4, Ch. 6, where Bonatti speaks specifically about observing these hours when going to war; see also Tr. 9, Part 3, 12th House, Ch. 7). But I do note that this is not what the printed editions of Sahl say: the 1493 edition of Sahl uses *duodecima*, while the 1509 edition uses Arabic numerals (12.). So it is possible that Sahl wants us to observe the *duodecimae* or "twelfth-parts" of the Moon (see Tr. 9, Part 3, 12th House, Ch. 6; also Tr. 5, the 89th Consideration).

[478] Al-Rijāl, p. 321.

[479] See al-Rijāl, p. 322, but also Sahl *On Elect.*, Ch. 27.

[480] There seem to be some missing words. Based on Bonatti's usual style, I would expect this to read: "…about which I have made *mention* to you. *And you ought to* adapt…"

[481] This must mean that winner will be he who has a nocturnal nativity and has Mars in a prominent place or rulership or signification above the horizon–since Mars belongs to the nocturnal sect and would therefore be in his *halb* if not in *hayyiz*.

And he said that they will perhaps be pacified or set the war aside, namely if the march to war of either of them were good.

On the revolution of the year of the chief of the army to be considered

And if the nativity of the king or captain of the army were to be known, it is necessary to look at his revolution: which if it signified victory for him over his enemies in that year, all doubt that his side will win, is banished. If however it were to signify the contrary for him, in that year he must be removed and another substituted in his place.

Chapter 4: On the discovery of the combust hours[482]

However, you could discover the combust hours this way. Consider the hour of the most recent, past conjunction of the Sun and the Moon, and its minute, and begin from that minute, and count up to 12 complete hours. Because those 12 hours are combust,[483] in which it is to be feared, according to what al-Rijāl said.[484] Because if someone were to begin wars then, and especially in the first four of those hours, defeat is to be feared for him, and the loss of his body and spirit, even if we were otherwise to have a good election for going off to war. And sometimes many ignorant people are deceived in this, whence deception comes to them, because they do not consider the combust hours. Indeed in the remaining eight hours it borders on danger, but not on the ultimate one.

And after these 12 combust hours are 72 incombust hours, in which men can do their business. And after those 72 incombust hours are 12 combust ones. And after those 12 combust hours are 72 incombust ones. Whence, by reckoning thus from the minute of the conjunction up to the hour and its minute in which you are, you could know whether the hour in which you wished to begin the war is combust or incombust.

And if the adversaries were to begin to do battle in those incombust hours, the same misfortune will happen to them. Nor will they be contrary to those against whom the battle was begun. But on account of the ever-present impossibility of the adaptation of everything said above, and because men at a [given] time cannot expect that all of their elections will be destined [to success],

---

[482] Again, these seem to be the *al-bust* hours (see Tr. 4).
[483] Due to the speed of the Moon's motion, she would be approximately 6° separated from the Sun after 12 hours.
[484] Al-Rijāl, p. 322.

as was said, it is necessary for the astrologer to do what he can, if he cannot do whatever he wants.

You, therefore, when you elect for the aforesaid, act so that you make the Ascendant one of the domiciles of one of the superior planets; which if they were [not] so disposed or so fit that the domicile of one of them should be made the Ascendant, make Leo the Ascendant, and make the Sun fortunate and strong; and weaken Saturn whenever you can, namely by making him retrograde or combust, or in Leo or in Cancer or in Aries; nor let [Saturn] aspect his own domicile nor a planet who renders his light to it; and weaken Jupiter [as] the significator of the helpers of the side of the adversaries, and make Mercury (the significator of the helpers of the one for whom you elect) strong.[485] And if you can, adapt Mars so that you have him well on your side; indeed, if not, make it so that the enemies do not have him on their side; nor let him be in the 7th or the 8th, nor should he aspect one of them, nor one of their Lords; and always weaken the 7th and the 8th and their Lords.

May you understand the same with Saturn and Jupiter, and may it always be your concern to strengthen the Ascendant and the 2nd and their Lords; because, as the Philosopher testifies,[486] a multitude cannot be killed, and thus there is no victory against a multitude; whence an election is weak against a multitude, nor is its aid clearly perceived.[487] If the side for which you elect is equal to the other, or a little less, you should elect for the equal or not particularly weaker one. If it were less, let it be by one-fifth or by one-fourth or by one-third, because from thence onwards it is unnecessary. And you will render fear to the side[488] which you favor.

And beware lest you put the Moon on the side of the enemies; and if she were the significatrix [of the enemy] (namely that the Ascendant were Capricorn), weaken her according to your ability, and strengthen Saturn as much as you can, so that your side wins.

And it seemed to certain ancients that retrograde superiors were stronger than direct inferiors—but it is not purely and simply so. But if the superiors were retrograde near their second station, they will be stronger than direct inferiors that are near their own first station.

---

[485] Again, if Leo is the rising sign, then Saturn will rule the seventh (adversary), Jupiter Pisces and the eighth (adversary's helpers), and Mercury Virgo and the second sign (inceptor's helpers).

[486] This seems to be a reference to a passage in Tr. 7, Part 1, Ch. 5.

[487] *Nec sentitur manifeste ipsius iuvamentum.*

[488] Reading *partae* for *partem.*

If however you could not adapt the aforesaid just as I have told you, put off your election while you can adapt.[489] If indeed he who consulted you did not want to put it off, you should not elect for him lest perhaps you should fall into ignominy–and not by your own fault, but he would make it so that it will seem possible to him. Perhaps it will be that the root of his nativity is so strong, that he will win; and perhaps it will be possible that the contrary will happen to him, which seems more likely, nor is it surprising.

Chapter 5: On raising military flags or large banners or pennants

To certain people it seemed that this chapter should be put before the preceding one, because the raising of military flags belongs to the matters leading to battle. To others it seemed that [the preceding chapter] ought to precede, and this one follow, because even though the raising of military flags is a sign that leads to battle, still it does not make the battle happen; indeed men can carry military flags and do battle, and carry them and not do battle. However, doing battle does not happen unless there *is* a battle. I however put no significance in this [debate].

The raising of military flags or other signs for battle is three-fold: for either it is the giving or confirmation of the standard of the king, or of another great man below the king, or of a city or other group of people; and if there were more [ways], they would be found subordinate to these. For if the king wished to raise or establish his own military flag, it is necessary that he raise it with his own hand, or that he commit it to another who would raise it in his name. And raising and confirming differ from one another. For raising is when the military standard is newly given to him who is not used to having it. Confirmation is when it is confirmed for him who then has it or to whom it has already been given.[490]

Whence, if someone wished that you would elect for him the hour fit for this, adapt the tenth and its Lord, and put the Moon in Scorpio, joined to Mars by an aspect of friendship, with the conjunction or aspect of some benefic; and let Mars be free (namely fortunate and strong, nor impeded). And if you cannot put the Moon in Scorpio, put her in Aries (but Scorpio is recommended more),

---

[489] I.e., provided that the inceptor has allowed enough time to wait for a good election.
[490] Perhaps the distinction being drawn is between (a) raising a flag to claim a position before it is fully secured, and (b) raising it in confirmation *after* it is secured.

and let it be near the end of the lunar month if it can be done[491]—however, always let the Moon be sound.[492] And if the 10th house [domicile?] could be Scorpio while the Moon is in it, and the Sun in Aquarius in the [geographical] region in which Aquarius is then the 1st house, and Saturn sound, it would be good. If however Capricorn were the 1st house, it would not be so secure. If for instance it were the military flag of another great man below the king, and he himself were the master of the war, it will be good if the Moon is in Scorpio when you elect for him, on account of the strength of Mars in it; and let the Ascendant be Scorpio, as was said, and let [the Moon] be free, joined to Mars by a praiseworthy aspect.

If however it were the military flag of some city or some group of people or a great man who is not the master of the war (namely that it is not his own war, but he is carrying it out for someone else), let the Moon be in the domiciles of Jupiter, cleansed (namely, made fortunate and strong, free from impediments); and let Jupiter be made fortunate and strong, free from every impediment. Nor should the Moon then be in Cancer, nor in the domicile of some malefic; and this has a role to play[493] when a specific battle is expected after the raising of their flag, even if perhaps afterwards the banner followed after the raising that cities and the other aforesaid people are wont to do. And if all of these cannot be done, [then] of whatever sort the raising of the military flags were, the Moon should be put in the domiciles of Mars as was said, and she should always be sound and free of impediments; or let her be put in Leo, joined to the Sun by a praiseworthy aspect. May you understand the same concerning the purchasing of the aforesaid signs[494] and about their cutting, conjoining, and adaptation.[495] May you understand the same about clothing pertaining to war (when the Moon is in Leo) with which men act for only that reason and not another, given that making or handling of the clothing of one of them for common use is then prohibited by the wise.[496]

But if you could not adapt all of these things, adapt those of them that you can; adapt at least the Moon and the Lord of the Ascendant. And if you can give

---

[491] Altogether, this would mean that the battle ought to take place in late fall or early winter, when the Sun is in Sagittarius or Capricorn.

[492] *Salva:* safe, unhurt, well. In other words, unafflicted, in a strong house, *etc.*

[493] Lit., "a place" (*locum*).

[494] I believe Bonatti means the flags, since the flags are signals. See also the next sentence.

[495] I.e., cutting, sewing, and preparation.

[496] In other words, battle clothing ought only to be worn for battle, and so its making and use should be elected.

the Part of Fortune to the Ascendant,[497] it will be good for the side of him for whom you are electing. And you will weaken the seventh and its Lord as much as you can, and the planet to which the Moon is joined, if you can; and strengthen him from whom she is being separated, if you can do it. Nor should you ever give the Part of Fortune to the adversary[498] if you were able to take it away from him.

Chapter 6: On arms or war horses or other instruments pertaining to procuring for war

Just as the raising of military flags seems to some that it ought to precede going out to war, so it seems to them that the procuring of arms ought to precede the raising of military flags. But it seemed to others [that] those two ought to precede, and this third [topic] should follow, because doing battle is the most powerful part of war or battle.[499] Whence, if you wanted the hour fit for this for someone wishing to procure arms (both to procur defensive arms and offensive ones–I say defensive, like cuirasses, shields, helmets and the like, or horses, solely with the intention and reason of doing battle with them), or for someone wanting to create the aforesaid arms or [that they be] painted or be adapted in some other way, you will adapt the Ascendant and its Lord, the Moon also and the Lord of the domicile in which she is; and make Mars free in one of his own dignities, and let the Moon be joined to him from an aspect of friendship; nor should the Moon be in increased light then, but [rather] in the defect of her light, in the last half or near it (provided she is not under the rays, nor going toward combustion). And if you could not help but make the Moon increased in light, keep her from the aspect of Mars and from his corporal conjunction. And let her be otherwise free from impediments. And if you cannot adapt all of these, at least adapt Mars as was said, and make him free (namely fortunate and strong).

---

[497] I believe this means, "elect the chart so the Part of Fortune is in the rising sign." This could only happen when the Moon were just outside of the Sun's beams.

[498] Again, if Bonatti is saying what I think he is, this would be the case if the election were near the Full Moon.

[499] I have reversed the clauses in this sentence, else it would have appeared to be a redundant repetition. In my version, Bonatti is reporting another reason for the alternative ordering of chapters.

On the procuring of horses

However, in the procuring of a horse you can make the ascending sign a common one; and let the Moon be in Taurus or Leo, and let the planet to which she is joined be ascending, [in] direct [motion]: for this signifies that the horse will increase in body and price. If however it were ascending retrograde, it will decrease in body, even if it were to increase in price. If however it were descending [in] direct [motion] it will decrease in price, even if perhaps it would increase in body. But if it were descending retrograde, it will decrease by both. You may understand the same about all other horses.[500]

Chapter 7: On the reconciliation of enemies or who (on the other hand) have made war

Since mention was made (in the preceding chapters) of war and of those things which pertain to war, it seemed[501] to the Master al-Rijāl that a speech on the concord or the reconciliation of enemies ought to follow immediately after those things which were said about war and the fighting of enemies.[502] Whence if you wished to elect the hour fit for this for someone wanting to be reconciled with his enemies, you will adapt the Ascendant and its Lord; make him fortunate and strong; the Moon also, if you can, and the Lord of the domicile in which she is. And weaken the seventh and its Lord; however, put the Part of Fortune [there], even though you will weaken [the seventh], and make it so that it[503] is joined to the Lord of the Ascendant by a trine or sextile aspect, or at least let him aspect the Ascendant by the same aspect.

And ʿAli said:[504] and let the Lord of the 12th be weak and cadent. And he said if the 12th house itself were impeded it will be good, and it must be done with the 12th and its Lord just as with the 7th and its Lord; and that the Lord of the 11th must be adapted, and its Lord. And he said the Lord of the Ascendant should be in the Midheaven or going toward it, and it should be as strong as it can be; likewise the planet in whose domicile it is, and in the best strength and fortune it can be.

---

[500] I believe by "ascending" and "descending," Bonatti means "in its epicycle"

[501] Adding *est* to *visum*.

[502] Al-Rijāl does not actually say this; he simply follows the chapter on war with one on making peace (p. 322).

[503] Probably the Lord of the seventh.

[504] I have not found this statement in al-Rijāl.

If indeed the Lord of the 12th is of those planets which are friendly with the Lord of the Ascendant, it will be better. And he said[505] if the degree of the Ascendant and the degree of the 12th were of one strength[506] it will be better than it could be in the adaptation of the houses. And he said, if he who makes peace were the king, the things that are to be adapted are whose which were recalled in the introduction of this chapter; and let the Lord of the Ascendant be transiting above the Lord of the 12th (which if the signs by which the significators[507] are taken are fixed or of direct ascension, it will be better). If indeed the harmony were by the hands of legates or by charters, Mercury will have to be adapted. If however it were by acts and the words of those present, Jupiter will have to be adapted, and the Lord of the Ascendant, in signs of direct ascension; also the Lord of the seventh and the 12th in signs of crooked ascension.

And al-Tabarī said[508] if it were the intention of him for whom you elect, to deceive the adversary by advancing upon him cleverly, let the Moon be in Aries or Taurus or Gemini or Scorpio or Sagittarius or Capricorn or Pisces; and let the Moon be joined to one of the benefics, or let one of them be in the Ascendant; nor let the Lord of the Ascendant be cadent from an angle, but let him aspect the Ascendant by an aspect of friendship; and let him be in the aspect of a benefic; and it is necessary that the Lord of the twelfth be weak.

Chapter 8: On the hour to be elected for expelling or ejecting phantasms or some malignant spirit (which is called the Devil by certain people) impeding or infesting some place or a home or some person; or to tear down the [place of an] oracle of idols or the like

And if someone wished to eject or expel phantasms or some harmful spirit (which is called the Devil by certain people) from some place or home, or some harmful thing either terrible or infesting the inhabitants of that place, or [if] in some person there were some violent motions (which is called demonic), and you wished to administer some medicine or perform some exorcism or the like, and you wanted to elect for him the hour fit for it, adapt the Ascendant and its

---

[505] I have not found this statement in al-Rijāl.
[506] As I cannot find Bonatti's source text in al-Rijāl, I am unsure what exactly al-Rijāl might have meant by this.
[507] Reading *significatores* for *significatore*.
[508] Again, I am not sure of the source, or whether this is al-Tabarī's own opinion or al-Rijāl's version of al-Tabarī.

Lord, and beware lest the Ascendant be Cancer or Leo or Scorpio or Aquarius; nor let the Moon be in one of those signs; let the Ascendant be whatever [other] one you wanted, and its Lord free;[509] and let the Moon be in any one of them,[510] joined to some benefic, nor let her be impeded. However in the destruction of homes in which idols are cared for, or in which there is some prayer which is not divine, it is enough for you to weaken Venus and make her unfortunate.

Chapter 9: On the purchasing of all things generally, both of movable and immovable things, under which the aforesaid chapter on the purchasing of animals may be comprehended

The other chapters on buying can be comprehended under this one and subordinated to it. Whence if someone wanted to buy something and wanted that you should elect for him the hour fit for doing this, adapt the Ascendant and its Lord, also the Moon, and put her in the first or the tenth, and, if you can do it, let the 1st and the 10th be a feminine sign; however the 10th is recommended in this case more so than the 1st; or let her be in the 11th. Even let the Lord of the domicile in which the Moon is, be sound and free from impediments; and let the Lord of the Ascendant be decreasing in in number, so that in one day it goes less than its average course [by speed]. And let Mercury and the Lord of the 10th be sound and free from impediments.

And al-Rijāl said[511] if the Moon were with Mercury, it will be useful; and if Mercury were even decreasing in his course, it will be good.

And ['Umar] al-Tabarī said[512] the crooked signs are good for buyers, and even seem to help sellers. If however the Lord of the Ascendant were increasing in number, and in signs of direct [ascension], it is bad for the one buying. Likewise if the Moon were in signs of direct ascension, and were increasing in course, it will be worse, because it makes dear whatever someone were to buy, and it will lose value so that harm could follow from it. If however she were in crooked ones, and were decreasing in course, she makes cheap whatever

---

509 This clause could also be read, "Let the Ascendant (whichever one you wanted) and its Lord be free."

510 I believe this is an error on Bonatti's part. Al-Rijāl (p. 312) says the Moon should *not* be in the above stated signs (Cancer, *etc.*).

511 Probably al-Rijāl (p. 306), though al-Rijāl seems to be paraphrasing another author. He mentions their conjunction again on p. 307.

512 Al-Rijāl says this on p. 306, but he does not name al-Tabarī as his source.

someone were to buy then, and it will become more valuable[513] so that wealth could follow from it; [and] I maintain what was said above in the chapter on procuring arms and a horse (both for wars and otherwise).[514]

And al-Rijāl said a certain person[515] had said buying and selling in the first quarter of the lunar month is useful for both (namely for the one buying and the one selling); indeed in the second quarter it is more useful for the seller than for the buyer; indeed in the third quarter, it is more useful for the buyer than for the seller; indeed in the last quarter it is very agreeable for the buyer. And he said[516] that certain people did not disapprove of the Moon being joined to Saturn—which seems to me to be commendable in the selling of heavy things, like of lands and other estates, both rustic and urban, and which it is hoped will remain for a long time with the buyer. However in the buying of movable things, and of those which we expect will be transferred quickly [to others], it does not seem recommendable to me.

You however, if you could not adapt all of the aforesaid, adapt what you can. Adapt at least the Moon, and use the quarter of the [lunar] month (as was said) if you can, and the crooked signs. If however it was the buying of an animal that the buyer intended to fatten up, like pigs, young chickens, and the like, let the Ascendant be a common sign, and [let] the Moon be in Taurus or Leo or at least in a common sign; and let the planet to which she is joined (or will first be joined) be ascending [in] direct [motion]; and this if he were to buy an animal in order to resell; if however he were buying not so as to resell it, but only to fatten it up for his own use, let the planet to which the Moon is joined be direct; nor will you care whether it is ascending or descending.

Chapter 10: On the buying of seeds for fields or gardens, *etc.*, like grain, barley, beans, winter wheat, cabbage, and the like

If someone wished to buy some sowable seed whose usefulness and a great amount[517] are expected, and you wished to elect for him an hour appropriate for this, adapt the Ascendant and its Lord; however let such an election be in the

---

[513] Reading *valescet* for *arescet*.

[514] Bonatti is recalling his statement about the ascending/descending and direct/retrograde conditions of the planet to which the Moon is joined.

[515] Al-Rijāl (p. 306) is paraphrasing Theophilus of Edessa (whom he calls Nufil, as is common in medieval works).

[516] Al-Rijāl, p. 307.

[517] Lit., "multiplicity" (*multiplicitas*).

first quarter of the lunar month; and let the Moon be in increased number, if it can be done; and let her even be in crooked signs (which are called the "increasing ones"), and in one of the masculine quarters (which are from the 10th up to the Ascendant, and from the 4th up to the 7th), because they likewise increase; and let even the Lord of the first be in one of those places; indeed let the 10th and its Lord be free from the impediments of the malefics.

And 'Alī said[518] the Moon should even be with Mercury, and him oriental, free, in his own fast motion; the which opinion I very much approve if it can be observed completely; but if it cannot be observed, let it be observed at least completely [enough] so that the Moon is adapted.

Chapter 11: On the taking and loaning of money

This chapter[519] seems to be contrary to the chapter on the loaning of money; whence it is necessary that he who elects, employ certain things contrary to those which he uses in that chapter; wherefore if someone wished to take out a loan, and he were to inquire of you so that you would elect for him an hour fit for this, adapt the Ascendant and its Lord, and put the Moon in Leo or Libra[520] or Scorpio or Sagittarius or Aquarius, and let her be in little light, and let her be in the aspect of Jupiter or Venus or Mercury; and let the Ascendant be one of the aforesaid signs, and let the Lord of the first and the Lord of the seventh be free of impediments. And if it can be done, let them be in harmony with or receiving one another,[521] from some of their dignities (whether great or small).

And al-Rijāl said that certain people hated the hour of Mars[522] and the hour of the Sun in this.

Chapter 12: On the hunting of birds, wild beasts, and fishes, by land and water

Just as was said elsewhere, there are two methods of hunting: one on the land and by land, the other in the water and by water. The one that is on land is

---

[518] I have not found this in al-Rijāl.
[519] By "this chapter," Bonatti must mean the chapter of equal length and content in al-Rijāl (p. 307), entitled "On the accepting of capital." But Bonatti's paraphrase is not quite accurate (see footnotes below).
[520] Al-Rijāl says Virgo, not Libra.
[521] Al-Rijāl does not mention reception.
[522] Al-Rijāl says Saturn, not Mars.

divided: for either it is on the mountains and by mountains, or it is on flat land and by flat land. Lisewike the one that is in the water and by water is divided: for either it is on the sea, or in rivers or in lakes or in hollows or in brooks.[523]

Again, the hunting that is on land, is either for wild animals or it is for birds. Again that which is for wild animals is either for wild animals that wound by biting or claws (like bears, wolves, foxes, and the like), or it is for other wild animals sharing something with domesticated [animals] by chewing the cud or [having] cloven hoofs (like hares, roebuck, deer, boars, and the like).

Again, that which is for birds is either for aerial birds (like eagles, hawks, sparrowhawks, kites, and the like that snatch up living [birds]); or for doves or *agatias*,[524] or cranes, or great grey partridges, or starlings, or blackbirds, or sparrows, or ravens, and the like; or it is for terrestrial birds like pheasants, partridges, terns,[525] *qualiae*,[526] quail, and the like. Or it is for marsh birds and [those] in water and which spend time near water (like geese, swans, ducks, diving-birds, and the like). Indeed that which is in the water is either with a hook or with a net or other clever instruments put in the water, like a wicker-trap, coverings, *nermelli*,[527] and the like.

Whence, if you wished to go out on a hunt, or you wished to elect the hour fit for this for someone wanting to go, adapt the Ascendant and its Lord, and let the seventh [sign] or at least the Ascendant be of the nature of the kind of hunting which the hunter intends to hunt [by]: however it is better that the seventh [sign] be of that nature, than the first [sign].

For if it were a hunt by mountains and for wild animals that wound, let the Ascendant be a fiery sign (of which the last half of Leo is better, and even Sagittarius, but it is below Leo [in effectiveness]; and Aries is below Sagittarius), and let the Lord of the Ascendant made fortunate and strong, and even the Lord of the sixth.

If however the hunt were for other cud-chewing or cloven-hooved wild animals, let the Ascendant be one of the quadrupedal signs, or of the other earthy ones. And if you cannot have it so, you should have whatever kind you can of the other quadrupedal ones (but the aforesaid have greater power than

---

[523] Bonatti's punctuation makes his distinction unclear: he is probably distinguishing between ocean/salt water fishing on the one hand, and landbound/fresh water fishing on the other.
[524] Perhaps magpies (*agausea*)?
[525] *Sternae.* This could be a misread for *sturnus* or starling, which does nest on the ground.
[526] This word also means quail, just like the following word *coturnix.* But I do not know what distinction Bonatti is trying to draw, so I have left it untranslated.
[527] Unknown word.

the others), if they can be had. If indeed it were a hunt for wild animals on flat land, whatever kind they were, let the Ascendant be an earthy or quadrupedal sign, and the Lord of the Ascendant[528] made fortunate and strong; likewise the Lord of the sixth.

If however the hunt were for aerial birds (whether it were in the mountains or on a flat plain), let the Ascendant be one of the airy signs; also [let] the Lord of the Ascendant be made fortunate and strong in a common or airy sign, and likewise the Lord of the sixth (or at least one of them). If indeed it were for terrestrial birds, let the Ascendant be an airy sign, and the Lord of the Ascendant in an earthy sign; also let the Lord of the sixth be in an airy sign, or let them both be in airy signs if you cannot [do] better. Indeed[529] if the hunt were for marsh birds, let the Ascendant be an airy sign, and the Lord of the Ascendant in a watery sign, or let the Ascendant be a watery sign and the Lord of the Ascendant in an airy or earthy one, and likewise the Lord of the sixth if it can be done. If however it cannot be done, let this Ascendant and its Lord, or either of them, be in an airy sign.

Nor should you forget always to adapt the sixth and its Lord, as well as you are ever able to. For the sixth [sign] signifies dogs and birds and spearing and other instruments with which men hunt every prey, both terrestrial and aquatic. And it likewise signifies every place deputed over hunting, like a snare or covering,[530] a trap, baskets,[531] bird-netting,[532] and the like. And if someone wanted to set up one of these instruments, namely a net, or any other one of them, or he wanted to teach a dog or bird to hunt, or to prepare one of these places, and you wanted to elect for him an hour fit for this, adapt the Ascendant and its Lord; also the sixth, and adapt its Lord not less than the first [sign] if you can, and weaken and make unfortunate the seventh and its Lord, and likewise you will weaken the Moon as much as you can, and make her slow in course, and make it so the Lord of the first or the Lord of the sixth is the one who makes the Lord of the seventh or the Moon unfortunate; however, there it is better (if you cannot make it so that the Lord of the first or of the sixth makes them unfortunate) that Mars make them unfortunate, and [that he be] strong and made fortunate (and Mars even has a role in every hunt by land, both flat

---

[528] Reading *ascendentisque dominus* for *ascendensque dominus*.
[529] Reading *quidem* for *quidam*.
[530] *Nassarium vel cucularia.*
[531] *Formaria*, from Gr. *phormos*, a basket, related to woven matting.
[532] *Pantheria*, from Gr. *panthēra*, the "whole catch," and according to Liddell and Scott, the equivalent to bird-netting. I take this to be a large net designed for birds, but I am not sure.

and mountainous); and make them to be joined together if you can: for the conjunction of the Lord of the seventh with the Lord of the first signifies getting it [the prey] with the labor and pursuit of the one hunting. If however the Lord of the seventh is joined to the Lord of the first, it signifies getting the prey with ease and little exhaustion; and the more strongly so if the Moon is joined to it.

However on a hunt on water (or fishing), if it were a hunt with a hook, adapt the Ascendant and its Lord, and make the Ascendant a common or watery sign; and let the Lord of the seventh and the Moon be made unfortunate and weak, and let the Lord of the first or the sixth or Saturn or Mars make them unfortunate–even though Mars is prohibited from a hunt on water. But in a hunt on water, whether fishing with a hook or *floximae*,[533] someone can use [Mars] on account of the wound which follows from a hook and *floxima*. If however it were fishing or hunting on the sea, let the Ascendant be a common sign, but not a fiery one. However [let] its Lord [be] in a watery sign, and let the Moon be joined with the Lord of the domicile in which she is, provided that she is otherwise made unfortunate and weak by the aforesaid method. If indeed it were a hunt on other waters outside the sea (whether it is in a river or brook or lake or a hollow), and it were with a hidden instrument put in the waters, let the Lord of the Ascendant be strong and joined with Mercury, and the Lord of the seventh and the Moon weak, as was said for the others. And in each and every one of the aforesaid [cases], may you always understand that the Ascendant and the sixth [sign] and their Lords are to be made fortunate and strong; and if you could adapt the fourth and its Lord, it would be good; and [make] the seventh and its Lord, and the Moon, unfortunate and weak.

And even if the Moon is put on the side of the prey, still the hunter always has something to do with her: whence she is not ever to be made void in course, for then that would signify the labor of the hunt to be deceptive and empty, and the hiding of the prey from his eyes. One must even beware lest she be cadent from the angle, because it would signify the loss of the prey after getting it (and likewise the Lord of the seventh).[534] Still, it is better that the Lord of the Ascendant make the Moon unfortunate than [that] the Lord of the sixth do so. Because even though the Moon does not signify the prey, still she always has something to do with the prey. Whence if the Lord of the sixth were to make

---

[533] Unknown word, but it might be related to Gr. *phlox* (flame, flower), in which case it might mean a lure tied with hairs or feathers.
[534] I.e., if it were cadent from an angle.

the Moon unfortunate, it could possibly happen by chance that the dog or bird with which one hunts (or one of the hunting instruments) might wound the hunter.

And let it always be your concern to adapt the Lord of the hour of going out to the hunt (and on all journeys). And you must consider, in making the Moon unfortunate, that the Lord of the first or the Lord of the sixth or the Lord of the second or of the eleventh, or the Lord of the Part of Fortune, makes her unfortunate. And if the Lord of the fourth were to make her unfortunate, [success] could be preserved; [but] she should not be made unfortunate by the others; but let her be weakened by whatever other means she can be weakened. I say this for the safety of the hunter, because he always has something to do with her, as I said. Her weakening always works for the hunter; indeed making her unfortunate does not always do so, unless she is made unfortunate by the aforesaid significators or by one of them. However, making the Lord of the seventh unfortunate always works for the hunter, and it is in his usefulness and favor.[535]

And beware lest the Lord of the eighth or of the seventh or of the twelfth make her unfortunate; [but] by the Lord of the third or the fifth or the ninth or the tenth, you will not worry about the loss of the prey after getting it (likewise the Lord of the seventh).

And beware of Mars in hunting by water, because he is bad, just like Saturn in hunting by land. For Saturn, if he impeded the Moon in fishing, or were joined to her by an aspect of enmity, would be to that extent successful;[536] and if the Lord of the first or the sixth were to impede her, and it will increase the [catch of] the hunting or fishing. Likewise in putting together the instruments for fishing, provided that Mars does not aspect her then.

And adapt the Part of Fortune in every fishing or hunting trip, by putting it in the first or sixth or fourth, or joined to their Lords. Likewise the Part of Hunting, which is taken from the Head of the Dragon to Saturn, and projected from the Ascendant.[537] And even adapt the Lord of the hour in every hunting trip and in every preparation of the hunting instruments. If however you could

---

[535] See earlier footnote and passage in Part 1, Ch. 7.

[536] *Tantum valet.*

[537] This is not correct. This is really al-Qabīsī's Part of Poisoned Things (*pars venenatorum*). But Bonatti's own edition of al-Qabīsī (who calls this the Part of Poisoned Things) must have misread *venationum* ("of hunts") or *venatorum* ("of hunters") for the correctly spelled *venenatorum* ("of poisoned things"). Here he calls it the *pars venationis*, "Part of Hunting." I do not know if there is really is a Part of Hunting. See Tr. 8, Part 2, Ch. 18.

not adapt all of the aforesaid by the method which I have told you (because it seems practically something impossible), adapt the Ascendant and the sixth and their Lords, and the house of hunting (which is the 7th); and let it be a sign of the nature of the prey which the one going out to hunt intends to hunt: like if it were his intention to hunt quadrupeds, let the house of hunting be an earthy sign; if it were his intention to hunt birds, let it be an airy sign; and if it were his intention to fish or to hunt quadrupeds naturally spending time in the water (like beavers, otters, and the like), in whichever waters it was, let it be a watery sign. And if it could be done, let the Lord of the seventh be likewise in signs congruent to the prey; and let it be weak and unfortunate, and let the Moon be [so] by the aforesaid method, so she is not in the angles. However the cadents are worse than the angles; but let them be in the succeedents to the angles, of which the second [sign] is more useful; then the fifth [sign]; and the eleventh [sign] is below the fifth, and the eighth [sign] below the eleventh.

Indeed let the Lord of the first be fortunate and strong, and let him or the Lord of the sixth, or Mars (on land) or Saturn (in water), make the Lord of the seventh unfortunate; and let the planet from which the Moon is being separated, be aspecting the one to whom she is joined (if it can be done). And let the Sun be adapted, because he has power in hunting. Even put the Lord of the seventh in the first or the second or the sixth, or make him retrograde or stationary in his first station; and make it so that he is not in the seventh, nor should he aspect it by an aspect of friendship; even let the Lord of the seventh be decreasing in number, and let him aspect the Lord of the first. And if the hunt were on the sea or in any other [waters], let the Ascendant be a common sign, of which Pisces is better than the others.

And al-Khayyat said,[538] let the Lord of the seventh be in one following the angle, nor let him be cadent; because it would signify the flight of the prey from the hands of the hunter. And he said that if the Lord of the seventh did not aspect the Lord of the first, it is to be feared that we will not catch the prey; and let he to which the Moon is joined, be cadent or in his own fall, and the Lord of the first elevated above him.[539]

Which if you cannot adapt all of these, adapt the Ascendant and the sixth, and their Lords, and make them fortunate and strong, and weaken the Moon and the Lord of the seventh according to your ability. And put the Part of

---

[538] Unknown source.

[539] This could refer to it being in a more northerly ecliptical latitude, but it could also refer to the Hellenistic "overcoming." See Introduction and footnote to Tr. 3, Part 2, Ch. 20.

Fortune in the first or the sixth, or with their Lords; and likewise the Part of
Hunting if you can; and adapt the Lord of the hour. And again if you cannot do
these things, adapt the Lord of the first for the protection of the body, and the
sixth for the animals and instruments of hunting. Which if, again, you could not
adapt these, because sometimes they cannot wait for that long (and hunts often
happen by day, and few by night, except perhaps hunts by water and snares for
quadrupeds that wound, and the like), at least adapt the Lord of the hour, and
weaken the Moon for the one wanting to go on the hunt, as was said, and he
will be successful (even if not so much as the hunter wanted).

Chapter 13: On games with dice,[540] which in another way are a cause of gaining wealth

If someone were to go out to a game of dice or to another game from which
it were his intent to gain wealth, it seemed to certain ancient sages that the
Ascendant should be a movable sign, and that the fixed signs are not useful.

And al-Rijāl said[541] that it is evident through their words that the common
signs are in between both [types of signs],[542] that is, neither very useful nor very
unuseful: like if the Ascendant were a common sign, and its Lord were of good
condition, it signifies good; if however it were of bad condition, it signifies evil.
And it is necessary that the Lord of the Ascendant be well disposed and of good
condition; indeed let the Lord of the seventh be weak and impeded; and if it can
be done, let the Lord of the eighth be in the second or in the first, received by
the Lord of the second or the first; nor let him receive the Lord of the second.
And especially if he were to approach the game in order to begin to play, let
even the Moon be separating herself from a free benefic, joining herself to
another benefic, and let her be above the earth, and facing the one who intends
to play,[543] and let her be made fortunate and strong. If however she were made

---

[540] In 1491 and 1550 there is a strange word *hel* that appears before the comma. It does not
seem to be Latin, and may be a misprint.

[541] This passage is based on al-Rijāl (pp. 325-26), who is more thorough.

[542] Al-Rijāl does not actually say this–at least in the chapter in question. Perhaps he made this
comment elsewhere in his work.

[543] Al-Rijāl attributes this view to Māshā'allāh (p. 326). Al-Rijāl's Māshā'allāh is more
thorough: "Māshā'allāh said, if you wished to gamble, look to see in which direction the
Moon is, and if she is in the east or the west or south or the north. And place yourself sitting
so that your face is against the face of the Moon, and you will win money. Know that the east
helps the north, and the west [helps] the south. Likewise if you saw two gambling, and you
wished to know which of them will win, look to see which of them has his face against the
face of the Moon, because he will win."

unfortunate, it is to be feared lest she be made contrary by him who had his face against her; and let her be on the rising side [of the chart], if he is seeking another to play. If indeed he himself were the one sought, let her be in his face on the setting side [of the chart]. And for whomever you elect so that he can play in order to gain wealth, always let his face and breast be toward the Moon.

And if not all of these could be done, let at least the Ascendant be a movable sign when he goes out in order to play, and [let] the Moon be facing him when he plays. And again, if not all of these can be done, let the face and breast of the player be toward the Moon, and he will win.

Chapter 14: How something can be known about something that is said or handled between two people speaking secretly[544]

If you were to see some people speaking secretly between themselves move apart from one another,[545] and you were suspicious about their deliberations, lest perhaps it might be harmful to you or another, and you wished to know something from it, consider the first and the seventh and their Lords: because the first [sign] and its Lord, and the planet from which the Moon is being separated, belong to the one who first began to speak about the affairs with which they dealt. Indeed the seventh [sign] and its Lord, and the planet to which the Moon is joined, belong to him with whom he began to speak. And the one of them who had his face toward the south [or the west][546] will be the one beginning, and he who had his face toward the east or toward the north will be the other. The tenth [sign] and its Lord signify him or those who discourse amongst themselves or between others, to whom [or to which] that which is then adapted pertains more.[547]

And if that with which they dealt were a lawsuit or contention between them, the tenth [sign] and its Lord will signify victory, and the victor will be he whom the Lord of the tenth aspects more;[548] indeed the fourth [sign] and its Lord, and the planet in whose domicile the Moon is, will signify the end to which it is handled. But the planet in whose domicile the Moon is, will be stronger in the

---

[544] This seems much more like a horary topic than an electional one.

[545] Reading *semotim* as a variant on *semote*.

[546] Note Māshā'allāh's comment in the footnote above, that the south and west "help each other."

[547] *Ad quos illud quod tunc aptatur magis spectat.* This apparently strange clause is explained in more detail below.

[548] This must mean "aspects more closely."

signification than the Lord of the 4th domicile.[549] Whence, look then at the Lord of the tenth, and see how it behaves with the significators (namely with the Lord of the first or the seventh): because if it were more favorable to the Lord of the first than to the Lord of the seventh, he who were to undertake [the action] will win. If however it were more favorable to the Lord of the seventh than to the Lord of the first, he against whom it was undertaken, will win (the which significators you will know from the aforesaid).

After this, you will look to see if the Lord of the first is of the truth-telling planets: he who undertakes the matter or for whom someone undertakes it, acts truly and legally. Indeed if it were of the false-speaking planets, he is acting with a lie, and falsely; it must be said likewise about the Lord of the seventh. If however the Lord of the tenth were of the truth-telling planets, the one discussing or handling the business will act with truth and legality toward him to which he were favorable; and *vice versa* if it were of the false-speaking ones. And if the Lord of the 4th domicile or the planet to which the Moon is joined, were of the truth-telling ones, that which is handled will be ended with truth and legality; and if it were of the false-speaking ones, it will be ended with lies and fraud and falseness.

Likewise, look at the planet which would signify the full completion of the matter, [to see] to whom it is joined after its perfection. For if it were joined to a good planet (or even a malefic not impeding and receiving it), he who obtained usefulness and good will follow from from the full completion or perfection.[550] If indeed it were joined to a malefic not receiving it, or an impeded benefic, the contrary will follow. You would be able to consider the same thing about the other matters whose end you desired to know.

Chapter 15: If you wished to search for a thief[551]

If someone wished to follow or track down a fugitive or some low-class person, or even his own attendant, it is necessary that the Moon be made

---

[549] *Domus.* I use "domicile" because Bonatti had just spoken of this planet as being the Lord of the fourth sign.

[550] *Sequetur ex complemento seu perfectione illa ille qui obtinuerit utilitatem atque bonum.* I think the oddness of this phrase has to do with Bonatti's often unclear use of the word *sequor* (see especially Tr. 9). The meaning is simply that if it will be joined to a good planet, *etc.*, good things will follow; if bad, the contrary.

[551] This short chapter is garbled in some of its details, but the main point is that one must impede the Moon.

impeded, namely in the same degree with the Sun, so that there is more than 16' between them (nor should this be in Aries or Leo);[552] or let her be in the last half of Libra or in the first [half] of Scorpio; or let her be with the Head of the Dragon or its Tail (namely by less than 12° before or 7° after); and if she could not be placed thus, she should be put in the Ascendant (according to al-Ṭabarī);[553] or she should be in the conjunction or the opposition or the square aspect; or let her be in their trine or sextile aspect without reception;[554] and let her be impeded by them; or let it be before the hour of a lunar eclipse by three days or after it by one day. And if her eclipse were in those days, and the Sun is free and cleansed of defects and of the impediments of the malefics, and of other impediments; and [let] one of the benefics [be] in the 10th and especially in front of the line of the 10th by 5° or beyond it by 3°;[555] and however more you impede the Moon, by that much more will the fugitive be impeded (or someone whose impediment you wanted to create, and particularly of the aforesaid ones, because she signifies them naturally, and even all common people).

Chapter 16: When it is the intention of the pursuer to harm him who flees

This chapter can be subordinated to the other one discussed above, because in it is treated of the things which are comprehended under the other–namely concerning a fugitive. But in this one they differ from one another, because in that one it was treated of the tracking down of the fugitive. In this one it is treated of how someone is able to harm the fugitive.

Whence al-Rijāl said[556] if it were the intention of the pursuer to harm the fugitive, namely to wound him in his person, let the Moon be in her own fall and in her own weakness (just as was said in the preceding chapter), and likewise the 12th and its Lord. If however it were not his intention to wound

---

[552] This implies that a conjunction of the Sun will not be as bad if he is in his own domicile or exaltation.

[553] Source unknown.

[554] Since the Nodes are not planets and cannot receive, Bonatti must mean that *she* should not receive *them*. This would be so especially if they were in Cancer or Taurus, because then they would harm her domicile or sign of exaltation–which seems to be the point here.

[555] In this case Bonatti is thinking of her primary motion. By "in front of," he means "in a later degree than the cusp's, moving toward it by primary motion"; by "beyond," he means "in an earlier degree than the cusp's, having passed beyond it."

[556] Al-Rijāl, p. 324. Al-Rijāl does not speak of hurting, but speaks of cases where the fugitive belongs to a class of enemies besides rebels.

him in his person, but only to catch or detain him, let the Moon be joined to a malefic and impeded; but she should not be put in the 4th (nor the planet to which she is then joined). And let the Lord of the first be joined with the Lord of the 7th. And one must beware lest the Moon be joined to some planet which is in the 12th, because it signifies that the fugitive will not be captured; and if he were captured, he will flee from the hands of the pursuer or of him who caught him.

Chapter 17: If someone wished to track down something from a thief or detained person, or someone else who is held suspect of something or some matter that was committed

If someone wished to track down something from a thief or from someone else that is made public (that about which it is asked, or whether he is guilty of the thing in which he is held suspect), let the Moon be put then in Libra, and likewise the planet to which she is joined. And al-Rijāl said[557] Abū Ma'shar had recommended this opinion.

And he said[558] everything that he said must be done after the adaptation of the roots of the elections, and [the roots] of those things which follow them [or are dependent on them]. And he said, one must beware of everything that he said must be avoided, and to work with those things which are discussed above. And he said that the 7th signifies everything that was said before about thieves and fugitives, just as the 12th signifies animals (namely larger ones). And he said that thus we ought to adapt the 7th and its Lord to the contrary of the aforesaid, along with what is signified by them, just as we adapt the 12th and its Lord in the buying of animals along with what is signified by them.

---

[557] Al-Rijāl's Abū Ma'shar says "rational signs," not just Libra.
[558] This passage seems to be a general summation by Bonatti based on a number of general principles on elections, as I do not find it in al-Rijāl.

ON THE EIGHTH HOUSE

Chapter 1: On the election of the return of someone absent

In this chapter we must make remembrance of returning.[559] And it seems to some that this chapter should be comprehended under the 10th house, because it immediately follows the 9th (which signifies a journey), and not under the 8th house, since that precedes the 9th–while returning does not happen before a journey. But because the 8th is given to one absent, and returning would not exist but through an absent person, it is deservedly considered and taken from the 8th and not from the 10th. And wherefore even the 2nd, which precedes the 3rd, is adapted and looked at in the affairs[560] of returning.

Whence if you wished to elect the hour fit for the return of someone absent, you ought to adapt the 2nd and its Lord just like Ptolemy [said] in the *Centiloquy*.[561] Beware of malefics located in the 8th in a journey, and in the 2nd for someone returning.

However, returning is made diverse in an entrance in accordance with the diversity of persons. For if it were the return of some citizen or inhabitant of some place, over whom another person who is the master of that land rules, his entrance is signified when he enters the boundary of the gate of his home or of another place in which he lives, or in which those people subject to him revere [or fear] him. Indeed the entrance of a king or prince or other magnate who rules and is master of the city or land, is when he enters the gates of the city or castle or other land over which he rules like a lord. If, however, after he went outside that land, and were returning to it, al-Rijāl said[562] that we will not be worried about his return (namely so that he might know the things which ought to happen to him from the hour of the return up until he goes again outside the land, as men are wont to do–both great men and others). For the return is just like a revolution of the years of nativities for nativities: wherefore if the nativity were good and the revolution good, the good will increase. If however the revolution were bad, it subtracts from the good that is signified by the nativity, even if not by much. And if the nativity were bad and the revolution bad, it will increase the evil. And if the revolution were good, it decreases evil, even if

---

[559] Bonatti is reminding us that (at least some) absent people are signified by the 8th in Tr. 6, which is background for the argument that follows.

[560] *Facto.* This could also mean "action," "situation."

[561] Aph. 41.

[562] This seems to be Bonatti's own elaboration on al-Rijāl's comments on p. 327.

moderately. Likewise it happens in the return from the aforesaid journeys: if the first entrance were good, and the return good, it will increase the good. And if it were bad, it decreases something of the good. And if the entrance were bad and the return bad, it will increase the evil; and if it were good, it takes away something of the evil; and this will last until the next time he goes outside the land, because then the signification will expire, just like what is signified by the revolution of the year expires when the next year of the revolution is revolved.

It seemed to certain people that we ought [not][563] to consider the entrances into cities of a traveler passing through them: because a traveler does not do [anything] in the cities he enters, except like [he does] in the other parts of the road by which he goes.

Chapter 2: On the adaptation of an election of inheritances

If you wished to elect the hour for the adaptation of some inheritance,[564] al-Rijāl said[565] that it is necessary to keep the 8th house one of the domiciles of Jupiter or Venus, free and fortunate, and likewise its Lord free and fortunate, and following an angle (of which the best is the second [sign]). And let the second [sign] and its Lord be free of the presence of the malefics and their opposition and square aspect, unless the malefic who impedes it is the Lord of the 8th house [domicile?], or of its exaltation, or he had two of the lesser dignities in it; and let him be free from impediments.

It would even be good if the degree of the 8th house were to fall in a bound of the benefics, either [that of] Jupiter or Venus; even the Moon should be free and made fortunate, and she should aspect the 8th or its Lord by a trine or sextile aspect. You will even adapt the first and its Lord, and all the other things you can (of those which are considered in elections). And if all of these cannot be adapted, let the first [sign] be adapted, and the 8th, and their Lords, also the Moon and the Lord of the domicile in which she is; or at least let the 8th and its Lord and the Moon be adapted; nor should you forget this.

---

[563] Adding *non*, otherwise the last two clauses contradict the first one. Read this way, the meaning is that we needn't elect for the entrances into cities when we are merely passing through them and not undertaking special actions in them.

[564] This might mean, "for the proper use of an inheritance."

[565] Al-Rijāl, p. 327.

Chapter 3: On making a will or codicil

If someone wished to make a will or codicils or to arrange any other last wish, and he wanted that you should elect for him the hour for doing this, make the Moon deficient in number and increased in light (because this signifies that the will will be perfected and changed, but it will remain firm just as the testator arranged it). It is even recommended that the Moon and the Lord of the Ascendant (or either of them) be joined to Saturn out of friendship, because it signifies the perfect completion of the matter, and that it will not be changed after it is once perfected, neither by the testator, nor after his death. And Sahl said[566] that it signifies the prologation of the life of the testator, even after making the will.

You may say the same (what was said about Saturn) if the Moon were joined to Jupiter or Venus. And let the Ascendant be a fixed sign, and the Moon likewise in a fixed sign: because if it were movable, or the Moon in a movable sign, it signifies that the will will be changed, and will not remain firm. One must even beware lest the Moon be joined to a planet appearing under the rays, nor let her be joined to Mars by body or by opposition or by a square aspect. Nor let Mars himself be in the Ascendant, nor should he aspect it or its Lord by an aspect of enmity: because this signifies that the will will be changed and will not remain firm, and that the life of the testator will be shortened, and he will not escape from his illness, and that the wishes of the testator will not be fulfilled, but rather the heirs and commissars will strive to pilfer what is adjudicated, and everyone will strive to extort for his own uses whatever sort of survivors there were, even if they[567] were religious.

---

[566] *On Elect.*, Ch. 29. In fact this whole chapter is based on Sahl.
[567] I.e., the heirs and commissars.

ON THE NINTH HOUSE

Chapter 1: On the entrance into some city or other place

Even though in this chapter mention is not made of the 9th house, still [the chapter] is comprehended under [the 9th], because it signifies local motion, both of those who are moved from far away and that of others.[568] Whence if you wanted the hour adapted for this purpose for someone, whatever kind of entrance it was (whether into a city or another land, or an entrance into the habitation of a home in which he was not already used to living for a long time), adapt the Ascendant and its Lord, also the Moon and the Lord of the domicile in which she is, and let her be in increased light. Even adapt the 2nd and its Lord (the adaptation of which is that it should be in the Ascendant, free from impediments, made fortunate and strong).

And Sahl said,[569] therefore make him[570] a benefic, and let him be above the earth (namely in the 9th or in the 10th or the 11th); and never should you put him below the earth (namely in the 4th or 5th or 6th): for he said that it is horrible in pilgrimages and in the work which you seek in that region (whether he were a benefic or a malefic). And let the Lord of the Moon[571] be with the Lord of the 2nd above the earth; nor is it recommended that he be below the earth unless that which you seek be a matter which someone wanted to hide until it is perfected. And he said, let the Moon be with the Sun [then],[572] so that between them there is from 12° up to 15°, and it will be better if she is going away from the Sun than when she is made fortunate, near the going out from under the rays by 3°.[573] And this is recommended in every occultation,[574] (however the

---

[568] Bonatti seems to be making this comment because the chapter is heavily indebted to Sahl, who recommends that we strengthen the whole sign houses (*etc.*) that pertain to the kind of travel it is.

[569] *On Elect.*, Ch. 31.

[570] I believe Sahl is speaking about the Lord of the second sign (see repetition of this passage below).

[571] Reading *lunae* (with Sahl) for *domus*.

[572] I.e., in cases where the matter is to be kept secret.

[573] Sahl says: "And beware in this, so that the Moon is made fortunate until she goes out, while under the rays up to 3°."

[574] It is unclear whether Bonatti is referring to the combust degrees around every New Moon, or journeys that are hidden. Earlier he said that the New Moon is good for hidden things generally, so maybe there is no difference.

Ascendant is more useful than the 10th or the 11th; and if the Moon were joined to [the Ascendant], and were made fortunate, it will be better).[575]

And beware lest you put him[576] below the earth, or joined to a planet located below the earth who is a malefic or made unfortunate or impeded. And let the Ascendant be a fixed sign. However, let the Lord of the tenth be free from impediments and from the malefics, nor let him aspect the 11th by an aspect of enmity. Let even the fourth [sign] be a fixed one, if it can be done.

And if the Moon could not be adapted, let her be cadent from the Ascendant. Let even one of the benefics be aspecting the 4th and the 10th (or either of them)–however the fourth [sign] is better than the 10th. And if in addition you could put Jupiter in the second it will be the ultimate, because he naturally signifies what is sought, and the increase of substance.

And if it were the intention of him who is entering the land or place, to leave from there later with prosperity and wealth, let the Lord of the 7th be made oriental [and] increased in number; and if in addition the Moon were increased in number, and the planet to which she is joined, it will be better.

And 'Ali said[577] one must beware lest the Lord of the second commit his disposition to the Lord of the 4th, 6th, or 8th or 12th. And he said that it would be detestable if he were to commit his own disposition to one of their Lords from one of those places; and the more strongly so if this were in one of the aforesaid places in the revolution of the year of the world, or of the nativity of him for whom you elect. Because it would be very detestable. Which if you could not adapt all of these, adapt the Ascendant and the second and their Lords, and the Moon, and the planet to which she is joined. And if again you could not adapt these, let it be your concern at least to adapt the second and its Lord (and especially if someone enters into the business district[578] of some city or some region).

And Sahl said[579] if you wished to enter a region or city, or you wished to enter any kind of land, it is necessary for you to adapt the second. And he said that when you have done this, you have already adapted the region; and that you ought to make the Lord of the second fortunate, if you can, in the 9th or in the

---

[575] This parenthetical comment seems to be Bonatti's own.

[576] I believe Bonatti is referring to the Lord of the Ascendant, but perhaps he is giving his own opinion about the Lord of the second sign.

[577] I have not found this in al-Rijāl.

[578] *Districtum. Districtus* means "stretched out" and "busy, occupied," hence Bonatti must mean the busy areas of a place.

[579] *On Elect.*, Ch. 31. Note that this is partly a repetition of a previous paragraph.

10th or the 11th. And he said that you should never put him below the earth (namely in the 4th or 5th or 6th), because that is horrible in pilgrimages and in the work which you sought in that region. Let him always be above the earth, whether he were a benefic or not. And he said, strive to put the Lord of the domicile of the Moon with the Lord of the 2nd above the earth; and if you could not adapt its Lord (namely of the 2nd), put at least Jupiter in the 2nd, not impeded; and he will be successful at least in wealth and in conserving his substance.

Chapter 2: On the beginning of general journeys not pertaining to war

In this chapter we must treat of journeys which happen to men every day, except that in it will not be treated of journeys pertaining to war. And even though journeys differ from each other, still they all take place either by land or by water.

Whence if it were a journey by land, let the Ascendant be an earthy sign. If indeed it were by water, let the Ascendant be a watery sign. And let the Moon be in the 11th, going toward the 10th; and you should never put her below the earth. But if you could not avoid this, put her in the 3rd or the 5th, cleansed of the malefics, and free from impediments. And if the journey were by land, one must beware lest the Moon be joined to Mars by body or from any aspect, unless perhaps by a trine or sextile aspect with perfect reception (unless Mars himself were in one of the houses of the journey); nor should he aspect the Ascendant or its Lord, nor should he himself be the Lord of the Ascendant nor of the 3rd or the 5th or the 9th (because then he will not impede his own domicile if he were to aspect it by a praiseworthy aspect).[580]

If indeed the journey were by water, let the Ascendant be a watery sign; and beware of Saturn in the water, unless Jupiter (who can break his malice) aspects him, by all of the stated methods and conditions,[581] just as I have told you about Mars on the land.

---

[580] This seems to be an awkward parenthetical comment. Bonatti seems to be saying that we should only allow Mars to be aspecting or play a rulership role *if* he aspects the relevant planet or domicile by a sextile or trine, with reception—because *then* he will not damage the planet or domicile involved. For a malefic planet will not harm its own domicile or anything in it, provided that it does so by a praiseworthy aspect.

[581] I presume this means that there should be a trine or sextile with perfect reception (see previous paragraph).

And Sahl said,[582] beware of Saturn lest he be in a watery sign, and lest he be fixed[583] in the Ascendant of the departure or with the Moon. Which if you could not avoid it, let the Moon be joined to him with a strong benefic, or in his trine or sextile aspect or from an angle, so that he takes away the malignance of Saturn from shipwreck or impediment and severe tempests.

You even ought to adapt the Moon, and the Lord of the domicile in which she is, in all journeys, both by land and by water, since she has signification in them above the others, except perhaps for the Lord of the hour in the matter of business (both in short and medium journeys as well as in long and longer journeys, and the longest ones). You will even adapt the Lord of the hour in the beginning of every journey from which usefulness or wealth is hoped.

In all significations of journeys you will adapt the Ascendant to the place from which the traveler leaves; and you will adapt the second for the protection of his things. Whence Māshā'allāh said[584] if a malefic were in the 2nd house, who did not have testimony there, it signifies that an impediment will happen to those things which he leaves behind him. If it were Mars, it signifies contentions, or wars, or fires, or sheddings of blood, since he is disposed to that. If it were Saturn, it signifies impediment by thieves, or flooding, and the like (just as was said above).

Indeed you will adapt the seventh to the place to which he goes, [and] the eighth for the wealth which he intends to make there, but the tenth and its Lord for the accidents which ought to happen to him on the road. You will adapt the fourth and its Lord for the end of the journey. And it is necessary for you to adapt all the angles, if you can, and chiefly the seventh. And make the Moon increased in light and number, nor should she be cadent. Let even the Lord of the first and the Lord of the domicile in which the Moon is, be going out of combustion; and let them be in angles or in their succeedents.

And al-Rijāl said[585] the increase [in light] of the Moon signifies that the traveler will arrive quickly at the place to which he intends to go. He even recommended that Mercury [already] have gone out of combustion, joined to some benefic, and especially in the journeys of those wishing to go for reasons

---

[582] *On Elect.*, Ch. 30.

[583] I am unclear on what this means (both in Bonatti and Sahl), but it may refer to a planet being "fixed" in a sign after it has traveled five degrees into it: see Tr. 5, the 58th Consideration.

[584] Source unknown, but Sahl does recommend adapting the Lord of the second in *On Elect.*, Ch. 31.

[585] Al-Rijāl, p. 327.

of buying or selling (because Mercury, as is said elsewhere, signifies objects and commodities, and particularly the mercantile dealings of merchants). If however the journey will be made different,[586] make the Moon joined to a planet signifying the object, or let her be in its domicile: like if it were a journey to a king, let her be joined to the Sun, or at least to the Lord of the 10th, by a trine or sextile aspect; and if it were with reception, it will be better. And let the Sun be in a good place (namely in the first or the 10th or the 11th): because if it were so, his journey will be useful and fruitful; it will be worse [if the Sun is] in other places. While if he were in the 3rd or the 5th or the 9th, it signifies that the journey will be of little use, and great labor. If he were in the 7th or the 4th, it signifies little use, and labor, namely with great delays.[587] However,[588] beware that you do not put the Moon (in a journey of someone wanted to go to the king) in Aquarius, because the king will not care about him on account of the fact that Aquarius is opposite Leo, which is the domicile of the Sun (who naturally signifies kings). Nor should you put her in Pisces, because the king would not want to see him, but will rather avert his face from him (because Aries is of the signs which have a signification over kings, and Pisces is the the twelfth sign from Aries, which signifies detriment and grief).

And if the traveler for whom you are electing were to go to warriors[589] or to bellicose men, make the Moon be joined to Mars by a trine or sextile aspect; and let both of them be of good condition. And Sahl said,[590] beware of her conjunction [with Mars] from angles and from the square aspect, and from the opposition, and let Mars be in those following the angles.

If indeed his journey were to bishops or to other religious men, of whatever sect they are, or to noble men, or to men that are not bellicose, and peaceful (and not using arms in the manner of warriors), or to judges, or doctors of the law or decrees, or similar men, make the Moon [be] joined to Jupiter by body or by a trine or sextile aspect, or at least the square

---

586 I.e., "for a different purpose."
587 Al-Rijāl says: "Likewise if he were in the 7th or in the 5th, it signifies labor and moderate good. If he were even in the west [occidente] or the 4th, it signifies moderate good, and great and long labor." I am not sure why al-Rijāl mentions the 7th twice (the "west" is the 7th house).
588 The remainder of this paragraph seems to be from Bonatti himself.
589 Guerrarios.
590 On Elect., Ch. 30.

with reception from some angle or another good place from the Ascendant.

And if his journey were to old men, ancient things,[591] or to Jews, or to ignoble or low-class persons, or to some rigid man who does not want to acquiesce in the sayings of others, and he wants that whatever he said or does to be held as authoritative, whether it is good or bad (like the tyrant Ezzelino da Romano, who was at least 45 years of age), make the Moon [be] joined to Saturn by a trine or sextile aspect; and let Saturn be of good condition, free from impediments and in the succeedents to the angles (and especially in the 5th or 11th).

And let whatever planet to which the Moon is joined, be free from impediments: because her impediment signifies the impediment of the matter wherefore the journey exists.

And if his journey were to women (of whatever condition they are), let the Moon be joined to Venus by a trine or sextile aspect; and let Venus be in a masculine sign; and if you could put her in the angles or in the succeedents to the angles, and especially in the 5th, it will be good.

And if his journey were to true, literate men, apart from the aforesaid, or to writers or merchants, let the Moon be joined to Mercury by a trine or sextile aspect, and let Mercury be of good condition, free and cleansed of impediments.

For Sahl said[592] whenever the planet to which the Moon is joined, or the planet which is in opposition to the Ascendant or the 7th, is slow or retrograde or impeded, it signifies complications and duress in those ways.

And 'Ali said[593] that if the Lord of the seventh were in the Ascendant, or the Moon were joined to a retrograde planet receiving her, that for which he goes will happen to him on the road.

And al-Qabīsī said[594] a journey is to be put off whenever the Moon is in the second or third face of Libra.

---

[591] *Longaevus.* Since Bonatti has already mentioned old men, I have not translated this as "ancient men."

[592] *On Elect.,* Ch. 30.

[593] I have not found this statement in al-Rijāl.

And al-Khayyat said[595] one must beware of the aspect of the malefics to the Moon in journeys, for it is more severe if she [or the malefic?] aspects the Ascendant (and especially in pilgrimages). And he said that the signification of a journey is given to the Moon, and she has her own signification over every beginning, and therefore she is stronger.

And al-Rijāl said[596] if the nativity of the traveler were known, or his question were had, let the Ascendant of the journey be [that of] the house of his nativity or question, and let the Moon be in increased light or number, or let her be joined to benefics from the 9th or the 3rd. And if the Moon were impeded but we could not defer the journey, let the Moon be cadent from the Ascendant, and likewise the planet who impedes her; and we should adapt the entrance and concern ourselves with that.

And al-Tabarī said[597] whoever desires a quick and prosperous return should put Venus and Jupiter both in the square of the Sun and the Moon: that is, so that one of them is in the 10th from the Sun and in the 4th from the Moon, or *vice versa*. And let the Moon be between the two benefics, separated from one and joined to the other. And he said that the Moon should be in increased light and number. And he said that likewise if the Sun were in the opposition of the benefics, it signifies the speed of the return; and the malefics make the return slow down, and they impede with the greatest impediment. And he said if a benefic were with them, prosperity will follow. And he said that the Moon, if she were in the fourth, signifies a long stay; and this is according to the nature and quality of the journey.

And Sahl said[598] that you should not make the Ascendant of the nativity[599] and its Lord cadent from the Ascendant of his departure. And he said, let the Ascendant of the departure be the 10th of the Ascendant of the nativity or question, if you were to seek a kingdom. And if you were to seek a business

---

[594] I have not found this in al-Qabīsī.

[595] I have not found this in al-Rijāl nor in *JN*.

[596] This seems to be Bonatti's paraphrase of (and additions to) statements in al-Rijāl, p. 327. Al-Rijāl says we should elect "according to his nativity, and according to the revolution of his year, or according to the Ascendant of the figure of his question (if he did not have his nativity). Indeed, according to what was already said, adapt the Moon and the Ascendant of the nativity, or the Ascendant of the revolution or of his question, and adapt the house in which is the matter for which he goes." For example, if he is going to a king, make the sign of the native's 10th house be rising on the Ascendant for the election.

[597] I have not found these statements in al-Rijāl.

[598] *On Elect.*, Ch. 30.

[599] Sahl says "question," because he sometimes assumes that the election is made on the basis of a horary question.

deal, let the Ascendant be his 11ᵗʰ; likewise in every matter which you were to seek. And he said, make that sign his Ascendant, and let the Moon be in an angle or a succeedent to an angle; and if she were made fortunate, let her be aspecting the Ascendant. If indeed she were impeded, made her cadent from the Ascendant. And he said, let the Lord of the Ascendant and the Lord of the domicile of the Moon be in angles, and let the Moon aspect the Lord of her own domicile. And beware lest you put the Moon with the malefics or in their square aspect or opposition. And he said that you should never put her in the fourth; but if you were to put her below the earth, put her in the fifth, made fortunate: for it will shorten the labor of the journey, and will increase its profit [or success], and will act more to the salvation of the body of the one journeying. And he said that you should not put her in the Ascendant (because she is inimical to the Ascendant, and is in inimical to the one journeying, as is said elsewhere).

Nor should you put her in the second, for it signifies the taking away of substance, and its diminution. And the Sun is friendly to the Ascendant, whence if the Moon were in the Ascendant, it is feared there will be sickness in the journeyer's body, or the labor of a similar or equivalent illness. And you should never put her[600] in the sixth, because illness will be feared for him; nor in the 8ᵗʰ, because death will be feared for him, unless God averts it; and all the more strongly, if she were to receive some Lord of those houses [domiciles?].

And Sahl said,[601] in sailing on the sea you should not make the luminaries impeded: because if they were free and made fortunate, they signify safety and prosperity. If however they were impeded, they signify death or the loss of the journeyer. And he said, you should not sail the sea during a New Moon,[602] because is it horrible. And he said if you were to sail the sea on account of business, adapt Mercury and the Moon; and let one of them be aspecting Jupiter from Cancer or from Pisces. And he said that Scorpio is horrible in sailing the sea, on account of the role of Mars and his enmity. And always fear the bounds of the malefics, both in sailing on the sea and in riding on land. One must even fear to journey on land and by water when the Moon is in the last half of Libra, unless Venus were to aspect her by a praiseworthy aspect, and she [were] of good condition, or Saturn were to aspect her with a praiseworthy aspect on

---

[600] Reading *eam* for *eum*.

[601] *On Elect.*, Ch. 30.

[602] The 1493 edition of Sahl says *interlunio Saturni* (the New Moon of Saturn?); the 1506 edition says "lacking in light" (*carens lumine*).

journeys by land (if [he were] oriental, direct in his own domicile or exaltation or in two of his lesser dignities).

And Sahl said[603] if you were to seek a kingdom in that region, adapt the Midheaven and its Lord with the Lord of the 2nd from the Ascendant, and the Moon. You may understand the same about a position of civil authority and any office and any lay dignity. And if the authorities, when he went to the land because of the position or authority of other office, were to adapt the aforesaid, it will be useful for him.[604]

And Dorotheus said,[605] look at the place of the Moon in the signs, in a pilgrimage by water:[606] which if she were in the first face of Aries, it signifies the ease of the matter for which the journey happens, whether planets aspect her or not. If she were [in Taurus there will be] less[607] impediment on the sea. If however Saturn were to aspect her, it will impede [the traveler], and [Saturn] will make a shipwreck for him. And in the second face of Gemini it signifies delay, after which it will be solved. However in Cancer [it signifies] safety from every impediment. Indeed in Leo he says [it sigifies] impediment, and more strongly so if a malefic were to aspect [there]. In Virgo he says prosperity and delay and turning back. In Libra, when she has transited the tenth degree, you will not go on a pilgrimage by land or sea. In Scorpio, say sadness. In Sagittarius, say that before the journey is finished, he will return. In Capricorn, a little good at the beginning.[608] In Aquarius, say delay and safety (but do not let the journey be to a king).[609] In Pisces, say impediment and difficulty. And he said if a malefic were to aspect, the impediment will increase. If indeed a benefic were to aspect, it will reduce the impediment and increase the good.

---

603 *On Elect.*, Ch. 31.

604 This might mean, "if the authorities at his destination were to cast an election chart for his entrance into the city or the office itself." This statement is not in Sahl.

605 This is Sahl's Dorotheus (*On Elect.*, Ch. 31), based on Dorotheus (*Carmen*, V.25).

606 In what follows, the delays and hindrances refer to either being in the face of a malefic, or being in a sign with malefics' faces; the good statements refer either to being in the face of a benefic, or being in a sign with no malefics' faces.

607 Adding *in Tauro minus erit* from Sahl.

608 I.e., in the beginning of Capricorn (which is the face of Jupiter). Sahl phrases it more clearly.

609 This parenthetical comment is Bonatti's own.

Chapter 3: On singing lessons, either for musicians or others

This chapter could be comprehended under either house (namely the 9th and the 10th), but to me it seems more suitable that it be comprehended rather under the 9th than under the 10th, because the 9th house signifies church-singing (which singers employ in temples and other religious places) more so than the 10th. For the 10th signifies melodies which originate from the laity and those rejoicing, and who delight in secular and lay songs and games. Whence if someone wished to be taught how to sing [or to practice singing], and you wanted to elect for him the hour fit for this, make the Ascendant or the 10th one of the rational signs, and adapt Mercury first and principally in ecclesiastical singing, and Venus secondly. Indeed in secular and lay singing, adapt Venus principally, but Mercury secondly. But in playing musical instruments, adapt the one of them which you can. And let the Ascendant be Libra or Taurus, or at least Pisces in delightful singing; either Gemini or Virgo in ecclesiastical singing.[610] In whatever kind of singing, let even the Moon be in Cancer or Taurus or Pisces, separated from Mercury, going toward the conjunction of Venus, if it can be done. Let even Venus be in one of her own dignities. You may say the same about Mercury: let even Mercury be joined to Venus by body or a sextile aspect, if you can do it, unless one of those three (namely Venus or Mercury or the Moon) is cadent–unless it is in the 9th, because it is not to be condemned, provided that it (namely the one who is in the 9th) is otherwise made fortunate and strong: because it signifies the goodness of the matter which he for whom you are electing, wants.

And if you wished that the singer be perfect, and one whom no one might exceed in singing, let Mercury be direct, joined to a retrograde Venus in the domicile or exaltation or in two of the lesser dignities of either of them. If however their conjunction were outside those places, your work will be less [effective] than this. You may say the same in nativities with respect to singing and the composition of melodies.

And of whatever sort the ascending [sign] were, if its Lord were in the 9th or 10th, it will be praiseworthy, provided that it is made fortunate and strong.

And[611] certain ancients said if the election were for the sounding of musical instruments like lyres or hurdy-gurdys,[612] or the like, let the Moon be in

---

[610] Thus for lay singing, Bonatti recommends a rational sign ruled by Venus (Libra), and then the other signs ruled by Venus; for ecclesiastical singing, a rational sign ruled by Mercury (Gemini), and then the other sign ruled by Mercury.

[611] See al-Rijāl, p. 333. Note he lists fewer instruments.

Capricorn. If however the election were for the sounding of instruments of the laity, like the cithara,[613] the bowed rote,[614] and the like, pertaining only to the playful laity, let the Moon be in the last face of Cancer,[615] or in Scorpio, or in Pisces, because [these signs] lack a voice. And even for the aforesaid instruments only[616] having a sound, like the trumpet and the like, the aforesaid signs are to be adapted, namely Cancer, Scorpio, and Pisces.[617] Indeed in songs that are rhythmic and read off, the more useful ones are Virgo and Gemini on account of their formation[618] into images of men, and because they have more beautiful voices than the rest of the signs; and wherefore likewise they are called "winged."[619]

And al-Rijāl said[620] in this matter we should adapt the 9th and its Lord; but if our intention in these things were for something which might pertain to the works or kings or great men or the wealthy who are fit for a kingdom, then the 10th will have to be adapted, and its Lord, which can even be recommended in the beginning of any sort of matter.

---

[612] *Symphoniae.*

[613] A precursor to the guitar.

[614] *Rota.* This was a simple lyre with only a few strings, requiring little finger dexterity, and was played more by wide strokes of the arm (which must account for the name *rota*, or "wheel").

[615] Reading *Cancer* for *Leo*, as Leo is not a voiceless sign, and Bonatti explicitly repeats his list of these signs in the following sentence.

[616] *Solummodo.* Meaning unclear–perhaps that the trumpet does not have the ability to make chords, but only produces a single note at a time?

[617] Perhaps these "lay" instruments were used for dancing and free-form melody, but not to accompany singing? That would explain the point of assigning the voiceless signs to them.

[618] Reading *formationem* for *fortunationem.* Perhaps Bonatti is thinking of music accompanying ballads, which recounts tales and deeds, and requires more structure (and a fixed text) than free melody.

[619] See Tr. 2, Part 2, Ch. 20.

[620] Al-Rijāl, p. 333. Al-Rijāl recommends the 10th because it pertains to professions (or "masteries").

ON THE TENTH HOUSE

Chapter 1: On the election of kings and nobles, or of great men and the wealthy

It was spoken in the preceding of those things which pertain to the elections of the 9th house. Now however we must speak of those which seem to pertain to the 10th house. Whence if you wished to elect for some king or duke or similar people concerning those things which pertain to a kingdom or duchy, or to their concerns or what belongs to them,[621] adapt the 10th and its Lord, also the Sun and the Moon; and do not let the Sun (nor even the Moon) be joined with some malefic; nor let the Sun be going toward the conjunction of Mars or Saturn, nor to their square aspect or opposition (even if he were to receive him),[622] nor to their trine aspect or sextile without reception; but put him in an angle or in one a succeedent to an angle, or let him be in Leo, not cadent nor otherwise impeded. And if he were not in Leo, let him be joined with the one in whose domicile or exaltation he was, by a trine or sextile aspect. And if you could not avoid the square aspect, let it be with reception; however you will avoid the opposition in every way, both with reception and without reception, just as you avoid his trine or sextile aspect with the malefics without reception. And let him be in a masculine sign and in the 4th, masculine,[623] if it can be done. Let him even be in a sign in which he has some dignity, if it can be done.

Even consider if, in that year, there was or is going to be an eclipse of one of the luminaries, and you will avoid the sign in which it was or ought to be. Let even both of the luminaries be in the bounds of the benefics, aspecting each other from a trine or sextile aspect, if it can be done; and the Lords of those bounds in their own dignities, aspecting the luminaries (or at least one of them), and by however much more you were to adapt the luminaries or make them stronger or more fortunate, by that much more will it be good for the matter for which you are electing. And by how much less you were to adapt them, by that much more will the matter be less than what you wished.

You must even beware lest the conjunction or the prevention which was before the election, be made unfortunate: because if it were so, you must not

---

[621] *Pro illis.*

[622] It is unclear who Bonatti conceives of as doing the receiving (probably the malefic receiving the Sun); but since no reception would seem to be acceptable, it might not matter.

[623] *4. masculina.* I believe this means that we should try to put him in the 4th, and make the 4th a masculine sign.

elect for the aforesaid persons (unless it was after the aforesaid conjunction or prevention by fifteen days or more), if you can avoid it, even if the election were to seem otherwise fortunate. If indeed you could avoid this, your election will be more secure and better, and made more fortunate.

Chapter 2: On the promotion to a kingdom or duchy or other dignity pertaining to a kingdom or duchy, or any other one

If someone wanting to be promoted to a kingdom or duchy (or something similar) were to consult you to elect for him the hour appropriate for this, make the Ascendant Leo, and let the Sun be then in Taurus, in the tenth from the Ascendant. Let even the Moon be in the first, joined to Venus or Jupiter or Mercury, with them being made fortunate and strong, both in the election and in the receiving of the dignity.

Chapter 3: On the enthronement of the kingdom or duchy or other dignity, or the ascending to its seat

If you wished to elect the hour for the enthronement of a kingdom, so that he might ascend the throne or to that position or the duchy or of whatever other dignity, make the angles the fixed signs, and especially the first [angle] and the fourth [angle]. And let the Lord of the tenth be free from impediments; and let even the Lord of the Ascendant be in the Ascendant or in the tenth or the eleventh or the fifth, received. Even let the Lord of the tenth receive the Lord of the domicile in which he is, by a trine or sextile aspect. Even let the Lord of the fourth be free, in the aspect of a benefic. Which if you could not do this, make it so the Moon is received. And if you could not make the Lord of the fourth free and strong, prevent him from aspecting the Ascendant or its Lord, and make it so that one of the benefics aspects the fourth and the tenth, or at least one of them, if you are ever able to do it.

On a dignity pertaining to war

If however it were a dignity which pertained to war, like the command[624] of an army and the like, make the Ascendant Aries or Scorpio, and make Mars fortunate and strong, and make it so that he aspects the Ascendant by a praiseworthy aspect (and the trine is better than the rest).

And if the Ascendant were one of the domiciles of the other planets, let Mars be aspecting the Lord of the Ascendant by a trine aspect, and let [Mars] be free from impediments. And let the Ascendant be a fixed sign, or at least a common one.

In elections lasting for a long time, fixed signs are better; common ones less so than the fixed ones; the movable ones less so than the common ones.

And in any election of whatever kind of dignity, make the Moon be received, or at least joined to the Sun by a trine or sextile aspect, or at least by a square with reception. Even let the Sun be joined to Jupiter from Sagittarius or Pisces or Aries or Cancer or Leo, by a trine or sextile aspect, if it can be done. And if you cannot adapt all of this (as often happens), adapt those which you can, but your work will not be so perfect. For all of these things are to be observed in the elections of a king, and of all of his[625] children, and of other dukes, in all stable matters.

Indeed if the dignity or office were on account of the fact that copper coin was committed to someone for giving out to strangers–like chamberlains, mace-bearers[626] of some society [or fellowship], namely of a city or a castle, or the like, or the monetary tribute of a magnate. And likewise you will adapt the second and its Lord with the adaptation of the first and its Lord and the Moon. And if your election were for some scribe, adapt Mercury after the adaptation of the aforesaid things, namely so Mercury aspects the Ascendant by a praiseworthy aspect (for this signifies that he will be faithful and lawful in the matter committed to him, and that it will be useful to him).

---

[624] *Ducatus*, which I have translated above as "duchy." As usual the blending of civil and military roles in medieval times makes this word and relates ones (like *dux*, which might mean a duke or the leader of an army) difficult to translate with one English term.
[625] Reading *eius* for *eorum*.
[626] *Massarii*.

Chapter 4: If someone wished to go and stay with a king or duke or official[627] or with another such person, or to travel with him

If someone wishing to go to the king or a duke or prince, or official, or other great man to stay or travel with him, were to consult you so you would elect for him the hour appropriate for this, [then] whatever sort of Ascendant you were to establish for him, let Jupiter be in it, and make him be joined with the Lord of the tenth, if you can: because this will signify that the king will be agreeable and affable, and that it will go well for him from him. And if you were to make them be joined by a trine or sextile aspect (or even by a square with reception), it will be good. And if you could not do this, put him in the ninth, for this will signify that the traveler will find something good and useful on the journey, and whence he will rejoice and he will see pleasing things for himself. And better than this is if Jupiter were sound and free from impediments. And you will avoid putting him in the fourth, because even though the fourth [sign] signifies the end of the matter, still in this case you must avoid it, lest you put him in it. And make it so the Moon aspects him from the tenth, if Jupiter himself were in the first–or from the seventh if he himself were in the ninth. However, beware of the sixth and the twelfth. But if you could not avoid this, it will be less horrible in such a case than in the others. And if you could not do this, let Venus testify to him from the first or from the seventh or the tenth or the fourth, whether with reception [or not],[628] or from the sixth or the third with reception.

And beware of Saturn and Mars, lest one of them be in the first or in one of the angles. And beware likewise lest the Moon be impeded (and especially by the misfortune of combustion, or with the Tail or another one of the malefics or impeding [planets]). Because this signifies that there will be nothing of utility in the journey, but rather it is feared that the traveler will not return. Even if it were another journey, he will fear the same. And if he becomes sick, death will be feared for him; and if he were to go to battle, then he will succumb or perhaps be killed; and to put the truth to you in brief, it will be great and practically miraculous if he were to escape the aforesaid dangers.

---

627 *Potestate.*
628 Adding *sive non*, as is Bonatti's usual practice.

Chapter 5: If someone wished to make an enemy of the king or a duke or someone similar

Sometimes it happens that someone wants to have enmity with the king or a duke or other great man concerning those things which are appropriate for a kingdom or his children who are going to succeed him in the dignity or inheritance. Make the Ascendant one of the domiciles of Jupiter or Mars, and let the Lord of the Ascendant be strong and made fortunate, free from impediments; and let the Lord of the seventh be impeded and made unfortunate, and weak in a malign place from the Ascendant (of which the worse are the sixth [sign] and twelfth [sign] from it); neither let him aspect one of the benefics (or one of the luminaries), nor it him.

Chapter 6: On reconciling with a king or duke or similar men

Sometimes someone is inimical to a king or duke or similar men, and wants that the king should be reconciled with him, and he asks of you so that you might elect for him the hour fit for this.

Whence if you wished to elect it for him, make the Ascendant any sort [of sign], and make it impeded, and its Lord, and let [the Lord] be made unfortunate and weak. And let the Moon be impeded, and the planet from which she is being separated, and let her be in defective light and number. Let even the seventh [sign] be made fortunate, and likewise strong, and its Lord made fortunate and strong, and the planet to which the Moon is joined; and let the Lord of the seventh be in a good place from the Ascendant, free from the malefics and impediments: for this signifies the strength of the matter which you seek.[629]

Chapter 7: On the taking away of some dignity

Sometimes it happens that he who promotes someone to a dignity, on account of things which sometimes are wont to happen, strives and wants to remove him from the dignity; and even sometimes another person strives to do the same. However whether it is he who promoted him, or another person, and he were to inquire of you that you should elect the hour fit for doing this, you

---

[629] The purpose of these instructions is to make the inceptor weak and put him at the king's mercy.

will consider if his intent is to remove him from the dignity in his hatred or his favor. Because if it were in his hatred, the Moon will have to be made unfortunate and weak by combustion, with another great impediment. And let her be in little light and number by putting her in the sixth or the twelfth. And let her be in a fixed sign, in the domicile or exaltation of Venus or the Sun or Mercury,[630] with them being made unfortunate and weak; but with the Ascendant and its Lord being made fortunate and strong.

If indeed it were his intention to remove him in favor, namely so that he might be restored to this [position] in order obtain a greater position, or be promoted to a greater dignity, let the Moon be in Virgo or Sagittarius or Pisces, or at least in Gemini (but it will be below than the others); and let her and the Lord of the Ascendant be in increased light and number; and let her be ascending in the north; let even the Moon be in the domicile or exaltation of one of the benefics, the benefic itself appearing fortunate and strong (and the Lord of the tenth if it were a lay dignity, or that of the ninth if it were a clerical dignity). Nor is this contrary to what was said elsewhere (that the Moon is the significatrix of the business with the weakened Lord of the Ascendant), because here the Ascendant is understood to be free, and its Lord likewise sound and made fortunate, and since the Lord of the Ascendant will be the significator just as the signification pertains to the Ascendant and its Lord. Indeed the Moon will be the signficatrix of the matter which you intend to adapt; and she has her own separate signification from what is signified by the Lord of the Ascendant. And understand this in like cases.

Chapter 8: On the instruction of morals

If someone wished to be taught moral doctrines, [and] were to consult you so that you might elect for him the time fit for this, make it so the Ascendant is Gemini or Virgo or Libra, or the first half of Sagittarius, or Aquarius, and itself free and made fortunate; and the Moon made fit in one of [these] signs; and let the Lord of the tenth be in the tenth, its Lord of the nature of the Lord of the Ascendant or at least of its friendship. Even let the Moon be joined to Mercury by body or by a trine or sextile aspect; and let Mercury be sound and free from

---

[630] But Mercury does not rule any fixed signs.

impediments, made fortunate and strong. And if you could make it so that he[631] aspects the Lord of the Ascendant by an aspect of friendship, it will be good. Even let the Moon be in her own *awj*, or going toward it, nor let her be descending from it. You will even adapt the ninth and its Lord, if you can do it in some way.

And al-Rijāl said that in the instruction of writing, the 10th house [domicile?] must be adapted with all of these, because it signifies what is written. And he said that writing is science and work: and he said we should comprehend the methods[632] in this chapter.

Chapter 9: On lessons in fighting or doing battle or having contests

If[633] you wished to elect the hour for someone wanting to be taught to do battle or fight or have a contest, make the Ascendant for him to be Aries or Leo or Sagittarius; and make Mars strong and fortunate, and let the Moon be made fortunate and strong (and it will be better if she is in Taurus, provided she is otherwise made fortunate). And beware lest you put her in Scorpio or Capricorn, and especially in lessons in military fighting. Let even the Lord of the Ascendant be put in his own exaltation, and in a strong place. And beware lest he or the Moon be cadent from an angle or the Ascendant. And if you could not do this, put the Moon and the Lord of the Ascendant (or either of them) in the 10th, or going toward it.

And al-Rijāl said[634] that certain people had said, that the Moon should be in Gemini.

Chapter 10: On swimming lessons

If[635] someone wanting to be taught how to swim were to consult you so you might elect for him the hour fit for this, make it so the Ascendant is Cancer or

---

[631] Bonatti does not specify whether he means "he" (Mercury) or "she" (Moon); but the context suggests Mercury, as does al-Rijāl's explicit instructions in his parallel chapter (p. 333).

[632] Lit., "the ways" (*vias*). Bonatti simply means that al-Rijāl approves of the rules Bonatti has set forth. Al-Rijāl says, "in writing is the science [knowledge] and work of a profession, wherefore it should not be postponed in sciences and professions."

[633] Based on al-Rijāl, p. 339.

[634] Al-Rijāl, p. 339. See also p. 333.

[635] Based on al-Rijāl, p. 339.

Scorpio or Pisces; even let the Lord of the Ascendant be in the angle of the tenth[636] or going toward it,[637] not far from it by more than 15°; and let him be made fortunate and strong. Even let the Moon be in one of her own dignities, among which Cancer holds the principal spot (and Taurus is below Cancer, [and] her other dignities are below Taurus). Let her even be ascending in the north, and if it can be done let her be in her *awj* going toward the proper distance[638] to the contact of the line of the epicycle with the line of the eccentric.

Chapter 11: On lessons in all things generally

If your election were general, for the works which men are generally wont to engage in (like with mechanical tools and the like), [then] whatever sort of Ascendant you were to posit, adapt the tenth and its Lord, and likewise the Moon; and put [there] a planet naturally signifying the work which someone intends to begin, made fortunate and strong.

Like if the work were difficult and laborious or drawn out (like the cultivation of lands or works of water or those which happen near water, like bridges, mills, and the like), adapt Saturn.

And if it were work which pertains to judges or arbitrators wishing to judge justly, and the like, you will adapt Jupiter.

And if it were the work of a blacksmith or a butcher, and the like, you will adapt Mars.

And if it were a work of goldsmithing or a moneychanger, and the like, you will adapt the Sun.

And if it were a work of the ornamenting of women, adapt Venus, and make Mercury joined with her, and likewise to the others by body or by a fortunate and strong aspect: because he has participation in all of these.

---

[636] I.e., the Midheaven.
[637] The degree of the Midheaven.
[638] *Vadens ad longitudinem proprie.*

And if it were the work of painters or writers or those forming images, or the minting[639] of *denarii* and the like, and of similar things which work by the keenness of thought, like the astrolabe or quadrant, and the like, adapt Mercury, and make him be joined with the Moon; and let him be fortunate and strong, and well disposed.

And if it were a work which pertains to sailors (and chiefly to younger ones), like sailing and the like, you will adapt the Moon, and put her in increased light and number. Nor let her be descending from her *awj*.

And in all the aforesaid cases, let [the Moon] be joined to the planet signifying the matter which you intend to begin, by an aspect of friendship, received by it or even by another, and especially in the house [domicile?] signifying the matter; and let her be in one of her own dignities. Even let the ascending sign and the sign in which the Moon is, be suitable to the matter which is begun: like an earthy sign in terrestrial matters, and a watery one in watery ones, and a fiery one in fiery ones, and an airy one in airy ones, if you can ever do this. Which if you did not do this, your work will be less than what you intended, according to the diminution of those [factors] which I told you.

---

[639] *Stampas.*

ON THE ELEVENTH HOUSE

Chapter 1: On those things concerning which we have hope or trust of being praised and attaining a good reputation

It seems this chapter could be able to be comprehended under the 10th house, because it is of those people from whom good fame is acquired, which is acquired and follows from hope that is already had.

But it seems more appropriate that it be comprehended under the 11th. Whence, if you wished to do this, make the Ascendant Sagittarius or Pisces, or at least Cancer (but Cancer will be below Sagittarius and Pisces), and you will adapt Jupiter just as well as you can. You will also adapt the 11th and its Lord with all of your ability. And if you could put Jupiter in the 11th it will be very useful for your matter. And if you could not put Jupiter in the eleventh, put him in the first. Which again if you could not do this, make it so that he aspects one of them by a praiseworthy aspect; and make him fortunate and strong, and free from impediments. And if you could put the Lord of the first in the eleventh, it will be praiseworthy.

And let the Sun be in the tenth, free from impediments, if it could be done, or in the first, provided that he does not impede Jupiter or the Lord of the first or the Lord of the eleventh. Even let the Moon be joined to him by a trine or sextile aspect, or at least by a square with reception, and be free, fortunate, and strong; let her be separating also from Jupiter while she is joined to the Sun or to the Lord of the first or the eleventh, if it could be done, and it will be better; and the reputation and renown will be made more public and will fall into the ears of men, and into their praises; and by whichever one (of the significators) you could adapt, it will be better—and especially if you could make it so that the luminaries aspect each other; or the Lord of the first with the Lord of the eleventh by a trine or sextile aspect, or at least by a square with reception. And if you could make it so that they regard[640] each other, it will be better.

---

[640] *Respiciant.* I.e., "aspect." Bonatti rarely uses this variant on *aspiciant.*

Chapter 2: When someone wishes to seek from some person, so that he may love him

If someone wished to seek from some person so that he may love him, like someone [male] loves someone [female] by way of friendship (and not in a lewd way), and he were to consult you so that you might elect for him the hour fit for this, make the Ascendant whatever sort you wish, and put the Moon in the 11th house. And if you could put the Lord of the Ascendant there, it will be better; and make it so that all are joined with Venus, if you can. And if you cannot do that, make it so that Venus is joined with the Moon and with the Lord of the eleventh. Which again if you could not do that, make it so that the Moon or the Lord of the Ascendant is joined with the Lord of the eleventh (or with Venus) by a trine or sextile aspect, with reception; or that he receives either of them from Taurus or Libra or Pisces; and that she is free, fortunate, strong, and well disposed. And if again you could not do this, make it so that Venus is received by the Moon in Taurus or Cancer, and the Moon is received by Jupiter (or even by the Lord of the second) by perfect reception. And if again you could not do this, put the Moon in Taurus or in the first half of Libra, or Pisces, or in two of the lesser dignities of Venus, free, fortunate, and strong.

If however someone were to seek the love of someone for the purpose of making money, so that usefulness would follow from that, put the Moon in the first or at least in her triplicity, free, fortunate, strong, and received by the Lord of the domicile or the exaltation of the sign in which she herself then is, and likewise let the Part of Fortune be there.

If however it were his intention to acquire some inheritance or some estate, namely a house or land, or the like, let the Moon be in the eighth with the Part of Fortune, received. And if it were by reason of small animals, let her be in the 6th house. If it were by reason of horses or other large animals, let her be in the 12th. And understand in this way concerning any house [domicile?] according to its character,[641] and according to its signification; and let the Moon always be received and with the Part of Fortune.

If however you could not do these things which were said, you will observe this other method–namely, that if someone wanted to seek from some person that he might give him or make him something, make the Ascendant (of whatever sort it is) fortunate, and let it be a fixed sign or at least a common one. And let its Lord be with it or in its triplicity, aspecting it with a praiseworthy

---

641 *Substantiam.*

aspect (namely by the trine or sextile). And beware lest the Moon be joined to the malefics or impeded in another way; and make it so that she aspects the Lord of the domicile in which she is: because if she did not aspect him, the matter about which it is done will not be perfected. And let the Moon be in increased light and number in such beginnings, and joined to the benefics. Let also the Lord of the Ascendant be made fortunate and strong, free from impediments. Indeed if it were a benefic to whom the Moon is joined, in direct [motion], in increased number, it will be more useful: for it signifies that what is sought will be increased for the seeker.

And always beware lest Mercury be impeded or of bad condition. For it signifies impediment or its prohibition, unless he were received along with the impediment. For if he were received, it signifies the perfection of the matter, but with striving and inconvenience, and anxiety and labor and complications, and still it will hardly be perfected, if it were perfected; and that they will part from each other with a vile and foul separation. And always make the significatrix (who is the Moon) be joined to the planet signifying the matter about which it is done, just as I told you above: so it is the Sun in the affairs of great men, and likewise Mars in the affairs of wars (and understand thusly about all of the significators).

If you wished to elect for someone wanting to make friendship with some-one, make the Moon cleansed of the malefics, and particularly from their square or opposition; and make her joined to the planet that signifies the matter which you wish to do or someone intends, just as was said: like Venus in the affairs of women, and Mercury in the affairs of writers; and understand thusly about the rest of the significators. And let the Lord of the eleventh be aspecting by a praiseworthy aspect; and if he were to aspect its[642] Lord or the Moon, it will be better.

Chapter 3: If someone wished to seek some object from some person, whether it were promised to him or not[643]

If[644] someone were to propose to seek some object from some person (whether the object were already promised to him or not), [and] were to consult

---

[642] It is unclear whose Lord is being spoken of, but it probably means "if the Lord of the eleventh were to aspect the Lord of the domicile in which he is."
[643] Omitting a repetition of *aliqua persona rem* in 1550, to match 1491.
[644] Based on al-Rijāl, p. 340.

you that you might elect for him the hour fit for this, adapt the Ascendant (whatever sort you were to make it) and its Lord; also the Moon and the Lord of the domicile in which she is; and you will even adapt the second and its Lord, [and] even the eleventh and its Lord. The Lord of the Ascendant should aspect the Moon, too, or at least either of them[645] by a praiseworthy aspect, and should receive them or at least one of them; and the Lord of the house [domicile?] signifying him from whom the object is sought, should receive the Lord of the first,[646] and the Moon, or at least one of them: like if someone sought some object from his brother, let the Lord of the third be receiving the Lord of the first or the Moon; if from the father, let the Lord of the fourth be receiving the Lord of the first or the Moon; if from a child, let the Lord of the fifth be receiving one of them; if from a slave, let the Lord of the sixth be receiving one of them; if from the wife or a partner, let the Lord of the seventh be receiving the Lord of the first [sign] or the Moon, or one of them; if from a bishop or the like, let the Lord of the ninth be receiving them or one of them; if from the king, let the Lord of the tenth be receiving one of them; if from a friend, let the Lord of the eleventh be receiving one of them, as was said.

If however it were a petition to those who are signified by Saturn (like old men, Jews, or low-class persons), let the cusp of the 11th house be in Capricorn or Aquarius or Libra, or at least in another dignity of his. Indeed, if it were a petition to be made to a scribe or a boy, let the Lord of the eleventh be in one of the dignities of Mercury (the weakest of all of which is the face).[647]

And al-Tabarī said,[648] let Mercury be joined to Jupiter or Venus. And let him be going toward the Lord of the Ascendant, and always let the aforesaid significators signifying the objects which are sought, be adapted. And if there were no [planet][649] between him who seeks and him from whom it is sought (of the aforesaid), then the 1st signifies him who seeks and the 7th him from whom

---

[645] Bonatti seems to be getting this phrase from al-Rijāl, who is not himself very clear. He says: "adapt the 11th house [domicile?] and its Lord, the Part of Fortune and its Lord, and let both or either of them aspect the Ascendant..." Al-Rijāl seems to mean that either the Lord of the 11th or of the Part of Fortune should do the aspecting, but Bonatti substitutes the Lord of the Ascendant and then leaves the clause dangling without clear instruction.

[646] Reading *primi* for *septimi*, since the following examples all explicitly speak of the Lord of the first (*primi*).

[647] Al-Rijāl (p. 340) uses these same planetary examples, adding that one should make the degree [cusp] of the 11th house fall in a dignity of the planetary significator. I.e., when adapting Saturn for petitions to old men, put the cusp of the 11th on a dignity of Saturn.

[648] As reported by al-Rijāl, p. 340. Most of the the the rest of this paragraph is not from al-Rijāl, but see the following footnote.

[649] This may refer to not having a *malefic* planet between them, as al-Rijāl reports (p. 340).

it is sought. And always make the Ascendant cleansed of the malefics, and likewise the seventh, or at least [make] the seventh [cleansed] of their aspects. And if you did not avoid this, it signifies that the matter will be destroyed and be in vain, and annihilated, even after it will seem to be in order.

And if the sought object were money, or an object similar to it, then you will adapt the second and its Lord with the adaptation of the aforesaid ones you can. And let the Lord of the Ascendant be aspecting the Lord of the second; nor let one of the malefics be between them, nor its rays; even let the Lord of the eleventh and the Lord of the domicile in which the Part of Fortune is, be aspecting the second by a praiseworthy aspect, or either of them, if you can.

And al-Rijāl said[650] if it were a woman's object which is sought or [one] which pertains to the wedding celebration, let the seventh [sign] and its Lord be just as was said concerning the second and its Lord.

---

[650] Al-Rijāl, p. 340.

ON THE TWELFTH HOUSE

Chapter 1: On the racing of horses or other animals, both rational and others running to a finish line

If someone wished to make a horse or other animal run in a race or in another matter for the reason of acquiring or winning it, and you wished to elect for him the hour fit for it, adapt for him the Ascendant and its Lord; also the Moon and the Lord of the domicile in which she is, and likewise him to whom she[651] is joined, if you can; and likewise the Part of Fortune and its Lord; and so that the Lord of the first and the Moon (or one of them) aspect it [the Part]. And after you have adapted these, put the Lord of the hour in the Ascendant, when he takes his foot out from the front door of his house. You will even see how many animals there are who are running, from the second up to the twelfth,[652] so you can see how the animal for which you are electing will be disposed. For if you were to put the Lord of the hour in the first, as I said, he will come in first; if in the tenth, second; if in the eleventh, third; if in the seventh, fourth; if in the fifth, fifth; if in the ninth, sixth; if in the third, seventh; if in the second, eighth; if in the eighth, ninth; if in the sixth, tenth; if in the eleventh or fourth, he will come in last or equal to the last.

If however there were more than twelve animals, the others will come in mixedly, by means of the first signified ones observed. And if you could not adapt all of these, adapt the Lord of the hour and of the Ascendant, and the Moon. And if you cannot do this, let it always be your concern to adapt the Lord of the hour by putting him in the first, and likewise adapt the Moon.

And al-Kindī said[653] that the adaptation of the Moon is to put her in Sagittarius or in the first half of Libra.

And you must beware lest the Lord of the Ascendant or the Lord of the hour or the Moon be in its own fall, because it will be feared that the horse or he who rides him, may fall.

---

[651] By context, I am assuming Bonatti means the Moon.

[652] Both "animal" and "sign" are neuter, so it is unclear which Bonatti means; but in the end it doesn't matter, since his description of the technique is clear enough in what follows.

[653] As reported in al-Rijāl, p. 340 (although al-Rijāl only says "in the half of Libra"). I do not find this statement in this chapter in al-Kindī (*The Forty Chapters*, Ch. 36).

Chapter 2: On the buying of larger animals, both horses and others of those that are ridden or tamed

If you wished to elect for someone the hour for buying an animal, either for riding or taming, adapt the Ascendant and its Lord, and the Moon; and make [the Moon] be joined to some benefic in direct [motion], which is oriental, ascending in the circle of its *awj*, if you can do it, or at least let it be direct. And beware lest the benefic or the Moon be joined to a malefic by body or by aspect, because it introduces fears to the animal: so if it were a purchase, it will threaten harm, and that he will not have a good market price from it; if it were riding or taming, what someone intends will not follow from it, and that the animal will be avoided; and the more so if the impeding malefic were in the twelfth. However, see if the horse were already ridden, or another animal already tamed: make the Ascendant of the sale a common sign for him, and let the Moon be in Taurus or Leo; also make her be joined to a direct planet who is ascending in the north, or at least south (provided that it is ascending), for this signifies that the animal will be increased in price and body. For if it were retrograde, it signifies that the animal will be increased in price, but not so much, and will decrease in body. And if it were direct [and] descending, whether it were northern or southern, it signifies that it will be increased in body, but decreased in price. Likewise if it were southern [and] descending, it signifies that it will be decreased in price and body; and the more so if it were southern.

If by chance the animal were untamed, make the Ascendant for him a common sign, and let the Moon be in a movable sign, joined to one of the benefics, having considered the aforesaid conditions according to ascension and descension, or direction and retrogradation, as was said.

However it must be considered if someone wished to buy some animal, namely a horse or a cow, or a donkey or a camel, for reasons of making money or making improvements, with the Moon located in the beginning[654] of Cancer up to the end of Sagittarius: he will not make money from it easily, for he will buy high and sell low. If however he were to buy with her located from the beginning of Capricorn up to the end of Gemini, the contrary will happen: for he will buy low, and sell high, and this will happen not only from the aforesaid animals; it is even true of any object which someone were to buy then. However this is not to be overlooked: that the benefics are always responsible for and increase the good, and decrease evil. Indeed the malefics, on the contrary,

---

[654] *Capite.*

increase evil and decrease good, each one according to its own nature, and according to how it is its business to help or harm, to increase or decrease.

BIBLIOGRAPHY

Abu Bakr, *Liber Genethliacus* (Nuremberg: Johannes Petreius, 1540)

Abū Ma'shar al-Balhi, *The Abbreviation of the Introduction to Astrology*, ed. and trans. Charles Burnett, K. Yamamoto, and Michio Yano (Leiden: E.J. Brill, 1994)

Abū Ma'shar al-Balhi, *Liber Introductorii Maioris ad Scientiam Iudiciorum Astrorum*, vols. VI, V, VI, IX, ed. Richard Lemay (Naples: Istituto Universitario Orientale, 1995)

Abū Ma'shar al-Balhi, *The Abbreviation of the Introduction to Astrology*, ed. and trans. Charles Burnett, annotated by Charles Burnett, G. Tobyn, G. Cornelius and V. Wells (ARHAT Publications, 1997)

Abū Ma'shar al-Balhi, *On Historical Astrology: The Book of Religions and Dynasties (On the Great Conjunctions)*, vols. I-II, eds. and trans. Keiji Yamamoto and Charles Burnett (Leiden: Brill, 2000)

Abū Ma'shar al-Balhi, *The Flowers of Abū Ma'shar*, trans. Benjamin Dykes (2nd ed., 2007)

Al-Biruni, Muhammad ibn Ahmad, *The Chronology of Ancient Nations*, trans. and ed. C. Edward Sachau (London: William H. Allen and Co., 1879)

Al-Biruni, Muhammad ibn Ahmad, *The Book of Instruction in the Elements of the Art of Astrology*, trans. R. Ramsay Wright (London: Luzac & Co., 1934)

Al-Fārābī, *De Ortu Scientiarum* (appearing as *"Alfarabi Über den Ursprung der Wissenschaften (De Ortu Scientiarum),"* ed. Clemens Baeumker, *Beiträge zur Geschichte der Philosophie des Mittelalters*, v. 19/3, 1916.

Al-Khayyat, Abu 'Ali, *The Judgments of Nativities*, trans. James H. Holden (Tempe, AZ: American Federation of Astrologers, Inc., 1988)

Al-Kindī, *The Forty Chapters (Iudicia Astrorum): The Two Latin Versions*, ed. Charles Burnett (London: The Warburg Institute, 1993)

Al-Mansur (attributed), *Capitula Almansoris*, ed. Plato of Tivoli (1136) (Basel: Johannes Hervagius, 1533)

Al-Qabīsī, *Isagoge*, trans. John of Spain, with commentary by John of Saxony (Paris: Simon Colinaeus, 1521)

Al-Qabīsī, *The Introduction to Astrology*, eds. Charles Burnett, Keiji Yamamoto, Michio Yano (London and Turin: The Warburg Institute, 2004)

Al-Rijāl, 'Alī, *In Iudiciis Astrorum* (Venice: Erhard Ratdolt, 1485)

Al-Rijāl, 'Alī, *Libri de Iudiciis Astrorum* (Basel: Henrichus Petrus, 1551)

Al-Tabarī, 'Umar, *De Nativitatibus* (Basel: Johannes Hervagius, 1533)

Al-Tabarī, 'Umar [Omar of Tiberias], *Three Books of Nativities*, ed. Robert Schmidt, trans. Robert Hand (Berkeley Springs, WV: The Golden Hind Press, 1997)

Alighieri, Dante, *Inferno*, trans. John Ciardi (New York, NY: Mentor, 1982)

Allen, Richard Hinckley, *Star Names: Their Lore and Meaning* (New York: Dover Publications Inc., 1963)

Aristotle, *The Complete Works of Aristotle* vols. I-II, ed. Jonathan Barnes (Princeton, NJ: Princeton University Press, 1984)

Bloch, Marc, *Feudal Society*, vols. I-II, trans. L.A. Manyon (Chicago: University of Chicago Press, 1961)

Bonatti, Guido, *Decem Tractatus Astronomiae* (Erhard Ratdolt: Venice, 1491)

Bonatti, Guido, *De Astronomia Tractatus X* (Basel, 1550)

Bonatti, Guido, *Liber Astronomiae: Books One, Two, and Three with Index*, trans. Robert Zoller and Robert Hand (Salisbury, Australia: Spica Publications, 1988)

Bonatti, Guido, *Liber Astronomiae Part IV: On Horary, First Part*, ed. Robert Schmidt, trans. Robert Hand (Berkeley Springs, WV: The Golden Hind Press, 1996)

Boncompagni, Baldassarre, *Della Vita e Della Opere di Guido Bonatti, Astrologo et Astronomo del Seculo Decimoterzo* (Rome: 1851)

Brady, Bernadette, *Brady's Book of Fixed Stars* (Boston: Weiser Books, 1998)

Burnett, Charles, ed., *Magic and Divination in the Middle Ages* (Aldershot, Great Britain: Ashgate Publishing Ltd., 1996)

Burnett, Charles and Gerrit Bos, *Scientific Weather Forecasting in the Middle Ages* (London and New York: Kegan Paul International, 2000)

Carmody, Francis, *Arabic Astronomical and Astrological Sciences in Latin Translation: A Critical Bibliography* (Berkeley and Los Angeles: University of California Press, 1956)

Carmody, Francis, *The Astronomical works of Thābit b. Qurra* (Berkeley and Los Angeles: University of California Press, 1960)

Dorotheus of Sidon, *Carmen Astrologicum*, trans. David Pingree (Abingdon, MD: The Astrology Center of America, 2005)

Grant, Edward, *Planets, Stars, and Orbs: The Medieval Cosmos, 1200–1687* (New York, NY: Cambridge University Press, 1994)

Haskins, Charles H., "Michael Scot and Frederick II," *Isis*, v. 4/2 (1921), pp. 250-75.

Haskins, Charles H., "Science at the Court of the Emperor Frederick II," *The American Historical Review*, v. 27/4 (1922), pp. 669-94.

Hermes Trismegistus, *Liber Hermetis*, ed. Robert Hand, trans. Robert Zoller (Salisbury, Australia: Spica Publications, 1998)

Holden, James H., *A History of Horoscopic Astrology* (Tempe, AZ: American Federation of Astrologers, Inc., 1996)

Ibn Labban, Kusyar, *Introduction to Astrology*, ed. and trans. Michio Yano (Tokyo: Institute for the Study of Languages and Cultures of Asia and Africa, 1997)

Ibn Sina (Avicenna), *The Canon of Medicine (al-Qanun fi'l tibb)*, ed. Laleh Bakhtiar (Great Books of the Islamic World, Inc., 1999)

Kennedy, Edward S., "The Sasanian Astronomical Handbook Zīj-I Shāh and the Astrological Doctrine of 'Transit' (Mamarr)," *Journal of the American Oriental Society*, v. 78/4 (1958), pp. 246-62.

Kunitzsch, Paul, "Mittelalterliche astronomisch-astrologische Glossare mit arabischen Fachausdrücken," *Bayerische Akademie der Wissenschaften Philosophisch-Historische Klasse*, 1977, v. 5

Kunitsch, Paul, trans. and ed., "Liber de Stellis Beibeniis," in *Hermetis Trismegisti: Astrologica et Divinatoria* (Turnhout: Brepols Publishers, 2001).

Kunitzsch, Paul and Tim Smart, *A Dictionary of Modern Star Names* (Cambridge, MA: New Track Media, 2006)

Latham, R.E., *Revised Medieval Latin Word-List from British and Irish Sources* (Oxford: Oxford University Press, 2004)

Lemay, Richard, *Abu Ma'shar and Latin Aristotelianism in the Twelfth Century* (Beirut: American University of Beirut, 1962)

Levy, Raphael, "A Note on the Latin Translators of Ibn Ezra," *Isis*, v. 37 nos. 3/4 (1947), pp. 153-55.

Lilly, William, *The Starry Messenger* (London: Company of Stationers and H. Blunden, 1652). Reprinted 2004 by Renaissance Astrology Facsimile Editions.

Lilly, William, *Anima Astrologiae*, trans. Henry Coley (London: B. Harris, 1676)

Lilly, William, *Christian Astrology*, vols. I-II, ed. David R. Roell (Abingdon, MD: Astrology Center of America, 2004)

Long, A.A. and D.N. Sedley, *The Hellenistic Philosophers*, vol. I (Cambridge: Cambridge University Press, 1987)

Māshā'allāh *et al.*, *Liber Novem Iudicum in Iudiciis Astrorum* [Book of the Nine Judges], ed. Peter Liechtenstein (Venice: 1509)

Māshā'allāh, *De Receptione* [*On Reception*] and *De Revolutione Annorum Mundi* and *De Interpraetationibus*, in *Messahalae Antiquissimi ac Laudatissimi Inter Arabes Astrologi, Libri Tres*, ed. Joachim Heller (Nuremberg: Joannes Montanus and Ulrich Neuber, 1549)

Māshā'allāh, *On Reception*, ed. and trans. Robert Hand (ARHAT Publications, 1998)

Maternus, Firmicus Julius, *Matheseos Libri VIII*, eds. W. Kroll and F. Skutsch (Stuttgard: Teubner, 1968)

Michelsen, Neil F., *The Koch Book of Tables* (San Diego: ACS Publications, Inc., 1985)

Mantello, F.A.C. and A.G. Rigg, eds., *Medieval Latin: An Introduction and Bibliographical Guide* (Washington, DC: The Catholic University of America Press, 1996)

New Oxford Annotated Bible, ed. Bruce M. Metzger and Roland E. Murphy (New York: Oxford University Press, 1994)

Pingree, David, "Astronomy and Astrology in India and Iran," *Isis* v. 54/2 (1963), pp. 229-46.

Pingree, David, "Classical and Byzantine Astrology in Sassanian Persia," *Dumbarton Oaks Papers*, v. 43 (1989), pp. 227-239.

Pingree, David, *From Astral Omens to Astrology: From Babylon to Bīkīner* (Rome: Istituto italiano per L'Africa e L'Oriente, 1997)

Pseudo-Ptolemy, *Centiloquium*, ed. Georgius Trapezuntius, in Bonatti (1550)

Ptolemy, Claudius, *Tetrabiblos* vols. 1, 2, 4, trans. Robert Schmidt, ed. Robert Hand (Berkeley Springs, WV: The Golden Hind Press, 1994-98)

Ptolemy, Claudius, *Tetrabiblos*, trans. F.E. Robbins (Cambridge and London: Harvard University Press, 1940)

Ptolemy, Claudius, *Quadripartitum* [Tetrabiblos], trans. Plato of Tivoli (1138) (Basel: Johannes Hervagius, 1533)

Sahl ibn Bishr, *Introductorium* and *Praecipua Iudicia* [The Fifty Judgments] *De Interrogationibus* and *De Electionibus*, in *Tetrabiblos*, ed. Girolamo Salio (Venice: Bonetus Locatellus, 1493)

Sahl ibn Bishr, *De Electionibus* (Venice: Peter of Liechtenstein, 1509)

Selby, Talbot R., "Filippo Villani and his Vita of Guido Bonatti," *Renaissance News*, v. 11/4 (1958), pp. 243-48.

Seneca, *The Stoic Philosophy of Seneca*, ed. and trans. Moses Hadas (New York: The Norton Library, 1968)

Stegemann, Viktor, *Dorotheos von Sidon und das Sogenannte* Introductorium *des Sahl ibn Biŝr* (Prague: Orientalisches Institut in Prag, 1942)

Thomson, S. Harrison, "The Text of Grosseteste's *De Cometis*," *Isis* v. 19/1 (1933), pp. 19-25.

Thorndike, Lynn, *A History of Magic and Experimental Science* (New York: The Macmillan Company, 1929)

Thorndike, Lynn, *The* Sphere *of Sacrobosco and Its Commentators* (Chicago: The University of Chicago Press, 1949)

Thorndike, Lynn, "A Third Translation by Salio," *Speculum*, v. 32/1 (1957), pp. 116-117.

Thorndike, Lynn, "John of Seville," *Speculum*, v. 34/1 (1959), pp. 20-38.

Utley, Francis Lee (review), "*The Legend of the Wandering Jew* by George K. Anderson," *Modern Philology*, v. 66/2 (1968), pp. 188-193.

Valens, Vettius, *The Anthology*, vols. I-VII, ed. Robert Hand, trans. Robert Schmidt (Berkeley Springs, WV: The Golden Hind Press, 1993-2001)

Van Cleve, Thomas Curtis, *The Emperor Frederick II of Hohenstaufen: Immutator Mundi* (London: Oxford University Press, 1972)

Weinstock, Stefan, "Lunar Mansions and Early Calendars," *The Journal of Hellenic Studies*, v. 69 (1949), pp. 48-69.

Zoller, Robert, *The Arabic Parts in Astrology: A Lost Key to Prediction* (Rochester, VT: Inner Traditions International, 1989)

Zoller, Robert, *Bonatti on War* (2nd ed., 2000)

INDEX

Lightning Source UK Ltd.
Milton Keynes UK
UKOW06f0158060315

247337UK00001B/26/P